John E. Marshall (1932–2003)

JOHN E. MARSHALL

LIFE AND WRITINGS

JOHN E. MARSHALL

LIFE AND WRITINGS

John J. Murray

THE BANNER OF TRUTH TRUST

THE BANNER OF TRUTH TRUST
3 Murrayfield Road, Edinburgh EH12 6EL, UK
P.O. Box 621, Carlisle, PA 17013, USA

*

ISBN 0 85151 902 4

*

Typeset in 11 /14 pt Sabon at the
Banner of Truth Trust, Edinburgh
Printed in the USA by
Versa Press, Inc.,
East Peoria, IL.

Dedicated to
SUSAN MARSHALL
and CYNTHIA MURRAY,
our supporters in the work

CONTENTS

PART ONE: BIOGRAPHY

PART TWO: WRITINGS

ILLUSTRATIONS

'Chasing New College' – Balliol's First VIII. John Marshall is the 'stroke', facing the cox.   *Endpaper*

John E. Marshall (1932–2003).   *Frontispiece*

ILLUSTRATIONS (cont.)

PREFACE

It has been a privilege for me to write a short biography of the late John Marshall and to make a selection of his addresses for this volume. I have been happy to do so as a tribute to his memory and in thankfulness for his friendship to me.

Although coming from different backgrounds our association and friendship developed, as has been the case with others, through our mutual interest in the re-discovery of the doctrines of grace in the mid-twentieth century. God seemed to be at work in the lives of several young men in the early 1950s both by conversion and by bringing them to an understanding of the doctrines of grace. The vision given for reformation and revival forged men into a kind of 'Puritan brotherhood' and, although 'the vision waits its appointed time', we believe 'it will surely come' (*Hab.* 2:2–3).

I feel indebted to a number of people for their help: to John's wife, Susan, and to his family Jeremy, Deborah, Sarah, and Rebecca for supplying vital information; to John's sister, Mrs Margaret Woodley, for light on the childhood years; to the Rev. David Winch for the insights into student days; to Mr Colin Thompson and Mr Leslie Gibbons elders of the congregation at Alexandra Road for their impressions of the early days there; to Simo Ralevic and Roger Weil for assistance in the matters pertaining to Eastern Europe; to my friend and colleague the Rev. Iain Murray for general help and especially with some details in Chapter 5; to Dr Alan Thomas for his helpful input into the editing of 'The Christian and Mental Illness', and to other friends and colleagues whose contributions are included.

JOHN J. MURRAY
February 2005

PART ONE

BIOGRAPHY

I

CHILDHOOD IN CHINGFORD, ESSEX

John Marshall was a man who possessed a rare combination of qualities. Although in many ways he was the quintessential Englishman, his fighting spirit betrayed the presence of Irish and Scottish blood in his veins. As a Christian there was a similar combination of differing qualities: while gentle and kind, he was also a tough contender for the truth and no mean protagonist in debate.

PARENTAGE

John's Irish lineage can be traced back to his grandmother on his father's side. Ellen Lanagan was an Irish Roman Catholic who later became a Protestant. She had a hard life and died at the age of 76. John's paternal great-grandmother came from Scotland and her maiden name was Ferguson.

John's paternal grandfather was born into a fairly well-off London family. He went to Paris to study painting but did not finish the course. Disinherited on account of his artistic lifestyle, he started a family and named his son Joseph William Marshall. The latter was a sickly child and the parents were told that he would probably die before the age of ten. However, William, as he was known, survived his childhood ailments and fought in the First World War with the London Rifle Brigade. He served with this regiment on the front line during major battles when his battalion was twice reduced in numbers to around twenty men not killed or wounded. William Marshall did not emerge from the trauma of war entirely unscathed; bad experiences with doctors at this time gave him a life-long dislike of the medical profession. He preferred natural remedies to medical ones and believed that a healthy diet and lifestyle were the path to physical well-being.

At what point the Christian faith entered William Marshall's life is not known, but it was at Clapton Park Congregational Church in London that he met his future wife, Amy Loveday Evans. At the tender age of five she had lost her father through pneumonia. For the first part of their married life William Marshall worked as a civil servant, before taking early retirement. He then studied and passed exams which enabled him to become an official Lay Preacher in the Congregational Union. Thereafter he preached regularly in struggling churches, especially those in the East End of London. He also took on the superintendence of the Grove Mission, which had been successfully run by his uncle, W. B. Evans. Beside these responsibilities he ran a children's Christian Endeavour with the aid of his wife who also conducted a weekly women's meeting.

Speaking at his funeral service in 1968, the Rev. Derek Swann referred to William Marshall as 'Mr Valiant-for-Truth'. He was steadfast, loyal, determined, and courageous. Prior to 1914 he had seen the onset of theological liberalism and rejected it. A contemporary recalls how he made an impassioned plea not to touch the Bible when those in positions of leadership attempted to introduce a new creedal statement that would affect the authority of Scripture at the Annual Meeting of the Union of Congregational Churches in Westminster Chapel. Smartly dressed, paying careful attention to every detail, he was the type of man whom people would notice when entering a room. Although he had lacked a formal education due to his father's financial difficulties, he willingly paid for the education of his own large number of young siblings. A great love of reading ensured that he was knowledgeable on a wide range of subjects. He served on the local council as an Independent member and in 1938 was invited to become Deputy Charter Mayor when Chingford received her Charter from King George VI. His membership of the Cromwell Association, which he served at one period as the chairman, was also characteristic of his interests.

EARLY FAMILY LIFE

It was in the family home in Chingford, on the edge of the Epping Forest on the outskirts of London, that John Evans Marshall was born on November 18, 1932. He was the third child born into that home, David and Margaret preceding him. The Marshalls were a tightly knit and happy family. Recently Margaret has recalled: 'Our parents were very proud of us and, because they had been deprived of a good family life, did all in their power to create a happy secure home for us. Every year up until the Second World War we had a wonderful two-week family holiday at the seaside. Christmas was a joyous time and we had lots of fun and games together. In the summertime we went for rambles in Epping Forest, boated on Connaught Waters, and visited London.'

The Marshall home was characterized by firm discipline. At the same time the younger members were encouraged to debate and share in lively conversation with their parents. As both parents were strong characters it is not surprising that their offspring had some strong and sometimes obstinate traits. Margaret comments: 'We knew our boundaries and expected to be punished if we went beyond the limits. Any punishment was swift and just. John did have a temper and could be violent sometimes. One Sunday morning when John was about six or seven, and we were getting ready for church, father had to tell him off for something. Undeterred, he retorted, "When I grow up I am going to be a Roman Catholic priest and I shall give you a bottle of whisky for Christmas."'

John's sister also describes their family life on a Sunday: 'It was kept as the Lord's Day. Games were put on one side and we attended church together in the morning and Sunday School in the afternoon. Sunday was a happy day. Each of us had a small job to do to make it a day of rest for my mother. Sometimes my father would read from *Pilgrim's Progress* after lunch, and commonly he would tell us stories about Drake, Raleigh, or Cromwell in the morning before church.' Not surprisingly, G. A. Henty was to be one of John's favourite authors in his youth.

At the outset of the Second World War all the family remained at home. When the bombing of London began in September 1940 John remembered being taken to Pole Hill and seeing what seemed to be the whole of the London skyline burning. Margaret says of this period: 'We were all at home during the Battle of Britain in 1940 and recall well the day of the second "Fire of London". During that time raids were continuous and we spent every day and night in shelters. Our family re-arranged the dining room furniture and slept under tables, bookcases, or any other shelter. Later we were issued with a Morrison shelter which was supposed to withstand the weight of a house if it should collapse. We always tried to keep cheerful and made up quizzes or silly stories and played endless games of Monopoly and table tennis. When raids were few John and I went swimming in the open-air swimming pool. Through this time our mother kept calm, fed us, and tried to give us a normal life.'

But the danger and stress of war-time life so close to London led to Margaret and John being evacuated to Chelmsford at the ages of ten and seven respectively. Because David their brother was already at Bancrofts School, a public school in neighbouring Woodford whose pupils, unlike those of other schools, were not evacuated, he stayed at home throughout the five years of the war. Their parents went through agonies over the absence of Margaret and John and the evacuees themselves were not happy. Margaret did her best to look after John, and kept him company when he was turned out of his foster home on Saturday afternoons. The family still have a postcard that tells how unhappy John was because the lady he was staying with took away all his sweets!

John's father became depressed and despairing in the years 1939–45. No doubt the events of those years revived his own memories of war. Only when John was somewhat older did his father speak to him of his experiences in France, and in due course, John passed on those memories to his own children. His daughter Sarah recalls: 'He was especially impressed with stories that illustrated man's mortality and how unexpected death could be. When as a teacher I accompanied a trip to Vimy Ridge, I was able to tell story after story to enthralled (though usually very inattentive!) boys, which had been told to me by Dad about my Grandfather. He was extremely close to his parents and loved them both dearly. This is some comfort to us as his children, in that although I never met either of his parents, I feel as if I knew them, because Dad would so often speak about them.'

Another interesting factor from John's background was that, living in Chingford as he did, his local MP was none other than Winston Churchill. John made no secret of the fact that Sir Winston was his great hero. If he had not received a higher calling he might well have become a Member of Parliament. His cut-and-thrust debating ability would have made him a very effective politician on the floor of the House of Commons.

In the light of John Marshall's background it is not surprising that family history, war, and politics remained three great interests of his life.

2

STUDENT AT OXFORD

John followed his brother David and his cousin Basil Taylor to Bancrofts School. He was young for his Year and took 'Matric' at the early age of fourteen. His father promised him five pounds if he passed that exam and the amount was duly paid. As with all young men of that day, he was called up for National Service at the age of eighteen. After basic training he was commissioned in the Royal Artillery and served in Germany. Although, it seems, he was not yet a Christian, his parents' influence was still with him. Thus when tempted to go to a cinema one Sunday it was the thought of the pain it would cause his mother that prevented him from going.

Military service was followed in 1952 by entrance to Balliol College, one of the oldest and proudest colleges in Oxford. For his first degree he read 'PPE', a course that combined Philosophy, Politics, and Economics. In sports, it was rowing that had the greatest appeal for him; he joined the College Boat Club and in 1954 had the distinction of being in Balliol's First VIII which went 'Head of the River' in Torpids. 'Torpids' was the name given to the annual Spring races, dating from 1815, which attracted the attention of almost the whole university. Every College competed for the honour of winning, entering one or more boats with eight-man crews. The competition began with all boats in a line astern with a fixed distance between them. When a boat overtook and touched the one

9

immediately in front both pulled to the bank, and in the next race the boat thus 'bumped' changed order with the one that was behind. Ultimately the boat that went to the front won the challenge cup and was 'Head of the River'. John was 'stroke' in Balliol's eight, the man described by the textbooks as 'selected to set a good style to the men who are to copy him'. He loved rowing and for some years after leaving Oxford would pay regular visits to help coach Balliol crews.[1]

Although the ancient buildings of Balliol looked out on the Memorial to the Protestant martyrs of Mary Tudor's reign, that subject aroused little interest for John in his first student days; on the contrary, he put up some resistance to the Christian faith he had known in his home. But conscience would not leave him in peace. Once in an important boat race at Henley, as he waited for the starting pistol all he could think of was the words of John Newton:

> Solid joys and lasting treasure
> None but Zion's children know.

Part of his inner conflict revolved around the implications for his life if he became a committed Christian. He had always believed in the veracity of the Bible and in the existence of God, but he had the conviction that being a Christian would mean responding to a call he already felt to the Christian ministry. That was not the direction in which he wished to go. Yet when the evangelist Billy Graham came to Oxford on 23 May 1954 to preach at St Aldate's Church, John was among the students who packed the building. On that day, and from that day, his commitment to Christ was definite, and his whole

[1] Balliol's win in 1954 was specially commemorated on 1 March 2004, when John's widow and his son Jeremy were invited to attend a celebration dinner. Two of John's fellow oarsmen from that event attended his funeral.

view of his Christian upbringing and his own future was changed.[2] It is interesting to reflect that at this time God seems to have been doing a simultaneous work in a number of young men who were later to feature in the recovery of the doctrines of the Reformed Faith in the United Kingdom.

MANSFIELD

On completing his degree in 1955, the sense of calling to the ministry led him to Mansfield College, Oxford, which was the theological school of the Congregational denomination to which he belonged. Originally known as Spring Hill College, this institution had been established in 1838 when George Mansfield and his two sisters provided the funds for a building in the Spring Hill district of Birmingham. Later it removed to another site, and it was only after an Act of Parliament opened the universities to Nonconformists in 1872 that it reached its final location. Initially some of the more promising Congregational students were encouraged to graduate at Oxford or Cambridge before returning to take their theological course at Spring Hill. This did not prove satisfactory, so Spring Hill was closed and in 1886 re-established at Oxford as 'Mansfield' in memory of its original founder.

The attraction of Oxford to the Congregationalists was symptomatic of the great self-confidence in that denomination towards the end of the nineteenth century. The Congregationalists intended to be at the forefront of theological education. Thus Mansfield's curriculum came to be advertised as part of the Oxford theological programme, and its ethos and lecturers embraced the latest scholarship of the 'Higher Critical' movement. In 1955 Dr John Marsh was the Principal. He had come to the Congregationalists from the Plymouth Brethren and, like a number of his generation, believed that it

---

[2] Whether John was regenerated at this time, or whether he now gained assurance, is something about which he was uncertain. There were occasions when he wondered if he had become a Christian in childhood.

was possible to combine a devout Christian life with an acceptance of Modernist views.

It was in Mansfield College that John Marshall began his life-long battle for the truth. At first he found only two like-minded men, John Bentliff and David Winch. Recalling those days David Winch says:

> Among the Mansfield students 'Modernist' views of Scripture were generally taken for granted, except for a very small group of us. As evangelicals we met together for prayer and Bible reading before breakfast. A fine Welsh postgraduate, two Americans, one Latvian joined us for varying periods of time as evangelicals, with whom we enjoyed good fellowship. We tried to make an impact on the College for good and the weekly 'sermon class' was often an opportunity for defending the truth. Our views were listened to respectfully, but generally not accepted.

One thing that helped John was the fact that his brother David had studied at Mansfield before him and had been well respected.[3] His former army commission and his three successful years at Balliol also gave him a measure of prestige and advantage. John was evidently the originator of the College's evangelical group at that time. David Winch writes further:

> In my undergraduate days as a student at Oxford, during the annual evangelistic student mission (under the aegis of the Oxford Inter-Collegiate Christian Union) John noticed that I was attending the mission meetings night by night and invited me back to his College room at Mansfield for coffee. Questioning me regarding my own spiritual state, he startled me by asking whether I was assured of being a child of God.

[3] A tribute to David W. Marshall (1927–92) will be found in *The Banner of Truth* magazine, February 1993. After training at the London Bible College and Mansfield, he entered the ministry of the Congregational churches.

In response to my answer in the negative, John pointed me to John 1:12: 'But as many as received him, to them gave he power to become the sons of God, even to them that believe on his name.' We then prayed together and I returned to the digs I was lodging in at the time – but not to sleep. I was enabled to wrestle in prayer, and God graciously granted me that assurance. I look back to that night as pivotal in my Christian experience.

Another Christian brother at Mansfield at the time, John Bentliff, had also previously been helping me from an evangelical point of view, but under God it was John Marshall's timely help that was so crucial at that stage. I must confess that it brings tears to my eyes as I now write of it.

After two years John attained the Bachelor of Arts Degree in Theology and proceeded to Master of Arts in the customary way.

3

THE CALL TO HEMEL HEMPSTEAD

It was through his friendship with David Winch at Mansfield that John Marshall came to be called to his first and only charge, at Hemel Hempstead in Hertfordshire. In that town there were two rather small struggling congregations, Alexandra Road Congregational Church and Box Lane Congregational Church. Members of the Winch family were involved in both churches.

David Winch's father and mother had begun to attend Alexandra Road Congregational Church in the early 1950s and became members there in 1955. David Winch's uncle, Arthur, and his wife Muriel, had also settled in the area and joined the Box Lane Congregational Church. The Winch family were products of the twentieth-century Congregationalism that had embraced theologically liberal teaching.

The Box Lane congregation met in what was an historic building. It was first built in 1600, rebuilt in 1690, and restored in 1876. A door behind the pulpit, ready for the escape of the preacher in days of persecution, was still retained but the gospel that had once caused such opposition had been lost. The congregation in the 1950s consisted of a sad little group deeply affected by the unbelief of their liberal background.

The situation in Alexandra Road was more encouraging. Although a number of the members were similar to those at

Box Lane, there was a small eager group of members who met for prayer. David Winch takes up the story:

> At an early morning prayer meeting in the Alexandra Road Sunday School room, a group of us were gathering to pray for revival of true religion. It must have started about 1955. I cannot remember whether it was every morning or (more likely) once a week. But I well remember the early rising, cycling the five miles into Hemel, the excitement and air of expectancy. There was also the regular church prayer meeting every Thursday evening. At these meetings we pleaded with God for the man of his choosing, a true man of God to be called to the Alexandra Road church.

This account, of course, only refers to David's experience during vacation times. It was when he returned to Mansfield on one occasion that he realized that the answer to their prayers might be at hand. He writes: 'With John Marshall in his final year, the thought came to me that maybe he could be the answer to our prayers for an evangelical minister. And so I mentioned it to him. And he made it a matter of prayer too.'

When David Winch proceeded to introduce his friend to the two congregations in Hemel Hempstead it was by no means a foregone conclusion that the wish of the evangelical element within the congregations would prevail. It was only some years later that a new church secretary at Alexandra Road discovered correspondence from this date which showed that one element in the congregation had been in correspondence with Mansfield College over a possible call to John Marshall. The College questioned the wisdom of the churches in calling a man with such strong convictions as Marshall as their minister. In the event the evangelical voice prevailed, in part because there were some who, while not evangelicals themselves, considered that he was a good speaker, a talented man, and that a Mansfield training would ensure their Congregational inheritance. So they went along with the majority view.

THE CALL

John Marshall often referred to his 'three-times call' to become minister of Alexandra Road church. Initially he was ordained and inducted to be minister of the two congregations, Alexandra Road and Box Lane. This took place on 12 July 1958. An account of the occasion was included in the *Congregational Newsletter* of October/November 1958, written by Arthur Winch of Box Lane:

> It was good to see the Church nearly full with some people in the gallery. The singing was grand and the service proceeded smoothly under the able leadership of the presiding minister, the Rev. E. Harland Brine. We were glad to have with us our former minister, the Rev. J. K. Antrobus who read the first lesson. Two members of Mr Marshall's family – his father and his brother – also took part.
>
> The statement by the ordinand followed in which Mr Marshall gave a clear and concise account of his decision to enter the ministry and his subsequent acceptance of the call to Hemel Hempstead. One could not help being impressed by his obvious sense of vocation and utter sincerity.

Then followed the induction of the new minister. The charge to the churches was given by Rev. John Marsh, the Principal of Mansfield College. The charge to the minister was given by the Rev. G. W. Kirby, the General Secretary of the Evangelical Alliance. The writer sums up the occasion:

> The whole service was indeed a great inspiration and one came away feeling that we were entering upon a new era full of great possibilities for both churches.

It was not long before tensions arose between the new minister and the Box Lane congregation. An entry in the

Congregational Newsletter reveals that the Box Lane congregation had as their church anniversary speaker on 5 October
1958, the Principal of the New College, the Rev John Huxtable.
Here was a theologian who was decidedly opposed to evangelicals and especially to their belief in Scripture and a
substitutionary atonement. Most in the congregation would
have supported Huxtable. It was also quite acceptable to them
to have women office-bearers, women preachers, and activities such as dancing and whist drives.

The Box Lane congregation had agreed at the time of the
call to John Marshall to allow no dancing on church premises.
After the announcement of a church social at which dancing
would be included, a protest by John Marshall went unheeded.
The church officers said that without these things they would
have no young people. The fact was, there were none anyway.
In the light of this John resigned from the Box Lane congregation. Alexandra Road, however, confirmed their call to him to
be their minister, without the involvement of Box Lane, which
'second' call he accepted. While the March 1959 *Newsletter*
contained news of both congregations, the May issue contained
no reference to the Box Lane Church.

It was clear from the outset that John Marshall was not
prepared to compromise the gospel. His first pastoral letter
following his induction, expressed appreciation of the 'warm-
ness of the welcome' and 'the many kindnesses' before
proceeding to urge the systematic and regular reading of the
Scriptures. The rightness of his stance was later shown to be
correct. In an account of a Gift Day in November 1961, Arthur
Winch recorded: 'Mr Marshall came to us in July 1958 and by
his forthright preaching and faithful visiting he has endeared
himself to us all. We are now seeing some of the fruits of his
labours in an enthusiastic and growing fellowship.'

Nonetheless it is apparent that even after this there was
serious trouble at Alexandra Road for John resigned his pastorate there before the end of 1961. No record of what

happened has survived, save that a 'third' call was given to him which he was persuaded to accept.

SIGNS OF NEW LIFE

Those who knew Alexandra Road at this date say that the congregation consisted of a handful of mostly elderly people. A change took place in February 1961 when four leather-clad young 'rockers' appeared on the scene. Their appearance alarmed the congregation. The youngsters were Colin Thompson with his girlfriend Jean Howe, and Leslie Gibbons with his girlfriend Janet Thompson (who was Colin's eldest sister).

Colin Thompson and Leslie Gibbons were sons of publicans. They had no religious upbringing and Colin first heard the gospel from a lecturer at his College who also recommended him to Alexandra Road. The following are Colin Thompson's first impressions:

> The preaching was serious, as was the preacher. If I had any preconceived idea of Christianity, it was for women and children. But here was a man, a real man, who took his religion seriously. It was an exposition of the Bible applied to the heart, not that I understood the significance of that at the time.
>
> The first time I remember becoming aware of the marked difference between Mr Marshall's preaching and that of other 'evangelicals' was when my College lecturer took a Bible study at Alexandra Road. Part the way through his address he became unwell. John Marshall took over on the spot and, although he took up the Scriptures where the other man left off, in the way he explained and applied the passage I was startled at the contrast between them.
>
> Early on when I expressed concern over my spiritual state Mr Marshall said, 'You will never become a Christian unless God makes you one.' Whereas others were

telling me that all I had to do was 'to believe'. But God began to work and during the year 1961 myself, my wife, my two sisters, my brother-in-law and my mother-in-law were all saved by grace. They were followed by a number of others – family and friends.

These couples, who appeared so unexpectedly in February 1961, were married by John Marshall in 1962, and they remain happily together to this day. John Marshall believed that ministers had a great responsibility when they joined people in marriage. He would carefully examine couples and believed that a minister might not be guiltless if a couple he had married later separated. Both Thompson and Gibbons went on to be elders in the congregation and were a great support to their pastor.

But it was not only the young whose lives were changed. There were some rescued from self-righteousness in their old age. A striking example was a Miss Vercoe. She had been a great 'worker' in the church and regularly attended the services of worship, but she was not a converted woman, having been exposed to years of liberal teaching. Under the new minister's preaching she began to see that she was not saved by her own works as she had previously been taught, but still needed a work of grace in her heart. Slowly her eyes were opened to the truth of her need of dependence on the atoning work of the Lord Jesus Christ and she came to rest by faith solely in the work of the Saviour. During her last illness in hospital, though feeble and frail, she would recommend her Saviour to all that came to her bedside. On one of John Marshall's last visits to her, when she was in pain and near to death, she exclaimed to him with joy: 'Oh Mr Marshall, I had a wonderful dream. I dreamt I was in heaven and I was with thousands and thousands of people. There in the middle of us was the Lord Jesus and we were all singing the hymn "Stand up, Stand up for Jesus".'

Others of liberal persuasion in the Alexandra Road congregation responded very differently to the preaching they were now hearing. Their annoyance at the minister's 'continual talking about sin' and his 'long sermons' was not hidden, and church meetings became a monthly trial. Non-attending members turned up to add their objections, people whose faces were unknown to those who had recently joined the church. One issue raised in church business meetings was the question whether the congregation would support or oppose a document drawn up by the denominational leaders preparing the way for a merger of the Congregationalists with the English Presbyterian Church. When this proposal was defeated at Alexandra Road most members of liberal persuasion left the church although a small number remained for many years to come – 'like thorns in the flesh', as one member described them.

RECOVERY OF THE BIBLICAL FAITH
Although many of the churches of the Congregational Union were reaching a nadir when John Marshall began his ministry in 1958, a new movement was arising in which he would later become a key figure. In his student days at Mansfield he had often felt his theological isolation. His feelings resembled those of John Stott who was at Cambridge a decade earlier and has recalled: 'When I was an undergraduate at Cambridge University in the early 1940s (a vulnerable and immature evangelical believer, beleaguered by liberal theologians) there was no evangelical literature available to help me . . . there was virtually no contemporary evangelical theology and IVP had not yet come into existence.'

The signs of a revival of evangelical theology, first manifested prior to 1939, were hampered by the restrictions on book publication during the Second World War. It was in the later 1940s that evangelicalism began to grow in influence, noticeably among students. By that date Dr Martyn Lloyd-Jones was widely involved with the Inter-Varsity Fellowship.

At an IVF Conference in 1952 he gave an address on 'Maintaining the Evangelical Faith Today', which was later published as a booklet. Its publication drew a stinging response from Nathaniel Micklem. At that time Dr Micklem, then Principal of Mansfield College, wrote: 'The kindest thing to say about Dr Lloyd-Jones position is that it rests upon downright theological ignorance.' This reaffirmation of evangelical teaching, still more significantly, was accompanied by a re-discovery of the doctrines of grace. The preaching of Dr Lloyd-Jones, the work of the Evangelical Library, the formation of the Puritan Conference, and the renewed publication of Calvinistic literature – first by James Clarke and more fully with the Banner of Truth Trust – all created a new sense of direction for significant numbers of young Christians.

From these sources came the influences that were destined to shape John Marshall's life and work. The resurgent evangelicalism affected the Congregational Union to some extent and it brought about the formation of the Congregational Evangelical Revival Fellowship. In the Alexandra Road *Congregational Newsletter* we read of John Marshall attending the Southern Conference of this Fellowship, and drawing attention in particular to an address by the Rev G. W. Kirby on Psalm 85:6: 'Wilt thou not revive us again: that thy people may rejoice in thee?' By 1964 there was a strong emphasis on revival evident in the prayer meetings of the Alexandra Road congregation.

An indication of John's growing desire to bring his membership into the re-discovered doctrines of grace is the fact that the Savoy Declaration was serialized in their *Congregational Newsletter* about this period. By 1964 he had opened a bookroom in the church on Saturdays. A notice about this read: 'Christian literature is on sale in the choir vestry every Saturday from 2pm to 5pm. If you are unable to come please give Mr Les Gibbons or Mr Colin Thompson your orders.' By 1965 a new feature appears in the *Newsletter*: book reviews were included. The books reviewed were mainly those published by the Banner of Truth Trust – J. H. Merle d'Aubigné's *History of the Reformation*, Joseph Alleine's *Alarm* and Thomas Boston's *Human Nature in Its Fourfold State*. By December 1965 the bookstall was open from 11.00 am to 5.00 pm every Saturday.

John Marshall's continuing ministry at Alexandra Road was not without opposition. Difficulties still arose at church meetings. There was an incident he used to tell in that connection. It happened after a particularly gruelling church meeting at which he had been continually 'savaged' by one faction who attended the church at that time. At the close of the meeting, feeling bruised and generally sorry for himself, he was handed a note from an old lady (known as 'Queenie') who was a staunch supporter of the gospel and therefore also of her minister. Her father had been minister of the congregation in the 1920s and she had been brought up in the rambling Victorian manse next to the church. Queenie lacked any formal education and spent her entire life working at the paper mill in Apsley, near to Hemel Hempstead. Often after similar meetings in the past, she had a word of comfort for her minister or slipped him a note that contained an uplifting thought or a comforting text. So on this occasion Marshall returned to the manse holding this 'comforting' gem and waiting till he reached his study before he read its message. However the note on this occasion did not contain such words of comfort as he had formerly received from this wise and spiritual lady; instead he found a word of rebuke: 'If thou faint in the day of adversity, thy strength is small' (*Prov.* 24.10). Although it was not what he had anticipated he took the timely words to heart.

Having survived the opposition of liberals in his early years, he encountered opposition from some evangelical people in his later years of ministry. This was due to his increasing emphasis on full-orbed Reformed teaching and values. A characteristic of his ministry was his insistence on the necessity for biblical evidence for any proposal or course of action that would affect the life of the church. Superficial meetings of a Young People's Fellowship were replaced by a meeting for 'Instruction in Basic Doctrine' where the Westminster Confession of Faith, the Heidelberg Catechism, and John Calvin's *Institutes of the Christian Religion* were studied.

His convictions necessarily led him to oppose charismatic teaching and this produced another period of difficulty in the congregation until those members who had accepted the new teaching left the church. These contendings brought a certain isolation to the congregation. When the Congregational Union of England and Wales ceased to exist, the Alexandra Road church was not represented at the inaugural meeting of the Evangelical Fellowship of Congregational Churches. The congregation endeavoured to cement ties with other like-minded churches but was not very successful in so doing.

1. Joseph William Marshall and Amy Loveday Evans
(John's parents).

2. Balliol College and the Martyrs' Memorial, Oxford (Courtesy: Elizabeth Wickens).

3. John Evans Marshall and Susan Westcott on their wedding day,
16 September 1961, at Westminster Chapel, London.

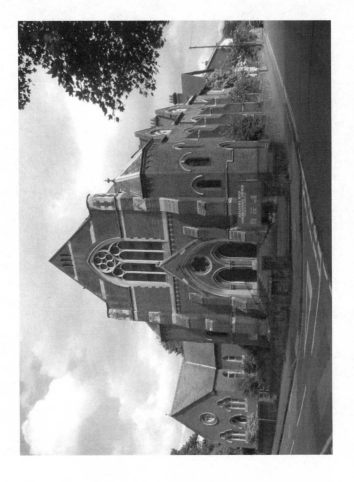

4. Alexandra Road Congregational Church, Hemel Hempstead,
where John Marshall ministered from 12 July 1958 until his death on 29 August 2003
(Photo courtesy of Andrew Doggrell).

4

MARRIAGE AND FAMILY LIFE

John Marshall came to the congregations at Hemel Hempstead as a bachelor and remained so for three years. A change in status was heralded in the Church *Newsletter* for November 1960: 'Members of the church were delighted to hear of the engagement of our minister the Rev. J. Marshall to Miss Susan Westcott of Chingford. We pray that the Lord will richly bless them both as they seek to serve him together.'

SUSAN WESTCOTT

Susan Westcott was from a Church of England background and went up to St Hugh's College, Oxford, in 1953. On her first Sunday she attended St Aldate's Church where the ministry of the Rev. Keith de Berry was immediately a help to her. Her spiritual interest awakened, Susan joined the Oxford Pastorate and the OICCU. The latter (a branch of IVF) had 'a good group in my College and they were a great help to me'. By the end of her first term in Oxford she was rejoicing in a new spiritual world.

Susan Westcott's first sight of her future husband was as the stroke in Balliol's 'Head of the River' boat in the Spring of 1954, and they were both in the packed service at St Aldate's that May when Billy Graham preached. It was not, however, until the September of that same year that they first met when they were both helping on a mission in Plymouth under Anglican auspices. To their surprise they discovered that their

25

respective homes were only a fifteen-minute walk from each other in Chingford. Thereafter they saw each other often, although Susan's immediate duty, after graduating in Mathematics in 1956, was to teach for five years at South Hampstead High School for girls. These were happy years for her; there were a number of other Christians on the staff and some, including Susan, attended the Friday night Bible Studies on Romans led by Dr Lloyd-Jones at Westminster Chapel.

It was at Westminster Chapel that the wedding of John and Susan took place on 16 September 1961, conducted by Dr Lloyd-Jones, assisted by the Rev Lance Vinall of Chingford. Dr Lloyd-Jones did not ask Susan's father to give her away and when asked in the vestry why not he replied: 'At twenty-six she is old enough to know her own mind.' John's brother, David, was the best man. The occasion was not without an embarrassing incident which Susan Marshall has recalled: 'The Church Secretary was elderly and had not informed the organist of the music we had chosen. I was to come in with my father to the music of "The Royal Fireworks" by Handel. The organist did not have the music so John's brother David, who knew the organ, went into the organ loft and played it on sight. None of the other music printed in the Order of Service could be played. And we still had to pay the organist.' The Reception was at the St Ermin's Hotel, where forty years later they were to celebrate their Ruby wedding anniversary.

On their return from the honeymoon a warm welcome awaited them in the congregation at Hemel Hempstead. On Sunday 15 October 1961 after the evening service members of the church gathered in the schoolroom to present the newly married couple with a gift from the congregation to mark the happy occasion. The following account is taken from the *Congregational Newsletter*:

Something quite unexpected happened when at the close of the service an electrical fault plunged the church and hall into darkness. Nevertheless after a short while plenty of candles were procured and placed around the hall giving a cosy and informal atmosphere. Mr Turner then welcomed Mrs Marshall into the fellowship and asked Mr Winch to make the presentation of an extremely comfortable-looking armchair and a bookcase, both of which were chosen by Mr and Mrs Marshall. Mr Winch said that before Mr Marshall came the church had been without a minister for three years. We have now had Mr Marshall for just over three years and the results of his ministry were now being seen in the spiritual growth of the church.

The Victorian manse next door to the church in Alexandra Road appears to have been in a poor condition when John first arrived. It was completely redecorated both outside and inside for the coming of the new bride. With the birth of Jeremy in 1963 the old house was filled with the sound of new life; the births of Deborah, Sarah, and Rebecca followed in due course.

THE CHRISTIAN HOME

John Marshall was a great family man and the home in Hemel Hempstead was not unlike the one in which he had grown up. It was first and foremost a Christian home. As his son Jeremy has said of his father: 'He was a man with strong biblical principles who based his whole life on the Word of God. For example, "Let not the sun go down on your wrath" meant that we never went to bed without having a dispute resolved. Dad "trained us up in the way we should go" but he also always respected his children's freedom of speech. There was strict discipline but debate and lively conversation were encouraged. The Marshall family life was built on lively arguments but these were loving discussions where Dad let us argue with him because he loved us and wanted to win our hearts and minds.' John always seemed to enjoy the intellectual exercise of argument and debate.

Friends of the Marshall children came into contact with the Christian influence of their home. Daughter Sarah has recorded these memories: 'The witness to visitors to the home was consolidated by family prayers, morning and evening, which we never ever missed. In the morning we would all read round as a family, after singing a hymn or psalm. In the evening Dad read from the Bible and asked us questions to make sure we were listening. Countless friends heard the Bible read, because no one was allowed to be in the house and not attend. Nor, when we were on holiday, would Dad ever consent to tone down the volume of the singing! He refused to even contemplate being embarrassed by singing God's praises!'

In connection with the spiritual impact he made on his children, Rebecca remembers her experience as a child:

I came under deep conviction of sin as a seven or eight-year-old listening to a number of evening sermons. I remember Dad holding out the promise so vividly that Jesus said 'Come unto me all ye that are weary and heavy laden and I will give you rest.' Even now as a thirty-one-year-old I can say that I have never felt closer to the Lord Jesus and more aware of his glory than on occasions when Dad was preaching – something I really miss.

Dad was always so wise and gentle with us spiritually and while he could be strict he would never pry into our souls or pressure us into showing signs of spiritual maturity. At the same time there was never any question about our participation in family prayers or attendance at church. Now as a parent I can see the wisdom of this gentle but exacting approach. He was my spiritual mentor as well as my father and I remember vividly waking him in the night to confess a lie I had told, or crying about a bad dream. I wanted him to pray with me and he was always so gentle and patient.

THE FAMILY MAN

John always had time for his children. Sarah recalls how 'he would while away hours telling us stories either of his own childhood or from history. I can particularly remember a time when we went walking on Dartmoor on a very cold windy day and I was completely enthralled as Dad explained all about Sir Francis Drake and the Spanish Armada and the beacons that had burned along the coastline to warn of the coming danger.'

There was no lack of a sense of fun and John loved to play games with the children. Sarah says she remembers 'telling a teacher at school how she was climbing on her Dad's desk one day. The teacher stopped me and said, "Does your father allow you to do that?" It apparently did not fit in with her image of my father. She would have been more surprised had she seen the large plastic spiders stuck to the study ceiling above his desk. He enjoyed the open consternation of young children who would come in especially to see the spiders, and also the adult visitors who would become distracted mid conversation by what they suddenly saw above the minister's head!'

In connection with that sense of humour Deborah says:

Some people may have thought Dad very serious, and although he did take life and particularly spiritual matters very seriously, he also had a sense of fun. He impressed many a child at our parties by 'eating fire'. He would sit them down, give them a solemn warning that what he was about to do was very dangerous and that they should never try it themselves. He would then set light to a big wad of cotton wool and eat it. Then he would allow the children to search in his mouth for evidence of the cotton wool afterwards. The look of amazement on the children's faces was hilarious: I always felt rather proud: I didn't know of any other Dad who could do such a trick.

We also came to know Dad as a loving grandfather. Who could forget him sitting with his grandchildren watching his favourite film from his childhood, *Gunga Din*, and all cheering together as the British Army arrived over the hill to relieve the beleaguered heroes! He said he loved naughty boys, as he was one himself.

John was interested in the character development of his grandchildren from an early age, especially if they displayed any 'Marshall' characteristics such as strong will and temper.

FAMILY EDUCATION

John Marshall sought the best in his children's education. Sarah says:

> Acting on principle as he did, Dad had more than a few strong disagreements with the school which we all attended. He would never remain silent on a point of principle and his filing cabinet is full of correspondence with the school about issues he objected to – particularly works of English literature being taught to his children which he considered to be corrupt or inappropriate. He said that people who met him in an educational context expected him to be a rather effete, bumbling cleric. This was not quite the man they met! Although strict with us in private about our behaviour at school, he was also lion-like in his defence of his children. I remember a time when I was in trouble at school and Dad left me sitting outside the headmaster's study while he marched in, defended me, and attacked the school for their mishandling of the situation. I knew nothing about this at the time and only found out years later.

Sarah continues:

> With a passionate interest in education Dad remained on the board of Governors at a local school for over twenty

years. When asked to give his opinion on disciplinary matters he seemed to keep just the right balance between sympathy with unhappy and disaffected pupils (of whom there were many), and the need to support staff who found their job increasingly difficult. Never one to do anything half-heartedly, Dad entered with great gusto and enthusiasm into the different roles of a school governor, challenging secular views over, for example, the school policy on relationships where he was outraged that marriage was not even mentioned.

OTHER INTERESTS

John Marshall was very fond of gardening and in the early years he looked after an allotment as well as the manse garden. Deborah recalls:

> We ate whatever was grown and the only disgruntlement we had was in the summer when we might be roped in to help do the watering. Lugging buckets around the allotment was not our favourite job. The plus side was that as Dad drove there on his day off (Monday), he would give us a lift to our secondary school. It wasn't far to walk, but a lift was welcome, and in the days before seat-belt laws, we extended the invitation to any children in the street who went to the same school. You never quite knew how many would turn up on a Monday morning, gym kit in hand, and all pile into the Volvo estate. You could fit at least six in the back and four in the boot. Of course Jeremy being the eldest, would lord it in the luxury of the front seat.

He supported the Woodland Trust and loved to try and plant trees wherever he could. His friends driving with him would sometimes be surprised to see him throwing flower seeds out of the car window on to grass verges and sometimes he actually planted bulbs in empty spaces. His son Jeremy believes, 'There is a bridge on the road to Cambridge which now has masses of daffodils which Dad planted.'

5

THE WIDER MINISTRY

During the 1960s John Marshall was comparatively little-known outside the immediate sphere of his ministry in Hemel Hempstead. One reason for this was that he did not belong to the circle of younger men which met monthly at Westminster Chapel, London, under the chairmanship of Dr Lloyd-Jones, and for whom 'the Doctor' was very much the leader. Commenting on his absence from this circle he was later to write:

> As a child my father took me to hear M.L-J. When I was in the army I used to go to Westminster Chapel on returning from a 48-hour leave. However although my first Banner Conference was in 1965, and I walked into the John Murray/M.L-J controversy, I did not join the Westminster Fraternal until the mid 1970s. There was no fundamental reason why I did not, except perhaps a certain perverse disposition in refusing to succumb to strong fraternal (literally!) pressure! I did not feel like proving my orthodoxy by joining the Fraternal. In the end I came to the conclusion I was causing my ministerial brethren unnecessary offence, and so I joined. Hence I was never among M.L-J's close associates, as was my brother. I think however in the end I have been

far more loyal to him than many who in early years were around him![4]

These words throw an interesting light on John's make-up. While ever respecting the minister of Westminster Chapel – who continued to lead the Fraternal till 1980 – he was not going to share in the element of hero worship that was undoubtedly indulged in by some others. The pressure he mentions refers, of course to his brother David (who became Assistant to Dr Glyn Owen, M.L-J's successor at Westminster). 'Controversy' is too strong a word for the difference he saw between M.L-J and Professor John Murray at the Leicester Conference in 1965. In short it had to do with how far explicit Calvinistic belief, and some Presbyterian distinctives, were necessary for securing a closer unity of churches. In the English context Murray would have been very much the under-dog on such points and John liked to take the side of under-dogs. In addition he not only admired John Murray as a speaker and theologian but came to know and esteem him personally. The Professor had a niece who lived near Hemel Hempstead and sometimes John would drive him there at the conclusion of Leicester Conferences where Murray was a chairman until 1971.

John had read Banner books from his early days in the ministry and it was through the new friends that he made at the Leicester Conference that he was led into a wider ministry. His presence and contributions at these conferences became increasingly valued and in 1975 it was his account of the conference that was printed in *The Banner of Truth* magazine. His first full addresses at Leicester were in 1976 and 1978 when he spoke on 'The Christian and Mental Illness' and 'The Christian Position in the USSR Today'.

Iain Murray, founding Trustee of the Banner of Truth Trust and its General Editor for many years, was especially aware of

[4] Letter to Iain Murray of November 23, 1988.

John's helpfulness in the work and, before he left for ministry in Australia in 1981, his fellow Trustees accepted his recommendation that John be invited to join the Board of Trustees. John was first present at a board meeting in the Spring of 1982; his company was immediately enjoyed and in the years that followed he was to give immense help to the work. His counsel at meetings was ever well thought-out and never weakly argued! He regularly read manuscripts offered for publication and gave them wise evaluation. In some instances it was his initiative that led to decisions on republications and these ranged from the reprint of Thomas Scott's little classic, *The Force of Truth*, at one end of the scale, and at the other, the massive facsimile of John Calvin's *Sermons on Job*. His enthusiasm for Calvin's sermons knew no bounds. In 1983 he also took on the position of Review Editor of *The Banner of Truth* and committed himself to that demanding department of the magazine for the next twenty years.

In John Marshall's many contributions at Banner Trustees' meetings there was one subject upon which he remained disappointed. Convinced as he was that the media in the United Kingdom were doing great damage to the nation he often pleaded that attention be given to the need for a newspaper that would report the secular world but from the basis of Christian and biblical principles. That nothing happened was not due to any lack of sympathy on the part of the Trustees but no way could be seen through the practical difficulties involved. The need certainly remains for God-honouring newsprint and for men capable to lead such an undertaking.

There was a side to John Marshall that was not known to the Banner Trustees in 1981, for he had been prepared for a role within the work that had not been anticipated. It concerned his summer vacations. For these he loved to travel with his family, and if a challenge or difficulty was involved then it was so much the better. From the 1970s, as we shall see in a later chapter, the family were several times at distant points in

Europe. In July 1982 they made a first visit to the United States, driving for three weeks in Colorado and Utah. His daughter Sarah recalls: 'Dad's interest in travel was marked by a particular keenness for extremes – the highest mountain, the longest river, and the furthest point were particularly appealing. After Dad died, when clearing out his study, Mum and I found a book on Alaska along with notes he had written. It was one of the "furthest points" he had always wanted to reach!'

This propensity for travel became of particular value to the Trust. He was at the Trust's office for the first time in Carlisle, Pennsylvania, in 1984, and thereafter was often present at the annual conference for ministers organized by Banner in the United States. No one from Britain was more warmly welcomed at those conferences than he was. His special friendships in the U.S.A. included the Banner Trustees, Ernest Reisinger, and 'Sonny' Peaster (at whose home in Yazoo City he was often to be a guest); and there was a wider circle of friends who first met him at the American conferences. The Rev. Michael Coleman, at whose Washington church he often spoke, writes:

> I first became acquainted with John Marshall through the Banner of Truth Conferences at Messiah College. For the first two years I just listened to him speak. I consider him one of the best preachers I ever heard. He was powerful, blunt yet very compassionate.

In 1988 the Marshall family's summer holiday was combined with work of the Trust when they drove 5,000 miles in South Africa and he preached and visited ministers in Johannesburg, Kimberley, Cape Town, Sharpeville (Vereeniging) and Kwa Zulu. His meeting with Flip Buys and elders in black churches in Sharpeville he especially appreciated.

But John's first love for travel was in the countries of Eastern Europe and it was here that his work for Banner was exceptional. It led not only to the wider circulation of literature in countries then cut off by the Iron Curtain,[5] but also to invitations to scores of pastors from those countries to attend the Leicester Conference. For many years John took on the responsibility of organizing the coming of these men; it was no small work and very often included meeting brethren who were entire strangers to Britain at London's airports and other locations. Probably hundreds of such men were thus introduced by John Marshall to the Leicester Ministers' Conference. One of the most moving and challenging sessions of the conference was the one devoted to these men who gave reports of the work of the gospel in their own countries. John normally chaired this and sometimes had to struggle with the difficulty of earnest men exceeding their allotted time. It would cause no little amusement to see John putting his hand on a shoulder trying to stop a man who was in full flow.

From the 1980s John shared with other Banner trustees who were ministers in chairing the Leicester Conference. Along with Iain Murray, he was invariably present. His generally unsmiling face could mislead the newcomer at first for he was a genial and lively chairman with a unique sense of humour. His exhortations to the assembled ministers came often as asides. A favourite way of introducing such rebukes would be, 'You will excuse me saying so but I think . . .' Other characteristic comments of his were, 'I must be very careful here', and, 'I am sorry if I am offending you. I don't want to offend you. If I am offending you perhaps you ought to be offended.' We still remember some of the addresses he gave to the Conference. Ian Densham has a reference to these occasions that gives an insight into the man: 'Time and again before preaching at the Banner Conference he would come into the room where I had

---

[5] For those who could read English he arranged the despatch of Banner books through the Book Fund operated by the Trust and at board meetings he frequently pleaded for funds to be directed to literature in the languages of Eastern Europe.

the recording equipment for a few moments of quiet. He often seemed distraught by the responsibility of preaching to his fellow ministers. Yet time and again we were lifted heavenward or challenged just at the right point.'

He had the ability to speak at short notice. One recalls the 2000 Conference when the appointed speaker for the first session was held up in a traffic jam on the motorway. John Marshall stood in with only thirty minutes notice. He spoke on 1 Samuel 4 and compared the spiritual situation in the United Kingdom to the defeat of the Israelites. The Israelites' so-called remedy in a crisis only led to a worse disaster and the verdict pronounced on Israel was 'the glory has departed'. Instead of indulging false hopes, he said, our attitude should be like that of Joshua after the defeat of Israel at Ai. He rent his clothes and sought the Lord. We needed to get down on our knees and find out why God had a controversy against us.

At Leicester, John usually arranged the leaders for the early morning prayer meetings which he regarded as so vital to the success of the Conference. After the conference sessions were over he would invite folk to his room for a chat and some good-humoured but heated debates took place on these occasions.

Once John entered the Westminster Fraternal (now more usually known as 'Fellowship') circle he was introduced to other agencies that soon looked to him for help. In the case of the annual Westminster Conference (previously the Puritan Conference) he was asked to speak in 1978 when Dr Lloyd-Jones was still the chairman. His subject was 'Puritan Use of Allegory, with Particular Reference to the Works of John Bunyan'. Later he became a member of the committee that organized this Conference.

In both the Fraternal and the Westminster Conference time was spent in discussion and John could usually be relied on to make sure it was not dull. He livened many discussions with inimitable contributions. On most subjects he had perceptive questions and decided views which he was ready to express vigorously. Once settled into combat with an opposing view he was not likely to withdraw.

The Rev. Graham Harrison, who became chairman of the Westminster Fellowship after the death of Dr Lloyd-Jones (1981), writes of John Marshall:

> John was a character! On that, all would be agreed! He never suffered fools gladly. Nor did he hesitate to call nonsense by its name. Forthrightness and ebullience were typical of him. Never slow to speak his mind, or to ridicule what he judged to be a perversion of the truth of Scripture, he sometimes could be misjudged as arrogant and uncaring. But in fact nothing could be further from the truth.
>
> In the discussion of the Westminster Fellowship you would rely on him to fasten on issues that were central to the point under discussion, even if others were not as quick as him to discern, or even agree, to their relevance. But if he could be sharp and vigorous in debate he expected others to respond in the same way and was not offended when they did so. Indeed if there were occasions when a chairman had to rein him in, or attempt to do so, there were many more when he became a chairman's best friend in that he guaranteed a somnolent gathering would suddenly be aroused into life and vigour by some provocative or incisive (sometimes both) comment that he had made!

John also became closely involved in two of the agencies which meant so much to Dr Lloyd-Jones, the Evangelical Library and the London Theological Seminary. Thoughts of a new theological College in England had exercised the minds of Reformed men since the early 1960s. For a time the Doctor doubted if it was needed, being firmly convinced that preachers are born not made. In the mid 1970s the practical needs of the situation convinced him that something had to be done.

He chaired the meetings of a sponsoring committee and, with a faculty of four ministers, the London Theological Seminary opened at Hendon Lane, Finchley on October 6, 1977.

Dr Philip Eveson, a subsequent Principal of the Seminary, has recalled:

> Soon after the Seminary began in 1977, when we were sorting out who should give occasional lectures on specific topics, I asked Doctor Lloyd-Jones if he had any suggestions on who could cover the subject of War and Violence. Without a moment's hesitation he said, 'John Marshall's your man.' And so John has spoken on that subject for us ever since and over a period which has witnessed Britain going to war with Argentina and Iraq (the Gulf War), besides the various violent scenes in many of our city and town centres and estates. In 2003 he was due to speak on this subject again – I wonder what he would have said about our further war with Iraq in the light of subsequent events? He also spoke at the Seminary on the Care of the Mentally Ill and preached for us from time to time.

In nothing was John more whole-hearted than in his commitment to the work of the Evangelical Library, speaking on occasions at the Annual Lecture and in all the behind-the-scenes work as a member of the Library Committee from 1991. When others sometimes despaired at problems the Library faced, he was resolute and ever pleaded that it should be given more support. His encouragement meant much to management and staff.

These agencies that had to do with the maintenance and propagation of the Reformed Faith were by no means all the ones to which he gave his aid. Others included the Sovereign Grace Union where he spoke regularly at their public meetings. There was also the Bible League. He joined the Bible League Trust in 1998 and entered enthusiastically into its witness. John Thackway, editor of the *Bible League Quarterly* says:

> He was a valuable contributor to the Trustees' meetings in London and preached at the 2001 Annual Meetings in Essex and Suffolk. We thank God for every remembrance of him, a brother beloved and a Mr Valiant-for-Truth.

6

VENTURES INTO
EASTERN EUROPE

The story of John Marshall's involvement in Eastern Europe has never been told. Apart from one article in *The Banner of Truth* magazine (December 1983) he put nothing in print. The reticence was due partly to his self-effacing nature and partly to the need for restraint about situations that could have had repercussions for others in the years when the Iron Curtain and the Cold War were realities.

Some of his journeys after 1981 had links with the work of the Banner of Truth Trust, as already noted, but they began well before that and all originated entirely with himself. 'As a child', his daughter Sarah writes, 'I thought that every family took the kind of holidays we did.' How far that was from being the case she only later realized. The motivation behind the ventures was her father's love of travel combined with a concern to contact Christians. Sarah continues:

> Wherever we went, one of Dad's first priorities would be to find a good church in the locality so that we could go and encourage God's people there. Obviously this was true in visiting Eastern Europe, but I also remember attending churches in Austria, travelling several hours to attend church in Carcassonne, and getting lost in Athens as we scoured Piraeus for a church.

After the initial summers visiting Eastern Europe in very Spartan camping conditions, in later years we had wonderful holidays in France, Italy, Greece, Yugoslavia, and on several occasions in America and Canada. Dad always managed to find the most amazing places to stay in – utterly obscure and out of the way locations which he loved!

BACKGROUND

There is a background to the Marshalls' first visit to Eastern Europe in 1974 that is too relevant to be missed. During the 1960s a Scot by the name of Colonel Robert Currie Thomson (1886–1967), who had served in the British Foreign Office, was looking eagerly for young Christian men who could carry on a mission that he had been conducting quietly and very effectively behind the Iron Curtain. In earlier years the kindness shown to his wife when dying of tuberculosis in a Polish sanatorium had established a bond with Eastern Europe and he knew its languages well.

In the summer of 1964 Thomson, then seventy-eight years old, took with him to Yugoslavia a young South African who worked at the Banner of Truth offices in London, Julian Sherman-Mouton. One of the most lasting contacts of that visit occurred in a Serbo-Croatian-speaking town where they gave a copy of a recently published Banner title, *A Commentary on Ecclesiastes* by Charles Bridges, to a young soldier who was later to write:

> After our dear guests had gone on their way I began to read and read and read. I had never had such an experience from any book before; I felt it fed my very soul! When I had finished I read it through again, and even today, now that I possess many hundreds of Reformed and Puritan writers, this book still occupies a very special place in my library and in my heart when I remember

that it was given to me by those dear brothers 'Uncle' Thomson and Julian.

The soldier was twenty-four-year-old Simo Ralevic. Born into a Serbian family in Kosovo, and belonging to the Orthodox Church, he had been converted two years earlier in the military barracks at Ilirska Bistrica in Slovenia. He left the army at the end of 1964, married and settled at Pec, where Colonel Thomson visited him again in 1965. With him was Roger Weil who takes up the story: 'We found Simo and his wife living in rather primitive circumstances in the small town of Pec where he had been born. He had felt God's call to return to this spot to testify to his family and numerous relations what great things God had done for him. Although he was able to support himself he believed that his real calling was to preach the gospel.'

FIRST VISIT
The friendship with Roger Weil led to Simo attending the Banner of Truth Ministers' Conference at Leicester in 1968 where he met John Marshall. It was Simo's invitation that first took John and his family to Yugoslavia in July 1974. With the whole family going – Susan and the four children (Rebecca was not quite two, Sarah five, Deborah eight and Jeremy eleven) – the family car was the only way to travel. At that time it was an Austin 1800 – known affectionately as the 'land crab' as it was nearly as wide as it was long. To prepare himself for the trip John bought a trailer and a frame tent. He had a practice run in Scotland where he left the tent poles behind! Son Jeremy retains vivid memories of the main event:

Dad packed up the Austin 1800 with masses of provisions of canned food – he never believed in too much exposure to the dangers of Continental cuisine – together with boxes of Bibles and Banner of Truth books.

We set out via Harwich and the Hook of Holland. On arrival at the Hook I remember it was raining heavily. In his inimitable style Dad had calculated that from there, if he drove 70 miles an hour for 10 hours, he could do 700 miles and accordingly had booked a place at a campsite 700 miles away on the Austrian/Yugoslav border. As happened rather often with Dad's optimistic plans – curious for a man whose character could be so pessimistic! – they had to be amended and about midnight, in pitch blackness, we found a campsite on the German/Austrian border. As bungling novices, we were helped by friendly locals – a type of event which occurred over and over again in our travels. At the worst times of disorganization and frustration some local would pop out of nowhere and save the day. He would be thanked in broken English, maybe with a few phrases from *Teach Yourself Serbo-Croat* and then disappear into the night – and it would usually be night – clutching some tins of spam, plus of course some suitable tract translated into approximately the right language. God certainly looked after us!

The stop the next night was near Split on the Adriatic coast and the story continues:

From the (relatively civilised) coast, we went on into the dusty and primitive inland, through Titograd, over the Cakor Pass (one lane with passing places, no crash barriers, hundred foot drops) to Pec in what is now Kosovo. Now at last our destination, Simo and his church, came into view. When we stopped the windscreen wipers had to be carefully removed as instructed by Simo (in case they were stolen) and then placed in Mum's handbag. They were too big for the bag so as we entered the church to meet the believers the ends stuck out. Simo was his wonderfully welcoming self, telling us in English what he was about to explain to the others in Serbo-Croat.

This was the first of several visits to Pec and conditions in Kosovo were not then as they later became. Jeremy has noted: 'Although Simo told us about the history and tensions, the area seemed normal – or as normal as Eastern Europe could be viewed from the eyes of the West. On subsequent visits, the atmosphere was more strained and one trip, in particular, I remember the central square was full of Yugoslav army armoured cars and conscripts.'

Referring to the mounting difficulties in Kosovo, John Marshall wrote in his one article on Eastern Europe (December 1983):

> Simo labours in an area which was controlled for many years by the Turks and today is 90 per cent Albanian Muslim. Looking around from a small rise on the outskirts of Pec one can count six minarets. Just recently there has been considerable trouble because many of the local population desire to set up some kind of independent state leading to closer ties with Albania. All seemed quiet when we were there but a number of Simo's congregation have moved away to the north of Yugoslavia. Simo, however, has resolved to stay in the area in the interests of his congregation, a very brave and caring action, giving evidence of how faith and love are powerful graces.

When the Iron Curtain eventually fell, the position of Christians in Kosovo only worsened. Roger Weil reported in *The Banner of Truth*:

> When talks between representatives of the European Union and President Milosevic broke down in May 1999, NATO was summoned to punish the Serbs by a prolonged bombing campaign, not only in Kosovo, but throughout Serbia itself. After three months, the Serb army and the paramilitary evacuated Kosovo leaving the remaining Serb civilian population exposed both to the Albanian Kosovo

Liberation Army (KLA) and to returning Albanian civilians seeking revenge for all they had lost and suffered.

In God's providence, Pastor Ralevic and his family
managed to escape to the north and to salvage from his
home in Pec (where some of the heaviest fighting of the
war had taken place) two-thirds of his personal library
and some items of furniture. However his literature ware-
house and office building just outside the town was totally
destroyed, as were the houses of his son, brothers, and
nephews in the village on the hill overlooking Pec.[6]

But the thirty years of Simo Ralevic's ministry at Pec bore
much fruit and John Marshall was privileged to play a part in
it. In 1971 Simo was persuaded to begin publishing his sermons (mainly evangelistic), at first only fifty cyclostyled copies,
but the number quickly grew to a thousand. This led to calls
for him to preach in many parts of Yugoslavia and to a much
more extensive publishing programme. In Simo's words: 'We
printed and distributed illegally thousands of New Testaments
and we printed about twenty-two books in Albanian and a
hundred different titles in Serbo-Croatian.' At one point he
would produce on average at least one title a year, with a print
run of five or six thousand copies. Roger Weil comments:

> Many hundreds of souls have been saved through read-
> ing his literature and a large part of his time was devoted
> to corresponding with those who had read his books and
> wrote to ask him for more. The Day alone will declare
> the full extent of his influence on Yugoslav Christianity.

Progress of this kind is never without opposition and Simo
had much to endure. His commitment to a Calvinistic understanding of the gospel meant an additional degree of isolation

---

[6] *Banner of Truth*, November 1999, p. 25. After many sufferings Simo and
his family eventually settled in Arandjelovac where he has a small church
and continues literature work.

in his own country. Sometimes the authors of the books he was reading were almost the only friends and teachers he had. John's own experiences of loneliness had prepared him to give sympathetic support, and from 1974 he stood behind Simo in a special way, sending books and arranging for him to come to the Leicester Conference on many occasions.[7] Simo devoured the books he received. Spurgeon's sermons, he would say, 'gave me the strength of a lion'. And the sermons of Lloyd-Jones and Albert N. Martin were not far behind, the latter through tape recordings.[8] Writing in 2003 by way of tribute to his dear friend, Simo recalled what John Marshall meant to him:

I was first introduced to the Banner Conference by my friend Roger Weil and to Banner books by Julian Sherman-Mouton. I started to come to the Conference thirty-five years ago. There I first met brother Marshall. Since that time we have been close friends in the Lord. He visited us in Pec several times. He was persistent. I don't remember much of his preaching but I do of our talks together. He was a very kind and humble person. In his character he was like his Master. He was a man of compassion and understanding. He never pressed his opinions on me but in love was interested in my opinions. . . . He made a great impact on my life. When I was persecuted he often called on the telephone to encourage me. When the U.N. bombardment started on Serbia he often called me to see how we were. . . . He was very gentle, but for the truth he was like a lion! And he did that in a very loving way. In

[7] Simo's regular attendance at Leicester Conference led to his speaking at churches in the UK, and this brought the needs of the evangelical churches in Yugoslavia vividly to the attention of his hearers.

[8] This is perhaps the place to set the record straight on Simon Ralevic's title, *The Tongue – Our Measure*, Banner of Truth, 1987. A Christian who heard these sermons in Serbo-Croat, and not realizing how much the preacher had benefited from Pastor Martin's sermons on the same subject, had them translated into English! Simo never hid the fact of how much his preaching depended on the work of others.

one word he was a man of integrity. I know that God has many choice servants but England became poor without John Marshall.

SOVIET UNION

The Marshalls' first visit to Yugoslavia paved the way for a longer and more hazardous journey to the Soviet Union. The decision to travel by car to and in that country with his whole family and a tent was one from which some of his friends tried to dissuade him. It was certainly a different proposition to Kosovo where he knew where to go and had in Simo a friend who could speak good English. What Susan Marshall thought of the proposition is not on record. Jeremy could later understand how the challenge appealed to his father's

buccaneering tendencies, doing something that others had not done, exploring in a dangerous if not hostile environment. Although appearing to others as the epitome of restrained Nonconformist rectitude, Dad's complex and multi-layered character – which he loved to endlessly analyse and examine – included a taste for adventure and even, dare I say, 'excitement' (for Dad felt that word was to be eschewed in Christian circles!) The adventure into Eastern Europe was a bold step.

At the same time John Marshall did not launch into Soviet Russia without careful thought and preparation. He was not irresponsible. 'Months before we travelled to Russia,' Sarah recalls, 'Dad would spend his Monday evenings (his day off) repeating incomprehensible Russian phrases to a Linguaphone. He was actually quite a good linguist. We were once travelling on an overnight train from Italy to France and happened to be sharing a carriage with a French girl and her boyfriend. I was studying A-level French at the time, but was completely lost when Dad got into a long conversation in French about the difference between Protestantism and Roman Catholicism after the girl had asked a leading question.'

Jeremy has given this account of their experiences in Eastern Europe:

> The arm of the State was everywhere, especially in Russia, which we went to twice. These were the longest and the most difficult of the visits. Firstly the border had to be negotiated. This would take several hours, as the whole car would have to be emptied and then driven away to be dismantled and examined. Every work of literature would be examined to see if it was suitable for Marxist-Leninist sensibilities. Several books – often quite unlikely ones, like a biography of Oliver Cromwell who as a republican and one would have thought quite acceptable – were confiscated. This was done, not in a brutal way, but along the lines of, 'We suggest we exchange this book for a biography of Lenin.'
>
> Dad was always open about the fact that he was bringing Bibles in English but that these were for personal use. Once, when doubt was expressed whether Becky at the age of four or five could actually read a Bible, Dad whipped one out and got Becky to read some verses from the Psalms. Then the whole car had to be put back together again. From then on our progress was closely monitored. Only a few roads were allowed to be used by Westerners. At each junction stood a police observation post complete with several militia or policemen monitoring the traffic. They would often stop us and say, 'Is this a British Volvo?' They had been told to look out for us but did not know what a Volvo looked like. By then the Austin 1800 had been retired!
>
> On several occasions with the terrible signposting – and it was all in Cyrillic – we got lost and would then be waved down by the police. On one occasion near the

Finnish border Dad had to disappear into a police post
for an hour and then sign a declaration in Russian acknow-
ledging his errors in going off the roads. At campsites
there would normally be a separate area for Westerners.
In Kiev, in the middle of this area, stood a little garden
shed in which twenty-four hours a day a watchman kept
guard over the Westerners. This was to make sure they
were not spreading counter-revolutionary ideas to the im-
pressionable local population! As we went around visiting
the Christians, in some cases people who had family members in labour camps, Dad was always convinced, rightly
I'm sure, that we were being followed by the police.

Deborah continues the story:

I went with my Dad from the campsite in Kiev to try and
find a Christian family. I felt quite privileged to have been
allowed to go on my own with Dad. We must have looked
obviously Western – indeed people often mistook Dad
for a German, an error of judgment which he always hastily corrected! We walked round a block of flats twice
before going in and I had a vague feeling of subterfuge.
We climbed many stairs in a dark, non-descript Commu-
nist block of flats, before knocking on a door. When it
was opened my Dad just said 'Christian'; the woman
looked at him a long time before letting us in. Maybe the
presence of a child with him suggested that this was OK.
On the way home we were walking at a brisk pace back
to the campsite when suddenly Dad knelt down with no
warning, as if to tie his shoe laces. I was holding his hand
and nearly fell over, a woman walked past us and after a
minute we carried on. Dad told me he thought she was
following us. I thought this was hugely exciting!
    Jeremy and I were taken with Dad to an unregistered
Baptist Church in Kiev one Sunday evening. We had a lift
with somebody else and seemed to drive for miles,

eventually ending up in quite a big building with at least 300 people there all gathering for worship. As we couldn't understand a word it seemed to be a very lengthy service. We had no way of knowing if we were near the end or not. To pray everyone knelt on the floor. The floor was very rough and I remember whispering to ask if it was OK to sit on the chair as my bare knees were suffering. I was given permission, and then felt a bit of a fraud when I realised the only other ones sitting up were ancient old ladies, who probably would never have been able to stand again if they had knelt.

Anyway, somebody spoke to Dad at some point and Dad whispered that we had been asked to sing. Russian families often sang in public and were very good. Dad was put on the spot. Here he was – unprepared, no piano to accompany us, a teenage son whose voice was breaking and a nine-year-old daughter and expected to sing to at least 300 Russians. Unlike the Von Trapp family we didn't have a singing repertoire up our sleeves. All we had were the metrical Psalms in the back of our Bibles. We duly stood up and sang the 23rd Psalm, or rather Dad stood up and sang the 23rd Psalm. Three hundred Russians looked back at us; stony faced and expressionless. What they must have thought! Dad cited this as his most embarrassing situation ever!

Deborah writes:

Travelling around Eastern Europe before the Iron Curtain came down was not very common, least of all in a tent with four children. Yet through the eyes of a child it did not seem strange at all. I, aged nine or ten, certainly had no concept of the dangers or anxieties that my parents may have had. It was just fun camping (most of the time), and meeting lots of people and being all together. Time was passed in the car with very few angry words being exchanged. My parents seemed to have endless patience telling stories; joining in our games or putting up with the music we played. There was no stereo system in the car, so we had a tape recorder and we each taped our favourite songs before we went and would be allowed to play our own tape for a certain amount of time. To conserve batteries we never used fast forward or rewind, but used a pen. We sang songs and all learnt the words of many traditional songs like, 'Green Grow the Rushes O!', 'O My Darling Clementine', 'The Skye Boat Song', 'The Ash Grove', 'You take the High Road', 'Bluebells of Scotland', etc. We were kept going by Dad's sweet tooth. He encouraged us each to save up sweets for weeks before so we each had a sweet tin which would last us a month.

John made one visit to Russia without his family in 1982. This time his travelling companion was Ray Birch and they flew on an official Intourist Tour. Deborah writes:

They took Bibles with them, and this time Dad had no place to hide them. He brought a large waterproof, quilted jacket, which had a lot of pockets inside and out. I don't know how many he took – Mum thinks it was about twenty. He put Bibles in all the pockets and there were so many it affected the way he walked even although they were paperbacks. When he was asked about Bibles, he showed his own. I don't know how these were distributed in Russia, but they visited Dushanbe (Tajikistan) and Samarkand (Uzbekistan). They stayed in hotels, and assumed, probably correctly, that the rooms were bugged. So when communicating with each other about churches etc, they wrote notes to each other. Dad's handwriting was dreadful, and Ray Birch couldn't read the notes!

Over a period of seven years John Marshall visited many churches in other parts of Eastern Europe, survived many searches and interrogations by border police, and brought much needed spiritual and practical support to small groups of Christians in Hungary, Romania, Poland, and Bulgaria. He genuinely wanted to make contact with Christians behind the Iron Curtain, to show Christian goodwill and to give some kind of encouragement and help where that might prove possible. Jeremy comments:

> Dad would say, when asked why he went, that even though the practical help – Bibles, money, literature – was of limited value, the fact that somebody in the West took the interest to visit these often obscure churches made the authorities realize that the Christians were not alone. Equally importantly, they encouraged the Christians themselves that somebody in the West was willing to take the time to go and see them.

When the Marshalls took their children with them on these ventures it had a further consequence John would not have foreseen. It took them into situations where the three girls and Jeremy had unusual opportunities to see the consistency of their father's character. Difficulties did not deflect him from God's work or subdue his witness. Every morning on Russian campsites there would be family prayers, complete with psalm singing, sometimes to the amusement of the locals. And when the only activities were those of travel and relaxation they remembered how he marvelled at the glories of God in his creation. As they stood in silence at a glacier in Canada on one occasion, with John lost in thought, Sarah asked him what he was thinking about. He replied, 'What an amazing Creation our God has made.' 'Above all', Jeremy was later to say, 'Dad was a man of God.'

5. John, Susan, Jeremy, Deborah, Sarah, and Rebecca on holiday in the former Soviet Union, 1978. Picture taken outside the Kremlin, Red Square, Moscow.

6. Leicester Conference, 1972 – John Marshall is in the centre, sixth row from the front.

7. (TOP) Simo Ralevic and John Marshall in conference at Leicester.
8. (BOTTOM) Speakers at Leicester, 1996 (L–R: Martin Holdt, Geoff
Thomas, John M. Brentnall, Paul E. G. Cook, John R. de Witt,
John Marshall).

9. Overseas visitors at Leicester in the mid-1990s with Iain Murray (front, first from right, kneeling) and John Marshall (standing, second from right).

7

PREACHER AND PASTOR

John Marshall had an exalted view of the ministry, of the preacher's call and the priority of the preaching of the Word.

HIS FLOCK
He considered that his first responsibility was to care for the flock that God had committed to his trust. Over the years John developed a method of preaching in which he would take a portion of Scripture and carry on each Sunday from where he had left off the week before – so the beginning of each sermon would consist of a brief re-capitulation of the previous week's sermon. In this way he was seeking to cover the whole of Scripture revelation, providing a 'balanced diet' for the regular congregation, morning and evening. He kept lists and records of his weekly sermon texts and also of the hymns and psalms sung lest he should be needlessly repetitive.

Although he had a comparatively small congregation he felt deeply responsible for them. His faithfulness to his own people over forty-five years can have few parallels in our day. For most of that time he laboured in comparative obscurity. Had his local work been larger it is probable he could never have achieved what he did elsewhere. He rested in the knowledge that God gives to every servant his own work.

In the last sermon preached at the Leicester Conference, when speaking of having to give an account of our ministry at the

Day of Judgment, he told of John Brown of Haddington's response to a minister who complained that he had only twenty-eight people in his church: 'You will find that quite enough to account for on the day of Judgment.' John Marshall saw to it that he kept in touch with his people. As well as visiting their homes, a regular component of his ministry on the Lord's Day was an 'open house' reception of any members of the congregation who wished to join him and the family in the manse lounge after evening service. A matter for debate might arise out of the preaching of the day or it could be a question introduced by one of the company.

Jeremy recalls, 'Although to some outside the congregation my father may have appeared to have been a stereotyped grim Calvinist, unwilling to allow any discussion of "the party line", the reality was the complete opposite.' He was always ready to prompt a lively discussion. Visitors were encouraged to share their views and sometimes conclusions were reached which rather surprised them. But the warmth of the handshake with which they departed was not to be doubted, it might well be accompanied with the gift of a book and such words as: 'I hope I wasn't too hard on you . . . I do so hope to see you again.' Jeremy adds, 'the "winningness" of his ways lay not so much in what he gave, or what he said, but in how he gave and said it.'

Preachers are born not made and this was certainly exemplified in John Marshall. He had a natural gift of oratory. He spoke with great enthusiasm and made his audience feel that what he was saying was well worth their hearing. In the presentation of his material he tended to be discursive rather than structured. This may have been due to the fact that he never wrote out his sermons and did not use notes in the pulpit. He often engaged a hearer by a very effective use of the rhetorical question. Irony could also be used to great effect although sometimes the reaction produced more laughter than he anticipated. As an avid reader of books on a wide range of subjects he had a fund of stories (some repeated rather frequently!) and illustrations.

An outstanding characteristic of his preaching was the way in which he would plead with sinners. This is illustrated in the testimony of Andrew Doggrell who sat under his ministry:

> It was when I was four years old that I can vividly remember the first words that the Holy Spirit said to me through Mr Marshall. I remember him saying, 'Children, did you know you can come to Christ?' Then he paused and his manner changed. With a stern look on his face he cried, 'Do you know you are a sinner? – lost, without God, bound for eternal punishment in hell – where the worm dieth not and the fire is not quenched, where there is weeping and gnashing of teeth?' He went on with words of entreaty that I cannot remember. This brought a tear to my eye, which I was quick to brush away for fear any member of my family might see. There was then another, deafening pause which I could not bear, as the silence gave my heart time to ponder eternity. Then he leaned forward in the pulpit and said softly, as he reached both arms out wide, 'Suffer little children to come unto me and forbid them not, for of such is the kingdom of heaven. Christ Jesus welcomes you to come unto him, did you know that? You, yes, you!' He concluded by inviting sinners to pray for a repentant heart and, as though reading our thoughts, he gave us this dialogue: 'Oh I want to come but I don't know how to pray!' 'Well, tell Almighty God – I am a bad, bad man, I hate all the wrong things I have done. I need you so much but I don't know you, help me Lord! I know you said whoever comes to you I will not cast out. Come to Him before it is too late.'

This is my earliest recollection of the impression upon me by the preaching of John Marshall when he was in his prime. He sought as best he could to bring the very youngest in his congregation to see their need of a Saviour. It was truly preaching to the whole congregation without regard to age or gender. I believe at four years old I was truly awakened, although not converted until twelve years later. Since then I have sat under the preaching of many capable and godly men but never heard the like of John Marshall.

John Marshall had supreme confidence in the ordinance of preaching. He saw it as the preacher's goal to convince people of the truth proclaimed and believed, and with Cotton Mather he heartily agreed that preaching was to 'recover the throne and dominion of God in the hearts of men'. The downgrading of preaching in the contemporary church he deplored, together with the 'lightness' adopted by too many 'grinning clerics'. A typical comment was, 'One does wonder whether Elijah, John the Baptist, and Paul were in the habit of grinning at their listeners in case it was thought their message was too serious and visitors might be put off by any evidence that they believed in hell and damnation.'

Such a change of approach on the part of preachers he saw as closely related to a change of appetite among the people. Many looked for music and entertainment instead of the Word of God. His scorn of all tendencies to entertainment in the churches was almost proverbial. He expressed it in an article in *The Banner of Truth* magazine, entitled 'Dance and Drama in Worship and Evangelism: A Contemporary Problem'. To those who insisted that a service must end by a certain time he demanded: 'Do you complain that your television programmes go on for too long? They go on for hours but some people say that half an hour is a long time to listen to the Word of God!'

That John was able to sustain a ministry in one congregation for forty-five years is in itself remarkable. Godliness nurtured by prayerful communion with the Lord was the secret strength of his preaching and ministry. The priority given to prayer in his own life was reflected in that of the congregation. Instead of the combined Bible Study and Prayer Meeting midweek, as is customary in so many churches, Friday evening was set aside for a Prayer Meeting.

It is not surprising that he was greatly loved by his people and that there are those who testify to the blessing received from his preaching and pastoral care. The following is the testimony of Iris Kinloch:

> I first attended Alexandra Road church in 1963, believing I was a Christian, but mostly by Mr Marshall's preaching I was challenged to reconsider my standing. My questioning also arose from his response to my request that our young child be baptized. He encouraged me to consider the reasons why I made the request. In my family background it was the tradition to have your baby 'christened'. Our discussion became a challenge to consider my standing before God. When I realized that I was not a Christian I rebelled and as a consequence had many years of trouble away from the church.
>
> Mr Marshall's preaching and the prayers of the folk in the church were not in vain, for I was converted and returned to Alexandra Road in 1984 where I was taught and greatly blessed. My husband and son, once very opposed, also came to sit under the ministry at Alexandra Road and it was a joy when our son was baptized as a believer. Before our son was converted Mr Marshall took a particular interest in him, encouraging him to seek either a job with better prospects or to go for further education. With this prompting he went on to college and then university, obtaining a good degree. It was through Mr Marshall's preaching, particularly a sermon on the conversion of the Philippian jailer, that my brother was converted. He also had strongly opposed my new-found faith but when listening to Mr Marshall preaching he had come to admit, 'He is right.'

Mr Marshall would visit my mother after the death of my father, when she was physically unable to get to church. She delighted in his visits. She had a great respect for him as he 'stood up for the truth'. When he went to see her in hospital, just before she died, although very weak she managed a smile for him. Mr Marshall was also concerned for our family who lived in Dorset. They had many problems and, when he heard that our daughter was unexpectedly in hospital, he dropped everything and in less than half an hour was driving us down to Dorset so we could look after the family and four grandchildren. When I went to him with problems and questions he helped me, not by telling me what to do or think but by getting me to think in the right direction, often with the help of one or more of his many books. I have many reasons to thank God for his ministry.

From the days of his conversion John Marshall sought to be a soul winner. The personal witness he began at Mansfield College, which so helped David Winch, he continued throughout his life. Readiness to speak of the Saviour was for him one mark of the Christian. If his forthright presentation of the gospel aroused opposition it also brought to salvation such individuals as the four teenage 'rockers' that suddenly came to the church in February 1961.

OPEN AIR PREACHING

It was concern for people that constrained him from his early years in Hemel Hempstead to take the gospel to the local open-air market. This practice he was to continue every other Saturday morning through most of his pastorate. Sarah writes:

His preaching in the market was something that was very much a feature of our childhood. As a child I did not appreciate the huge strength of character and faith which it took for him to stand there as he did week after week, but I came to find it awe-inspiring as an adult. At one point, some years ago, he tended to stop preaching if it started to rain, until one market trader – a regular listener – teased him about it, declaring that the traders had to keep going, even when the rain poured down. From that moment Dad refused to stop, no matter what the weather was like! On occasions there were torrents of abuse to bear, contemptuous remarks made and even rotten fruit thrown. He remained resolute and courteous at all times. Sometimes when he was heckled by one man, another would threaten to thump the heckler to shut him up. Dad always saw the humour in such situations and was encouraged by any kind of support.

In this open-air forum he loved to engage in debate with the local youths. Perspicacious as he was, it often took him only a few minutes to establish which local school they attended, and then to draw them into conversation. What I always found incredible was that, in spite of the fact that he preached there – as everywhere – without notes, repeated interruptions and distractions never prevented him picking up the thread of his sermon again, and carry on before breaking off again for the next passer-by. He was well acquainted with many of the local characters who used to sidle in and out of the betting shop as Dad preached and would often challenge them, or tease them about how much money they had lost!

Through more than thirty years the minister of Alexandra Road continued this open-air preaching and yet without knowing an instance of any saving response. While he deeply regretted that fact, he remembered that gospel proclamation had more than one effect and that thousands in Hemel Hempstead had been left without excuse. But there were consequences of this market-place ministry other than the conversion of non-Christians. Sometimes it led to far-reaching relations with believers from other parts who happened to hear him.

One Saturday in the 1970s as John was preaching as usual in the market a short dark man stood attentively right in front of him. When he finished the stranger introduced himself, he was Chuba Ao from Nagaland, who was then working at the local hospital as a porter. Over the next few months the church got to know him and his wife well. Within living memory his family had been headhunters in Nagaland, in the far north-east of India. Chuba Ao was involved in establishing the Nagaland Bible Institute and had a vision for the whole area which he shared with John Marshall. As a result, when he returned to Nagaland they corresponded regularly. Over the years John was to send him most of the entire range of Banner of Truth books and in gratitude Chuba Ao named the College library the 'John Marshall Memorial Library'.

Another Christian hearer of the market place ministry was a school friend of Jeremy Marshall's who became a missionary. After he had been away from Britain for a quarter of a century, he returned to a very changed homeland only to find John Marshall still preaching the gospel in the Hemel Hempstead market on a Saturday. It was a lesson to him on perseverance and he wrote to the preacher: 'For me it was a great encouragement to see after a twenty-five year absence from the United Kingdom . . . your faithfulness to the gospel.'

Who can say what other consequences followed this apparently unfruitful open-air preaching?

TRAFALGAR SQUARE

It would appear that as the years passed John's burden to reach the lost with the gospel increased and a new opportunity opened to him after he met and began a friendship with Sebastian Mani at the Leicester Conference in 1995. Sebastian was brought up as a Roman Catholic. He had been converted in 1983 after he had applied for a free Bible correspondence course advertised in the Indian newspaper he was reading. By this means the Bible came into his life and spoke to his heart, especially the words of 1 John 5:11–13 and Revelation 3:20. Later, when in Saudi Arabia, the attempt of Muslims to convert him to Islam had the opposite effect:

> That is where God called me, gave me a burden for the Islamic world and brought me to England. I began preaching in the open air from 1991, first at Tower Hill then at Speaker's Corner, Hyde Park, and wherever and whenever there was opportunity. In August 1995 I was present at a large Islamic rally in Trafalgar Square, and heard everyone asked to convert to Islam including the Queen, the Royal family, and others.

It was the latter event that prompted Sebastian to raise with John Marshall the need for open-air preaching in the heart of London. At Marshall's invitation, Sebastian attended the Westminster Fellowship where he met Rev. Geoffrey Gobbett of Hope Baptist Chapel and shared the same concern with him. This led to the first Gospel-Preaching Rally in Trafalgar Square on 12 October 1996. Hundreds of Christians including a number of pastors supported this meeting and all were encouraged with the response.

A second attempt met with disappointment due to various technical problems. Better planning was clearly needed and John Marshall suggested the need for an organization with the responsibility for arranging future meetings. Thus the 'Biblical Gospel Ministries' was established. Others co-opted were the Rev. Stuart Pendrich of Days Lane Baptist Church, Sidcup, Frederick Raynsford of Camberwell Evangelical Church,[9] and Joseph Pettitt of the Alexandra Road congregation who later agreed to become the Treasurer. From that time to the present these occasional meetings in Trafalgar Square have been continued.

---

[9] The friendship with Mr Raynsford led to his joining the Board of Trustees of the Banner of Truth Trust.

PASTORAL CONCERN

John Marshall's commitment to preaching was matched by his concern for the individual. Sarah writes:

> He was always keenly sympathetic and concerned about anybody with difficulties and would pray repeatedly for pupils I mentioned at home who had particular difficulties. An incident that occurred when Dad had to have his kidney removed illustrates this. At the time, I had been spending a lot of time talking with a girl called Ali, who was experiencing a very traumatic situation. I often used to talk the issues through with Dad and ask for his wisdom. I knew that he would pray for her. When we arrived to see Dad in the hospital after his operation he had just come round from the anaesthetic. As he opened his eyes and saw us all at the foot of the bed, he said something to Mum, then looked at me and said, 'How's Ali?' I was astounded, but it was typical of Dad.

One of his daughter Rebecca's special memories was of the way her father would visit an invalid aunt across the other side of London in Hackney. 'She became increasingly confused but Dad faithfully visited her weekly. I loved the car journeys with him as we would have great times to chat. He always showed his love and fulfilled any duty in such a practical way.'

The same testimony comes from a man whom John met only once:

> I met John Marshall in the South of France. It was the summer of 1993. He was holidaying with his family in a house in the mountains. I was depressed by my sinfulness and by difficult circumstances. John not only took my mind off my difficulties by talking about a book of literary criticism (I am an English teacher). He also enthused about a book which could help me through depression. Several weeks later I received a package through the post

which contained Thomas Boston's book, *The Crook in the Lot*. It helped me! What a delightful man. If the Lord Jesus can make a sinner like John Marshall, as kind, as thoughtful, as interesting – what must the Lord himself be like? I never met John Marshall again.

THE PASTOR'S PASTOR

To many it was as a pastor's pastor that John Marshall made his most lasting impression. He showed the sympathy of one who had himself been in the furnace and suffered in battles for truth and righteousness. He knew from experience what it was to fight against depression in his own life and that of others. His concern to help others also led him to the study of mental illness and he came to understand it well as a later chapter in this book will show. He would urge that if men would avoid mental trouble they must lead a balanced life. Hard work, rest, and recreation must all have their place if the mind is to be kept from a preoccupation with itself.

As a 'minister to ministers' he had a role given to few. Friends who rang the manse very often heard the recorded words, 'The number you are calling knows you are waiting.' It meant he was on a call to a fellow minister with words of encouragement. Jeremy Marshall recalls: 'Any beleaguered struggling pastor of a small cause, with his back to the sea and seemingly on the brink of defeat, like the British Army at Dunkirk, only had to call Dad and he would be on his way again. He had a tremendous ministry of encouragement to pastors, not least, as he knew himself what Dunkirk experiences could be like.'

The Rev. Ian Densham of St Ives, in a tribute to his friend wrote:

I first got to know John Marshall well in the mid-1970s. I had recently become the minister of a church in Oxfordshire and was invited along to a minister's fraternal by the Rev. Edwin King. This fraternal was held at the manse of Alexandra Road Congregational Church. For about six years while I was in the area, I attended this fraternal which was wisely led by John. It was the most profitable and spiritual fraternal I have ever attended thus far. John's counsel, advice, and insights into whatever passage of God's Word we were studying were full of rich spirituality and practical application . . . The fraternal was for me a spiritual oasis in what became very difficult years.

Sebastian Mani writes:

He was like a father to me as the apostle Paul was to Timothy. I understood him as one of the spiritual giants in wisdom and in the understanding of the Word of God. I wish I had spent more time with him, learning more. He was a man who spent time with God even when the days were so busy. Once I called him late in the night and asked if he might be getting ready to sleep. 'No, Sebastian, I am reading my Bible', was the reply.

An amusing incident can be told in connection with his concern to help others. When the present writer was going through a period of difficulty John was determined to make time to call on him when he flew to Edinburgh for a Banner of Truth Trustees' meeting. He wondered what he would bring to cheer the sufferer and decided upon a giant-size tin of chocolates. This he had carefully stored in the overhead locker above his seat in the plane only to forget it on arrival in Edinburgh. Only later in the day, at the Banner offices, did he receive a message from the airport informing him of the package he had left on the plane and that its discovery had caused the evacuation of the return flight to London! Understandably not everyone shared our amusement.

An overseas pastor whom John helped was Michael Coleman of Bowie, Washington. The latter writes:

I treasure the relationship I had with John. Not only the time we spent together on his visits to the United States, but also his phone calls to me from his home in England. We would discuss ministry issues, personal issues, and of course laugh a bit. Now that I am writing this down I see that John was really a pastor to me – a pastor to a pastor. What a great calling – what a great man!

John's view of his life was very different. Writing from Hemel Hempstead, he commented in a letter to his friend Iain Murray on 5 July 1984:

On Saturday I have my 26th Anniversary here. It is very humbling that I have achieved so little. Nevertheless it is only by God's grace I have survived the opposition I have encountered.

The loyalty of the congregation meant much to him. He had been particularly appreciative on his twenty-fourth anniversary when his people gave him a full set of Calvin's *Commentaries on the Old and New Testaments*. The pastor of the Alexandra Road Church had been given the abilities that would have fitted him for various successful careers: the one that satisfied him was the service of God's people in the place where God had put him.

8

THE LAST BATTLE

John Marshall belonged to a generation that did not complain about illness and never made a fuss about it. For many years his health was good; he rarely took a day off sick. When he was diagnosed with cancer in 1999 he was well aware of the implications but was accepting of God's will. His one concern was that he would be able to continue to preach as long as possible.

The following year he faced surgery for the removal of a kidney. He understood the seriousness of what was involved, and was helped by his respect for and trust in the renal surgeon looking after him. He was to refer to this event, with its possibility of death, in the last sermon he preached (on 1 Cor. 3.11) outside his own pulpit in Winslow, Buckinghamshire, on 28 June 2003. 'We are all dying souls', he reminded the congregation, 'and we must make sure of our hope for eternity. When faced once with a drastic operation I said to myself, "John, you better have got it right." '

The kidney operation took place on 14 January 2000. In the very early post-operative period it was also found that he suffered from atrial fibrillation. This led to a visit to a cardiologist who indicated that he would be taken into theatre next morning, his heart would be stopped and then restarted; this procedure the cardiologist assured him should cure the problem. John, never one to be hesitant or passive, immediately replied, 'Oh no, you won't'. The cardiologist was a little surprised by the reaction of his patient but agreed to an alternative course of action and after a few days humbly confessed that John's opinion had been the right one! He had had the irregular heart beat for years.

Following this his main concern was to know how long the recovery time would be. He was eager to get back to work, and with that in view he adopted a good regime of rest, gentle exercise, and increasing activity. This was closely monitored by his surgeon. There were regular CT scans and within a year these revealed secondaries in his left lung. The surgeon wanted him to consult an immunologist but as the treatment was experimental, with unpleasant side-effects and an unknown success rate, John declined. The surgeon consulted his colleagues and was satisfied with John's decision. Later check-ups showed that the secondaries were growing very slowly, but not increasing in number.

For two years he enjoyed reasonable health but he was reaching seventy years of age and was sometimes frustrated that he did not have the energy which he once enjoyed. Yet he did not want to sit back and become 'old'. Susan says: 'He disliked refusing offers to preach, especially from small and less well-known causes. He always wanted to continue to preach. He considered retiring but could obtain no guidance or peace about it. His family urged him from time to time to slow down.'

In the final sermon he preached at the Leicester Conference he shared his feelings with his fellow ministers: 'I am old, getting old anyway, and people say to me, "Why don't you seek a wider ministry?" I don't want a wider ministry. Who wants a wider ministry? I don't think I care at all for that. But at the same time we do get restless, don't we? But be careful about resigning. I don't say you should never change your position; I didn't say that at all; I say, accept God's ordained place for you. If he changes your position, well and good. It is God who ordains our situation.'

FIGHTING ON
John's daughter Deborah says:

> The extraordinary thing was that although we could see
> that Dad didn't have the energy he once had – it was
> obvious to us – yet when he preached you would never
> think anything was wrong. Despite being exhausted after
> preaching, so that sometimes he could not even eat for a
> while, seeing him in the pulpit you would never believe it
> was the same man. Dad said to me on many occasions
> that he had been called to preach and that is what he
> wanted to continue to do. He quoted the verse, 'I must
> work the works of him that sent me while it is day. The
> night cometh when no man can work.' He was a fighter
> in many senses, and to carry on, despite not feeling as
> well as he thought he should, was his life. 'I won't give
> up,' he used to say.

The spirit just described was exactly what we saw when he
spoke for the last time at the Banner of Truth Ministers' Conference at Leicester on 3 April 2003. Although he was not due
to preach till the closing session on the Thursday he arrived
for the opening of the Conference on the Monday as he had
always done for almost forty years. During those years he had
chaired many sessions, and given addresses and sermons that
were greatly appreciated. At the 2003 Conference there was a
particular anticipation among the men and speculation on what
he would take for his text. There was perhaps a measure of
surprise that he chose the familiar story of David and Goliath
and delivered its message to us with all his customary insight,
vigour, and tender encouragement. One could scarcely believe
there was anything wrong, yet afterwards he was utterly
exhausted and took a week to recover.

Back in his own pulpit on Easter Sunday, 20 April 2003, he
found that he could not physically continue preaching the sermon. Interpreting it as exhaustion, John and Susan went away

for two weeks rest. But he was no better and continued to lose weight. On return to Hemel Hempstead a visit to his GP and a blood test revealed he had a late onset of diabetes. A specialist then put him on medication and a strict diet. It was also found that his atrial fibrillation was not well controlled which would result in a lot of symptoms of tiredness. He was referred to a cardiologist who adjusted his medication.

A close ministerial friend of his was also suffering from cancer. Ian Childs was the Secretary of the Westminster Ministers' Fellowship. In spite of his own weak condition John visited him in his home and shortly after wrote some touching comments in the Alexandra Road *Congregational Newsletter* that were to become so true of himself:

> It is a most solemn thing to sit beside a man whom one has known in full vigour of health and usefulness and now his voice is weak, his countenance ashen, and he stands at the very gates of eternity . . . for the Christian the way to death is not always easy, nor for the Christian minister is the way to death always easy . . . We may reflect on the terrible predicament of those whose bodies decay and yet they themselves have no glorious Saviour to lead them to the gates of death.
>
> Let us reflect on the glories of our Saviour who never leaves us or forsakes us.
>
> > Jesus loves me, loves me still,
> > When I'm very weak and ill.
>
> How glorious is the Christian religion! – to know that not a hair shall fall from our heads, and nothing shall happen to us outside his divine purposes. How good that, as his family and friends looked upon their dying husband, father, and pastor, he was 'Safe in the arms of Jesus.'

Ian Childs passed away on 26 April 2003 and the funeral was arranged for 1 May. In spite of his increasing weakness

John was determined to be at the funeral service which he conducted with the Rev. Charles Sleeman. John preached on 1 Corinthians 15:22 and paid tribute to Pastor Child's faithfulness, ordered life, uniqueness, great strength of personality, and quiet thoughtful maturity. Deborah speaking of this occasion says 'He felt an utter duty to take the dear friend's funeral despite feeling so ill; and that was the kind of man he was, putting principles and duty first before his physical well-being.'

As already mentioned, the last occasion on which John Marshall preached away from his own pulpit was on Saturday, 28 June 2003 when he spoke at Benjamin Keach's Meeting House in Winslow where it is the custom to hold a special service each year at Midsummer. His text on that occasion was 1 Corinthians 3:11, 'For other foundation can no man lay than that is laid, which is Jesus Christ.' Pastor T. D. Martin, a trustee of the chapel, recalls the occasion: 'He preached with much force and power of spirit and in the Spirit, though with evident weakness – with a strong voice at the outset, yet scarce a whisper at the close. There was a solemnity and sweetness in that little chapel on that fine evening.'

He was destined to have only two more Sundays in his own pulpit. The last occasion was 13 July 2003. His text in the morning was Romans 8:15–16 and in the evening 2 Timothy 2:24–26. Deborah takes up the story:

> On the Monday after his last Sunday in the pulpit, he joined us on holiday in Devon for two weeks. He loved holidays and was looking forward to spending time with some of his family and recuperating further. On the Saturday he was so delighted and enthusiastic for us when we rang to say that, despite various car problems we were having, we were now leaving Preston as planned and were on our way to Devon where he would be joining us on the Monday. When he arrived he was obviously in pain

with his back and during the two weeks there he was very unwell. He admitted he didn't feel well, but again his attitude was typical. He didn't lie around complaining of feeling ill and lamenting lost holiday time; he just couldn't understand why he didn't feel better. We talked about retirement, and again he said he did not think that it was the right thing to do. I remember talking about how he was trying to slow down a bit, how he had stopped taking so many invitations to preach and how he had agreed to let others take a Bible Study once a month. He told me that he already had a couple of sermons prepared mentally. He was planning ahead, keeping on top of things. I still find it strange that he went to glory with sermons that he had not been able to preach.

After the holiday in Devon John and Susan went to Norfolk. In spite of great discomfort he attended worship twice on the Lord's Day at Cromer Baptist Church. David Ellis from Stowmarket, who was present that day, wrote later to Susan, 'Little did I know that when I spoke briefly with Mr Marshall at Cromer Baptist Church on Lord's Day 10 August, he would so soon be going home to glory. He looked unwell and commented on his discomfort but was with the Lord's people to sit under his Word. What an example and inspiration he has been to so many of us!'

David Ellis also wrote: 'Who would ever forget that inimitable style of preaching that was his? He will be sorely missed by all who love the truths to which he witnessed so faithfully and enthusiastically. When one heard him one wanted to glorify the Lord. His closing sermon at the Banner conference was an inspiration and encouragement to us all. Though I do not know you personally as a family, I do wish to express to you my deepest sympathy in your loss but also to rejoice with you in his gain. May the God of all comfort be especially near to you all at this time.'

LAST DAYS

On returning home he immediately went to see his GP. Three
days later he fell on the road outside the home and was admitted to hospital for what were to be the last two weeks of his
life. Deborah recalls: 'By this time, his physical needs became
great, as he was in a great deal of pain. I remember telling him
that his ultra-sound scan showed that he had cancer in his
liver. He and we already knew that he had secondaries in his
bones, causing the pain. His response was, "That means I
haven't got long then". As many friends were now concerned
for him, the family set up a website that would give regular
reports on his condition. This was widely appreciated and read
by many. The entry on 21 August read:

> Dad was admitted to hospital following a rapid decline
> in his health which culminated in a fall in the road on
> Saturday afternoon. He is in the West Herts Hospital
> which is very close for Mum and where he is being well
> looked after.'

Deborah continues:

> He asked that we should pray for him to have the strength
> to die, and he spoke about death being the last enemy.
> Having been a minister for forty-five years, and used to
> visiting people who were dying, he had some idea of what
> was ahead. He got weaker every day and we would read
> the Bible to him. Yet he still remained very much in con-
> trol, being involved in decision-making about his
> treatment and pain control. He was a very strong
> character and this was obvious to the staff, both nursing
> and medical. People facing death go through many differ-
> ent emotions; they can become angry or depressed or go
> into total denial. Dad seemed very accepting, he felt he
> was being well looked after in hospital and, as the hospi-
> tal was so close to home, visiting was no problem. His

character shone through when he must have been feeling so dreadful, taking an interest in other patients and the nurses; always interested in letters, phone calls, and messages that now came to us on the website. He was always unfailingly polite. He was greatly loved by his family and he loved them very much too.

As his condition deteriorated during this week he was able to see few visitors apart from the family. One of these was the church elder, Mr Leslie Gibbons, with whom he spoke about supply for the pulpit. Another was the Rev. Ian Hamilton who was a great support to the family at this time. After Ian's move from Scotland to Cambridge in 1999 John had come to value his fellowship. One of the very last friends to visit him was Dr Peter Golding who later recalled the time in a tribute in the *Evangelical Times*:

> He was weak to the point of exhaustion, breathless, emaciated, and hardly able to raise a whisper. But in spite of the pain and physical distress he was as ever strong in spirit. I reminded him of Arthur Pink's dying words to his wife: 'He doeth all things well, my dear. All things, not some things.' But after I had spoken a few faltering words of what I trust was encouragement, John gave me a final word, 'Be faithful to the end.'

Deborah resumes her narrative:

> Right up to twelve hours before he died, when he lapsed into unconsciousness, he continued to make decisions. He made it very clear that he wanted his family with him and during those last two days he was never alone. Some of his last words were calling on God to take him to heaven. He knew he was going to glory to be with the Lord Jesus Christ, his work was finished and he finally departed from us to go to be with Christ 'which is far better'.

On the following day, 29 August 2003, just before midnight he slipped away into the world to come. Jeremy recounted the last moments:

> As Dad lay dying in his bed in the hospital we asked Ian Hamilton, 'Does God send his angels to fetch his children to him?' 'Oh no', said Ian, 'When it's important family business the Lord Jesus comes himself.' I am *absolutely sure* that as I sat holding Dad's hand at just before midnight on the 29th August the Lord Jesus himself came and summoned his faithful servant.

On the website notice it was recorded: 'At twelve minutes to midnight on Friday 29th August our beloved Dad slipped peacefully in his sleep from us to glory, to the cry of Hallelujah from his family.'

How appropriate to think of Mr Standfast in *Pilgrim's Progress*:

> Then there came a summons for Mr Standfast . . . that he must prepare for a change of life, for his Master was not willing that he should be so far from him any longer . . . Now while he was thus in discourse, his countenance changed, his strong man bowed under him and after that he said, 'Take me, for I come unto thee', he ceased to be seen of them.

THE FUNERAL

The funeral was arranged for Thursday, 11 September 2003. Family, church members, and friends from near and far made their way to the church where the one they wished to honour had preached the gospel for forty-five years. That voice was silent but the worship and praise of Almighty God continued. The service, conducted by the Rev. Ian Hamilton, began with a rendering of Psalm 90:

> Time, like an ever rolling-stream
> Bears all its sons away;
> They fly forgotten, as a dream
> Dies at the opening day

The Scriptures were read by Joseph Pettitt and, following another hymn, there was a touching and memorable eulogy of his father given by Jeremy. In the words of a friend, 'He painted such a graphic picture of "Mr Stand-up-for-Jesus", that anyone who had not known John Marshall could have felt as if they had been well acquainted with him. Elder Leslie Gibbons paid tribute on behalf of the church. Ian Hamilton then preached from Revelation 7:9–17 on the white robed multitude who have come out of great tribulation. The committal was in Woodwells cemetery, on the edge of the country, as another dear friend and fellow Banner Trustee, Frederick Raynsford, led in prayer and the assembled congregation sang, 'Safe in the arms of Jesus'.

The affectionate interest shown in John Marshall and his family during the last traumatic week was deep and worldwide. Messages of support poured in. This was followed by letters of tribute and sympathy, many of them appearing on the website.

Dr Sinclair B. Ferguson, with whom John had served in the Banner of Truth work for several years, wrote to Susan:

> Earlier in the year, as John preached at the closing session of the Leicester Ministers' Conference – with such grace and unction – I was overtaken by a sense that perhaps the explanation for the unusual occasion it was might be that it would be the last time many of his friends would ever hear him preach. I do wish you could have been there to have heard him, such was the blessing of his ministry. It now seems to me to have been a little intimation of the Lord's love for him, when John himself seemed to grow

in grace, assurance, joy in proclaiming Christ, confidence in the gospel.

John was such a warrior – and now he has placed his sword in tribute at Christ's feet. Yet to me on a personal level he was full of kindness, friendship, encouragement, full of good fun, full of a seriousness of spirit that was a model to me. Thank you for sharing him with me.

Another long-standing friend was the Rev. Ernest Reisinger, also a fellow-Trustee of the Banner, whose biography had been published by the Trust in 2002 and who died in 2004. He wrote:

Dear Susan,

You have lost a devoted husband and I have lost a very dear friend, but our loss is his gain. As you know, I considered John one of my close friends. We shared many of the same desires for the kingdom of God. He had a wonderful catholic spirit and a heavenly zeal for God's truth and the propagation of it. He had a compassionate heart for poor, lost sinners. I will truly miss our phone conversations.

The last conflict is over and the last enemy subdued ('the last enemy to be destroyed is death' – 1 Corinthians 15:26). Death was not a calamity to your dear husband. I believe his soul marched in triumph to his chosen home, the scene of his abiding rest.

We do not weep for him but for ourselves. We are the sufferers; we are the losers. He has gained heaven, and his gain may also become our joy if we follow the example of his faith in Christ. He has now changed places of service, but he has not changed Masters. Revelation 22:3–4 says, 'And there shall be no more curse, but the throne of God and of the Lamb shall be in it, and his servants shall serve him. They shall see his face . . .' This being

true, what John did in this house he is now doing in the
higher house; and it is all one and the same – the same
service and the same Master.

'The good Husbandman may pluck His roses and gather
His lilies at any time that He chooses – they are all His.
He may transplant His trees from lower ground to higher
ground where there is no more sunlight. He may do this
at any season of the year. They are all His.'

Yes, you will miss John very much, but some of us will
soon be where he is. Yes, I expect soon to be with my
blessed Redeemer. My wasting strength daily reminds me
that the sands of time are sinking, and I often read my
own funeral hymn, 'The Sands of Time are Sinking':

Until the day dawns and the morning star rises in your
heart.

From your sympathizing friend,
Ernest C. Reisinger

A moving tribute was also to come from one of the younger
generation of ministers whose life had been touched by John
Marshall, the Rev. J. Philip Arthur:

Dear Mrs Marshall,
I only heard of your husband's entrance into glory early
this week and could not travel south for the funeral but I
wanted to say that while no one will miss him more than
you do, many others will certainly miss him. As a regular
at the Westminster Conference, I recall many delightful
occasions when his interventions had us all moving in a
moment from high good humour to serious reflection.
Your husband was a 'character' in the best sense, robust
and manly yet with the simplicity of a child. In particular,
I don't know that I will ever forget his closing address
at this year's Leicester Conference. Trials in my own

situation made it especially applicable and I have lived on the memory of it from April till now. Few sermons have touched me more. May the Lord comfort you as only he can! Will we ever see his like again?

HIS WIFE

The influence of John Marshall's life and ministry owed so much to his wife. In his striking address on *The Puritan Woman* at the 1994 Westminster Conference he began with the text 'Who can find a virtuous woman? For her price is far above rubies' (*Prov.* 31:10). He found her in Susan. They were a truly devoted couple and happily married for nearly forty-two years. Although they were different in temperament they complemented each other. John was pessimistic; Susan was an optimist. She was the quiet support behind all that he did. John was in turn fiercely protective of his wife. Susan coming as the young bride to the Alexandra Road manse had quickly to learn her role as the minister's wife. She was destined to bring up a family of four, give herself to hospitality in the home, and share in the difficulties of church life. After the children left home she became her husband's secretary and personal assistant. She handled all the typing of letters and the sending of faxes and e-mails. John joked that he was 'with it' when they went 'on-line' but, as his family would say, he probably didn't know how to turn the computer on! His favourite means of communication was the telephone, which according to the family, was 'always hot from overuse – calls in and out'.

In speaking on behalf of the family Deborah pays tribute to their mother:

When Dad's health deteriorated over the last year, Mum continued to minister to his needs with love and always putting him before herself. She tried to ease his workload by acting as chauffeur whenever possible for example and encouraging him. She must have been so worried seeing his health decline, yet she didn't try and tell him what she thought he should do, she was always a supporter. She accepted what he wanted to do (carry on preaching) and saw her role as enabling him to do that. When he was diagnosed with diabetes, she had to change a lifetime's eating habits, not an easy thing to do. Mum was only a little younger than Dad, and it would be easy for anyone in the same position to think that they should have the 'right' to retire and enjoy life a little, with less work. Like Dad, she acted on principle and duty and love to God foremost and to Dad secondly.

When Dad was dying, he continued to express concern for her and Mum continued to care for him even in hospital. We took all his meals up to him, and helped care for him there. Mum never expressed anger or resentment at the turn of events. Her years of faithfulness walking with God have meant that she knows who her 'safe stronghold and fortress' is.

THE GOOD SOLDIER

It was destined that from his early childhood John Marshall should be caught up in warfare. At first it was the sound of bombing as he became caught up in the London Blitz, and then the echoes of previous conflicts from the stories told him by his father. 'Had he lived in another age', says Iain Murray, 'he would have made a fine sea captain under Drake, or a fearless infantry officer on the North-West Frontier.' He loved king and country. He loved the history of the British Empire. He loved to read of battles; the exploits of our generals and admirals seemed to fire him and he passed them on to his own family.

As a Christian he soon became aware of the greater conflict that was taking place in this world. He could discern the way in which Christ's kingship over the nations worked out in

Britain's history. 'Them that honour me I will honour' is true
of nations as well as individuals. As he made clear in a Westminster Conference paper on the subject, he could see the hand
of providence in the great national deliverances like the defeat
of the Spanish Armada.

Donald Underwood in paying a tribute to John said: 'His
imagination may have been fired in part by G. A. Henty, but
much more by the Reformation and the example of the Marian
Martyrs. He is remembered for his slipping away from a daughter's wedding reception to stand in morning coat at the annual
commemoration at the Smithfield Martyrs' Memorial. He was
constant and fervent in prayer that the judgment of God upon
our nation for its abuse of its Protestant heritage might be
averted.'

But, above all, it was his membership of the spiritual army
of the great King that meant most to him. The words of William
Williams sung at the funeral service would be John's testimony.

> Onward march all-conquering Jesus,
> Gird Thee on Thy mighty sword.
> Sinful earth can ne'er oppose Thee.
> Hell itself quails at thy Word

In that service he wanted to remain active for his Master
until the end. And finally he 'placed his sword in tribute at
Christ's feet'.

The battle in which John fought continues. He has joined
the Church triumphant but calls us to continue the fight.
J. Gresham Machen, of whom John wrote in *The Banner of
Truth* in May 2001, has an article in which he memorably
described the apostle Paul as the man who could say 'No' and
the closing words seem appropriate to conclude this short
biography of another 'Mr Standfast':

> We know not in detail what will take place when the great
> revival comes, the great revival for which we long, when

the spirit of God will sweep over the church like a mighty flood. But one thing we do know – when that great day comes, the present feeble aversion to 'controversy', the present cowardly unwillingness to take sides in the age-long issue between faith and unbelief in the church – will at once be swept aside. There is not a trace of such an attitude in God's holy Word. That attitude is just Satan's way of trying to deceive the people of God; peace and church-unionism and aversion to controversy, as they are found in the modern church are just the fine garments that cover the enemy, unbelief.

May God send us men who are not deceived, men who will respond to the forces of unbelief and compromise now so largely dominant in the visible church with a brave and unqualified 'No'. Paul was such a man in his day. He said 'No' in the very first word of this epistle [to the Galatians] after the bare name and title of the author; and that word gives the key to the whole Epistle that follows. The Epistle to the Galatians is a polemic, a fighting Epistle from beginning to end. What a fire it kindled at the Reformation! May it kindle another fire in our day – not a fire that will destroy any fine or noble or Christian thing, but a fire of Christian love in hearts grown cold.

10. Celebrating John's seventieth birthday.

11. John and Susan Marshall.

PART TWO

WRITINGS

I

JOHN ROGERS: PROTO-MARTYR OF THE ENGLISH REFORMATION[1]

It is Monday, 4 February 1555, and Mary Tudor, commonly known as 'Bloody Mary', is on the throne. The French Ambassador, Count Noailles, sends a report to his sovereign back in Paris, informing him of the situation in London.

> This day was performed the confirmation of the alliance between the Pope and this kingdom, by the public and solemn sacrifice of a preaching doctor named Rogers, who has been burned alive for being a Lutheran; but he died persisting in his opinion. At this conduct the greatest part of the people took such pleasure that they were not afraid to make him many exclamations to strengthen his courage. Even his children assisted at it, comforting him in such a manner that it seemed as if he had been led to a wedding.

Thus died the proto-martyr of the English Reformation. Two hundred and eighty-two men and women were subsequently put to death as Mary sought to burn out Protestantism from her realm. At the stake Rogers was offered a pardon if he would recant, but he would have no parley with error, nor buy his life by selling the truth. He would seal with his blood the message he delighted to preach.

The noble death of John Roger greatly encouraged those who were soon to follow him. Nicholas Ridley said the news of Roger's death destroyed 'a lumpish heaviness in his heart'. John Bradford in a rather unusual metaphor wrote that Rogers broke the ice valiantly. Up until that time the question in many minds was whether the many who had preached and taught Reformation truth would be prepared to burn for the truth. By his death Rogers demonstrated that the truth of the gospel was more important than life itself and led the way for the many who would follow in his martyr's footsteps.

Before going into more detail of the life and significance of John Rogers, it is pertinent to ask why we should be studying this man.

REASONS

The first reason why we should study the life and death of John Rogers is that *the Bible gives significant space within its pages to history*. The Bible, it may truthfully be said, is full of history. God is a God who reveals himself in history, and through history. It has been well-said 'Weltgeschichte ist weltgericht' (World history is world judgment). In history God reveals his grace and his righteousness. Those who had little or no interest in history before their conversion are soon transformed into those who love history as they read their Bible. Ephesians 1:11 teaches us that God is he 'who worketh all things after the counsel of his own will.' In biblical and secular history we can observe God working out his own purposes. Every serious student of the Bible will to some degree be an historian.

Secondly, *the Bible specifically instructs us to teach our children history*. 'We will not hide them from their children, shewing to the generation to come the praises of the LORD, and his strength, and his wonderful works that he hath done.

For he established a testimony in Jacob, and appointed a law in Israel, which he commanded our fathers, that they should make them known to their children' (*Psa.* 78:4–8). If our children are to walk in ways of righteousness and show to the generations to come the praises of the Lord and his strength and his wonderful works it is necessary that we teach them church history.

Thirdly, *the Bible teaches us that the lives of God's faithful servants are to be examples to us.* Hebrews 12 teaches us that we are compassed about with a 'great cloud of witnesses' and that we are to be encouraged by their successes and strengthened as we read of their faithful endurance in the face of cruelty and dreadful adversities (cf. *Heb.* 11:32–40). If we are to learn from the likes of Daniel and Jeremiah in the Old Testament and the martyrs of the New Testament, why should we not be uplifted and empowered by the example of a man such as John Rogers who lived for God in the sixteenth century?

Fourthly, *it is right that we learn of John Rogers simply because many who should know about him are ignorant of him.* It is possible that this is due partly to Foxe's *Book of Martyrs* which, as J. L. Chester in *John Rogers, the Compiler of the First Authorised English Bible; the Pioneer of the English Reformation and its First Martyr* argues, concentrates attention upon Cranmer, Latimer, and Ridley rather than upon Rogers. Whatever the reason, the fact is that highly intelligent, well informed and sympathetic Protestants in the U.K. in 2002 have not heard of Rogers. Yet this man was burnt at the stake for upholding the truths we hold to be fundamental to the Reformation.

Finally, in an age when Reformed Evangelicalism is weak *this man should put some backbone into us,* faced as we are with the apparent irresistible tide of religious error and hostility to authentic Christianity. Hear Rogers praying for himself and Hooper: 'The Lord grant us grace to stand together, fighting lawfully in his cause, till we be smitten down together, if the Lord's will be so to permit it. For there shall not a hair of our heads perish against his will, but with his will. Whereunto the same Lord grant us to be obedient unto the end; and in the end, Amen, sweet, mighty and merciful Lord Jesus, the Son of David and of God! Amen! Amen!' We need strength and encouragement. We live at a time when the atmosphere of society and many of the leaders appears to be hostile to the gospel. People feel crushed and burdened; an atmosphere of hopelessness hangs over the church. John Rogers is an example to us of wise, patient, and courageous endurance.

Let us return now to a consideration of the significant events in the life of this servant of our Lord Jesus Christ.

HIS LIFE

We do not know a great deal about Rogers' life. He was born at Deritend in the parish of Aston, which is now part of England's second largest city, Birmingham. He graduated from Pembroke Hall, Cambridge, in 1526. Nicholas Ridley was also a member of this college. However, while a student in Cambridge Rogers did not seem to be affected by the vigorous Protestantism that was then beginning to be manifested in parts of the University.

On 28 December 1532 Rogers was presented to the London Rectory of Holy Trinity and Trinity the Less (now united with that of St Michael, Queenshithe). At the end of 1534 he resigned from these livings and went to Antwerp to act as chaplain to the English Merchant Venturers there. It was while he was in Antwerp that he came into contact with William Tyndale and we may assume that it was through this contact that John Rogers was brought to the Reformed faith. Sadly, this friendship did not have much time to develop. Tyndale was soon betrayed and arrested in the Spring of 1535 and on 6 October 1536 was executed by being strangled and burned. Before his death, Tyndale entrusted his friend with his incomplete translation of the Old Testament. During 1536 Rogers mainly occupied himself in the preparation of a new English version of the entire Bible, which would include Tyndale's translation of the New Testament (1526). It will be remembered that Tyndale's expiring prayer had been, 'O Lord, open the king of England's eyes.' God wonderfully answered the prayer of his dying servant and martyr. Henry's policy about an English Bible, no doubt under the power of God, changed, and Thomas Cromwell was able to persuade his sovereign to license the Matthew Bible. It is generally considered that the name Thomas Matthew not only concealed the name of John Rogers, but more significantly, the name of William Tyndale. At the end of the whole Old Testament there are the large letters, 'W T'.

It was presumed that Richard Grafton and Edward Whitchurch had financed this wonderful production. John Rogers was not the translator but rather the 'general editor' of it. Rogers used Tyndale's incomplete manuscript of the Old Testament together with the already produced translation of Miles Coverdale. The completed version was made up of Tyndale's Pentateuch, Tyndale's New Testament (first published 1525), Coverdale's Ezra-Malachi and Apocrypha, and Joshua-Chronicles in a version later shown to be Tyndale's. David Daniell writes 'What he (Rogers) did do triumphantly was to transmit the 200,000 words of Tyndale's Pentateuch, and the even longer New Testament, to a more influential English readership, and guarantee that Tyndale was the maker of most of the English Bible for centuries to come.' Rogers' own share in the work was largely confined to the prefaces and the marginal notes for which he leaned heavily on some continental Reformed sources. Indeed he seems to have adopted the French prefaces and chapter headings of Lefevre or Olivetan. Rogers was not original, but profoundly valuable.

Rogers used the Dedication borrowed from Lefevre and set forth his own view of salvation. As we read this, you will see his grasp of the Law and the Gospel, of sin and redemption, the gift of faith, and the ground of personal acceptance with God.

While the fathers looked for salvation and deliverance promised, because man's nature is such that he not only can not, but also will not confess himself to be a sinner, and specially such a sinner that hath need of the saving health promised, the Law was given [that] men might know sin and that they are sinners . . . And yet this Law was given to the intent that sin and the malice of men's hearts being thereby the better known, men should the more fervently thirst for the coming of Christ which should redeem them from their sins . . . In the New Testament therefore it is most evidently declared that Jesus Christ, the true Lamb and Host, is come to the intent to reconcile us to the Father, paying on the Cross the punishment due unto our sins; and to deliver us from the bondage of the devil . . . and to make us the sons of God . . . For that faith is the gift of God, whereby we believe that Christ is come into this world to save sinners: which is of so great pith that they which have it desire to perform all the duties of love to all men after the example of Christ . . . By that faith and confidence in Christ which by love is mighty in operation and that sheweth itself through the works of love, stirring men thereto, by that (I say) we are justified: that is, by that faith Christ's Father (which is become ours also through that Christ our Brother) counteth us for righteous and for His sons: imputing not our sins unto us, through His grace.

The identification of Thomas Matthew as John Rogers may shed light upon the question raised in Chester's biography of Rogers: 'Why did Bonner and Gardiner so hate Rogers?' Chester believes that Bonner and Gardiner's strong hatred of Rogers was mainly due to the latter's great popularity and staunch defence of the Protestant cause. Moreover, being the editor of the first licensed Bible in the English language would also set him up as a target for Roman Catholic hatred, as their leaders were so deeply opposed to the circulation of the Bible in the vernacular.

Mozley summarizes the arguments for the identification of John Rogers with Thomas Matthew as follows:

> No one with the name of Thomas Matthew is known as a leader of the Reformation at all, but John Rogers was the companion and disciple of Tyndale in the last months of his freedom. Rogers would treasure the unpublished translation of a substantial part of the Old Testament and may have been disappointed when it did not find a place in Coverdale's translation. He did not feel himself called to translate and he never engaged in such activity once the Matthew Bible had been published; but he was a Cambridge man and a good scholar, and he might well edit materials left in his hands and see them through the press. He would learn both French and German while in Antwerp, and this would be in full accord with the use of French and German sources in the Matthew Bible. It would not be wise to use the name of Tyndale, since he had been condemned and burnt; nor could he use Coverdale's name, since his share in the work was so much less. Least of all could he use his own name, for his own contribution was minute in comparison.
>
> No one can say why he chose the name of Thomas Matthew; perhaps the fact that the printer's name was Matthew Cron would put the idea into his mind. It is not strictly correct to say that Matthew is Rogers, though sometimes one can scarcely avoid that manner of speaking; rather Matthew stands for Tyndale, plus Coverdale, plus (to a very small degree) Rogers. Bale and Foxe both identify Thomas Matthew with John Rogers, and their statements have been confirmed by the official documents which dealt with the case of Rogers when he was in trouble under Mary. On August 16th, 1554, when the Privy

Council confined him to his house, he was described as 'John Rogers, alias Matthew'. This phrase was used in the sentence of condemnation pronounced by Gardiner on January 29th, 1555. There could be no reason for the second name of Matthew unless it was believed that he had been responsible for the Matthew Bible.

In 1536 or perhaps later, in 1537, Rogers married Adrianne de Weyden. Foxe wrote of her that she was 'more richly endowed with virtue and soberness of life than with worldly treasures.'

Sometime after his work on the Matthew Bible, Rogers moved to Wittenberg where he matriculated on 25 November 1540. Foxe writes 'He with much soberness of living did not only increase in all good and godly learning but also so much profited in the knowledge of the Dutch [Deutsch] tongue that the charge of a congregation was orderly committed to his care.' Rogers seems to have been particularly close to Melanchthon and translated some of his books into English (*Homilies*, *Locus Communes*, *In Danielem* and *Considerations of the Augsburg Interim*).

It seems that Rogers did not remain permanently in Wittenberg. Foxe speaks of Rogers in north-west Germany in a place called Dithmarsch. 'In this rude country of Dithmarsch, Master Rogers our countryman was superintendent at the time of the Six Articles, where he with great danger of his life did much good.' Mozley, who has researched this very thoroughly, says that on September 18th, 1543, Melancthon proposed the name of Rogers for the vacant living. Melancthon wrote encouraging Rogers to go.

Rogers remained in his German exile so long as Henry VIII lived. Henry died on 28 January 1547. However Rogers did not return until July 1548. The reason for this was probably his marriage. Foxe writes that had it not been for a law legitimizing priests' marriages Rogers might never have come back to England. We know that he did come back to his home country because he helped in the translation and publication of a tract by Melancthon called 'A Weighing and Considering of the Interim'. While written in Germany its translation was printed in England. The Preface of this tract includes these details: 'At London in Edward Whitchurch House by John Rogers 1st August 1548.' On 11 October 1548 Rogers was inducted to the rectory of St Matthias, Friday Street. In the 1548–9 session of Parliament a law was passed which gave grudging recognition to the marriage of priests and it thus became safe for Rogers to bring his wife and eight children back to England. In April 1552 he secured a special Act of Parliament naturalizing his wife and the children born to them while in Germany.

Once returned to England, Rogers' qualities were quickly recognized and his sphere of influence rapidly expanded. On 10 May 1550 Rogers was presented simultaneously to the rectory of St. Margaret Moyses and the vicarage of St Sepulchre, both in London and both Crown livings. Interesting enough is the fact that Nicasius Yetswiert, whose daughter married Rogers' eldest son, was patron of St Sepulchre *pro hac vice*. On 24 August 1551 Rogers was appointed to the valuable Prebend of St Pancras in St Paul's Cathedral by Nicholas Ridley, Bishop of London; with the Prebend went the rectory of Chigwell, but this had no monetary value. Ridley wrote of Rogers that he was a preacher 'who for detecting and confuting Anabaptists and papists in Essex, both by his preaching and by his writing is enforced now to bear Christ's Cross'. Later the Dean and Chapter of St Paul's appointed him divinity lecturer in the Cathedral.

Rogers was obviously a brave and uncompromising preacher of righteousness. In the *Dictionary of National Biography* it is said: 'But Rogers attitude to the government was not wholly complacent. The greed of the chief courtiers about Edward VI excited his disgust, and in a sermon at Paul's Cross he denounced the misuse of the property of the suppressed monasteries with such vigour that he was summoned before the privy council. He made an outspoken defence, and no further proceedings are known to have been taken. But at the same time he declined to conform to the vestments, and insisted upon wearing a round cap. Consequently, it would appear, he was temporarily suspended from his divinity lectureship at St. Paul's. According to an obscure entry in the 'Privy Council Register' in June 1553, orders were then issued by the council to the chapter to admit him within the cathedral, apparently to fulfil the duties of divinity-lecturer.

After the death of Edward VI on 16 July 1553, which was the day before Mary was proclaimed queen, Rogers preached by order of Queen Jane's council at Paul's Cross. Unlike Ridley who had preached on the preceding Sunday he simply preached from the set gospel for the day. On 6 August, three days after Queen Mary's arrival in London, he preached again and 'boldly set forth such true doctrine which he and others had there taught in King Edward's day, exhorting the people constantly to remain in the same and to beware all pestilent Popery, idolatry and superstition.' He was brought before the council for this preaching but defended himself by explaining that he was merely preaching the religion established by Parliament. Nothing immediately resulted from this examination, but Rogers was never to preach again.

LAST DAYS

Let us now proceed to the events that led to his martyrdom. After examination by Gardiner, and just five days before his martyrdom, Rogers and Hooper were placed in the prison of Clink, Liberty in the Manor of Southwark, which belonged to the Bishop of Winchester. They were held there until nightfall. When it was dark, they were led out of the prison by heavily armed sheriffs, and taken through the bishop's house, St Mary Overy's churchyard, into Southwark, over the bridge to Newgate, and into the city.

The authorities feared there would be a popular uproar on account of their actions and as a precautionary measure they darkened the streets and extinguished the very torches on costermonger's stalls. But the streets were lined with men and women holding lighted candles in their hands who cheered as the godly prisoners passed by.

When it came to his martyrdom, the same sort of thing occurred; he was led to Smithfield through streets full of people supporting and encouraging him. No doubt there were others reviling and abusing him, but as we have already noted, it seemed as if he were going to a wedding rather than to his own death!

How very different is the situation in our country today! Little more than one hundred years ago, the streets of south London were lined six or more deep as the funeral cortege of Charles Haddon Spurgeon, preacher of the gospel, passed by. Spurgeon was a faithful Christian and a nationally known figure. But can you imagine what would happen today if it was announced that such-and-such a gospel preacher had died? Our nation having turned away from God and the Bible have little interest in the gospel, the church, and its ministers.

John Rogers was a well-known preacher and was evidently loved and respected by the people to whom he preached. We can be in no doubt that he was also a wise scholar, a Cambridge graduate, fluent in Latin, skilful in French and German, and proficient in Greek, Hebrew and Aramaic. But he was not popular because of his scholarship. It was his evident love for God, love for the souls of men and utter faithfulness to the gospel of grace that won him a place in the hearts of the people of London.

Alas! today the sad fact is that too many ministers are confined to the walls of their own churches and are too little known in their surrounding areas. But the kind of preaching and teaching ministry Rogers exercised took him out among the people and when the clouds of persecution gathered over him the crowds knew who Rogers was and wished to encourage him.

Is there not a message here for evangelicals? We are still free to preach in the open air and should seize the opportunities while we have them. Then, at the very least, some of our fellow-citizens will know there is such a thing as the preaching of the gospel, and will hear about the Lord Jesus Christ whose name is above every name. John Rogers exalted Christ through his preaching and the crowd of ordinary Londoners who supported him in his hour of need was an incidental result of this.

On 16 August 1554 the Lord Mayor placed a number of men under arrest. Rogers was brought before the Queen's Council in the Tower of London, a minute of which cites his case:

> John Rogers, a seditious preacher, ordered by the Lords of the council to keep himself as present at this house at St Paul's without conference of any person other than such as [live] daily with him in [his] household until such time as he hath contrary commandment.

It is possible this house arrest was meant to give him opportunity to flee abroad, where of course he would find succour. However, while many Protestants fled, Rogers refused to flee. He was deprived of his income. Foxe writes: 'After he was called to answer in Christ's cause, he would not depart and for the trial of the truth, was content to hazard his life.'

Towards Christmas 1554 Rogers sent his wife who was 'great with child' and eight honest women to petition Gardiner for his release from house arrest. Gardiner, hard-hearted as ever, refused, and on 27 January 1555 he was transferred from his home to Newgate. In prison Rogers showed true Christian love in an extraordinary willingness to forego his two meals a day. Just one meal would suffice him so that his fellow-prisoners, less fortunate than himself, should also have something to eat. On 12 February Lady Jane Grey's execution took place and a few days later Bradford expressed the hope that God might spare them as he had spared Peter from the hands of Herod. 'Even so, dear Lord, break the dreams of thy combined enemies with us and save Thy servants, Latimer, Cranmer, Ridley, Hooper, Crowe, Rogers, Saunders, Bradford, Philpot, Coverdale, Barlow, Cardmaker, Taylor, "which are appointed to die" if thou by Thy mighty power deliver them not.'

As the end approached not only for Rogers but for those who would soon follow him to a fiery death, these martyrs kept in mind the suffering of believers as set forth in Scriptures and uttered many prayers to their God that he would keep them faithful unto death. At the end of his first encounter we hear Rogers praying 'that I and they all may despise all manner of threats and cruelty and even bitter burning fire and the dreadful dart of death'. He also prays for 'my poor honest wife . . . and all my little souls, hers and my children'. Rogers was under no illusion both as to his own weakness and the pains of a death by burning at the stake. Foxe records Rogers as saying:

The apostles were beaten for their boldness and they rejoiced that they suffered for Christ's cause. Ye have also provided rods for us, and bloody whips: yet when ye have done that which God's hand and counsel hath determined that ye shall do, be it life or death, I trust that God will so assist us by his Holy Spirit and grace, that we shall patiently suffer it and praise God for it.

On 20 January 1555 the old Lollard laws passed in the reigns of Richard II, Henry IV, and Henry V were revived. Two days later the first official proceedings began.

Gardiner introduced matters with an account of Pole's absolution of both Houses of Parliament and their recognition of the Pope as Head of the Church. 'How say ye?' He then asked Rogers: 'Are ye content to unite and knit yourself to the faith of the Catholic Church with us in the state in which it is now in England? Will ye do that?' Rogers replied: 'The

Catholic church I never did nor will dissent from.' But he was told that it was that Church which had now received the Pope as Supreme Head, and he replied: 'I know none other Head but Christ of His Catholic Church, neither will I acknowledge the Bishop of Rome to have any more authority than any other Bishop hath by the Word of God.' He went on to say that he had never allowed Henry VIII supremacy in things spiritual such as the forgiveness of sins, and they began to laugh. 'Yea', they said, 'if thou hadst said so in his days, thou hadst not been alive now.'

There was further word-play; then he was asked: 'What sayest thou? Make us a direct answer whether thou wilt be one of this Catholic Church or not with us, in that state in which we are now?' And he replied: 'My Lord, I cannot believe, that ye yourselves do think in your hearts that he is supreme head in forgiving of sin, etc., seeing you, and all the bishops of the realm have now twenty years long preached, and some of you also written to the contrary, and the parliament hath so long agone condescended unto it.' The Lord Chancellor offered Rogers either mercy or justice. Rogers said he would not refuse the Queen's mercy though he had offended in nothing nor was disobedient in any matter relating to his sovereign. Gardiner replied, 'If thou wilt not receive the Bishop of Rome to be the supreme head of the Catholic Church then thou shalt never have her mercy.' Sir Richard Southwell said, 'Thou wilt not burn in this gear when it cometh to the purpose, I know well that.' Rogers lifted up his eyes to heaven and said, 'Sir, I cannot tell, but I trust in my Lord God, yes.'

THE TRIAL
On 28 January Gardiner's Commission for the trial of imprisoned heretics began to sit. Hooper, Cardmaker, and Rogers were examined. Cardmaker temporarily weakened, although later he recovered his nerve and suffered a martyr's death at the stake. The hearing was public and many were

present. The examination went on all day and at 4 p.m.
Gardiner determined to adjourn the hearing saying he would
give Rogers time to repent and return to the true Catholic
Church. Rogers at once declared, 'I was never out of the true
catholic church, nor would be; but into *his* church would I by
God's grace never come.' Gardiner responded, 'Is our church
false and antichristian?' 'Yes', said Rogers boldly. 'And what
is the doctrine of the sacrament?', retorted Gardiner. 'False',
confessed Rogers once again. The sheriffs then marched them
to the Compter in Southwark, and such a great crowd thronged
all about 'that we had much to do to go in the streets', adds
Rogers.

On 29 January the next day's hearing was private, the public being kept at bay. Gardiner pressed Rogers to recant, but
he would not. There was uproar as Rogers sought to defend
himself by arguments from the Word of God. Rogers replied
at length, but was told to be silent.

Then Rogers' condemnation was read before the court. He
was styled 'John Rogers, priest, *alias* called Matthew' and was
condemned for 'two damnable opinions' namely 'that the
Catholic Church of Rome is the church of Antichrist; that in
the Sacrament of the Altar there is not substantially nor really
the natural body and blood of Christ.' He was therefore
excommunicated as an 'obstinate heretic' and was handed over
to the State for secular punishment. Rogers then spoke in
reply:

> Well, my Lord, here I stand before God, and you and all
> this honourable audience, and take him to witness that I
> never wittingly or willingly taught any false doctrine; and
> therefore have I a good conscience before God and all
> good men. I am sure that you and I shall come before a
> Judge that is righteous, before whom I shall be as good a
> man as you: and I nothing doubt but that I shall be found
> there a true member of the true catholic church of Christ,

and everlastingly saved. And as for your false church, ye need not to excommunicate me forth of it. I have not been in it these twenty years. The Lord be thanked therefor.

Rogers then made a plea that his wife be allowed to come to see him. Being a foreigner, she needed help and advice as to what was best for her to do to care for her large family of children. Gardiner refused and denied that she was his wife. Rogers replied that she had been his wife for eighteen years. Gardiner again refused. To which Rogers gave a most devastating rebuke to which no one dared reply. 'Then I have tired out all your charity. You make yourself highly displeased with the matrimony of priests, but you maintain open whoredom; as in Wales every priest hath his whore openly dwelling with him, and lying by him: even as your holy father suffereth all the priests in Dutchland [Germany] and in France to do the like.'

Foxe prints without comment a translation of the Latin condemnation read by Gardiner:

We, Stephen, by permission of God bishop of Winchester, lawfully and rightfully proceeding with all godly favour . . . having heard, seen, and understood, and with all diligent deliberation, weighed, discussed and considered, the merits of the cause . . . do find thou hast taught, holden, and affirmed, and obstinately defended divers errors, heresies, and damnable opinions, contrary to the doctrine and determination of the holy church . . .

In the five days between condemnation and execution Rogers wrote and concealed from his captors his own defence which he had no opportunity properly to prove.

. . . we be the members of the true catholic church, because we suffer for the same doctrine which John Baptist, James, the Israelites, yea Christ and the apostles, did teach

. . . we suffer the like reproach, shame, and rebuke of the world, and the like persecution, losing our lives, and goods, forsaking (as our master Christ commandeth) father, mother, sisters, brethren, wives, children and all that there is; being assured of a joyful resurrection, and to be crowned in glory with them, according to the infallible promises made unto us in Christ, our only and sufficient Mediator, Reconciler, Priest, and Sacrifice . . .

Rogers proceeds and prophesies God's judgment on our 'bloody Babylonian bishops'.

On Monday morning, 4 February 1555, Rogers was roused from a very deep sleep and told he was to die. He was finally degraded by Bonner and once more requested 'That I might take a few words with my wife before burning.' This was refused. Sherriff Woodroofe asked if 'he would revoke his evil opinions of the sacrament of the altar'. Rogers replied, 'That which I have preached I will seal with my blood.' 'Then, you are a heretic', Woodroofe exclaimed. 'That shall be known at the day of judgment', replied Rogers. 'Well', Woodroofe answered, 'I will never pray for thee.' 'But I will pray for you', said Rogers. Reading the 51st Psalm, Rogers was led by the sheriffs through the throng of ordinary Londoners to Smithfield, the place appointed for him to die. Foxe tells us that 'all the people wonderfully rejoiced at his constancy, with great praises and thanks to God for the same.'

The fire was put unto him; and when it had taken hold upon his legs and shoulders, he, as one feeling no smart, washed his hands in the flame, as though it had been in cold water. And after lifting up his hands unto heaven, not removing the same until such time as the devouring fire had consumed them – most mildly this happy martyr yielded up his spirit into the hands of his heavenly Father.

A little before his burning at the stake, his pardon was brought, if he would have recanted, but he utterly refused.

He was the first proto-martyr of all the blessed company that suffered in Queen Mary's time, that gave the first adventure upon the fire. His wife and children, being eleven in number, and ten able to go, and one sucking on the breast, met him by the way as he went towards Smithfield. This sorrowful sight of his own flesh and blood could nothing move him; but that he constantly and cheerfully took his death with wonderful patience, in the defence and quarrel of Christ's gospel.

[1] This address was delivered at St Matthew's Church, Cambridge, under the auspices of the Protestant Truth Society, October 2002. The term 'proto-martyr' could be objected to, since William Tyndale, Thomas Bilney, and others had already suffered martyrdom in the cause of Reformation in England, but Mr Marshall was thinking of the Marian martyrs, among whom Rogers was the first to suffer.

2

THE PURITAN WOMAN[1]

'Who can find a virtuous woman? For her price is
far above rubies' (*Prov.* 31:10).

A virtuous woman glorifies God. She is a blessing to her
husband and her children, a fountain of blessedness to
the society of which she is part, and an ornament and honour
to the church of Christ. But where shall we find such a woman
or, to be more precise, such women? To go back to the Puritan
era on our search for this type of woman is no disparagement
to modern Christian womanhood. However, surrounded as
the modern woman is by the strident voice of feminism and
cries for women's rights, it would be folly if we ignored the
kind of Christian women produced by the revival of biblical
Christianity of the Reformation and Puritan eras.

In the Puritan era there was a remarkable unanimity of opinion as to the characteristics of a good wife. This cannot be
said of our present time. It is not only that the world is racked
with the ideas of feminists of varying hues, but also the evangelical constituency itself is not free from significant differences
over the role of women in the family, the church, and society.
From some perspectives the church in our land (and evangelical churches in particular are not free from this) has a perilously
effeminate air about it. Women (whether *de jure* or *de facto!*)
have exercised such a controlling influence over the church

that outsiders have increasingly come to view it as an institution suitable only for children, women, and old people. Whilst of course we are not to be governed by the world's opinion of the church, yet it would be foolish to ignore how much such a view can hinder men from hearing the gospel.

Antonia Fraser cites the description of Elizabeth Cavendish, Countess of Bridgwater, who died at the age of thirty-seven, as 'a most affectionate and observing wife to her husband, a most tender and indulgent mother to her children, a most kind and bountiful mistress to her family . . . in a word she was so superlatively good that language is too narrow to express her deserved character.'

She then adds a most perceptive comment:

> There was indeed a remarkable unanimity in the nature of such tributes. For all the religious differences which bedevilled the structure of society, the qualities which were to make up a right royal 'crown to her husband' were not much in dispute.[2]

EXAMPLES OF PURITAN WOMANHOOD

Where shall we begin? First, let us hear part of a letter:

> I have now sent you my dear sister Katherine, a book, which although it be not outwardly trimmed with gold, or the various embroidery of the artfullest needles, yet inwardly it is more worth than all the precious mines which the vast world can boast of: it is the book, my only best and best beloved sister, of the law of the Lord: it is the Testament and Last Will which he bequeathed unto us wretches and wretched sinners, which will lead you to the path of eternal joy; and if you with good mind read it, and with an earnest desire follow it, no doubt shall bring you to an immortal and everlasting life; it will teach you to live and learn you to die . . . my good sister, and more

again let me entreat thee to learn to die; deny the world, defy the devil and despise the flesh, and delight yourself only in the Lord: be penitent for your sins and yet despair not, be strong in faith, yet presume not; and desire with St Paul to be dissolved and to be with Christ with whom even in death there is life . . . Farewell once again my beloved sister, and put your only trust in God who only must help you. Amen.'[3]

Secondly, let us hear part of a prayer by the same person:

O Lord, thou God and Father of my life, Hear me, poor and desolate woman, which flyeth unto thee only, in all troubles and miseries. Thou, O Lord, art the only Defender and Deliverer of those that put their trust in thee and therefore, being defiled with sin, encumbered with miseries, vexed with temptations, and grievously tormented with the long imprisonment of this vile mass of clay, my sinful body, do come unto thee, O merciful Saviour, craving thy mercy and help, without the which so little hope of deliverance is left that I may utterly despair of my liberty . . . Suffer me not to be tempted above my power, but either be thou a Deliverer unto me out of this great misery, or else give me grace patiently to bear thy heavy hand and sharp correction . . . Hear me, O merciful Father, for his sake, whom thou wouldest be a sacrifice for my sins, to whom with thee and the Holy Ghost be all honour and glory. Amen![4]

Thirdly, let us consider part of an account. The date is Monday, 12 February 1554; the place the Tower of London; the subject of the account a young woman of sixteen years of age. Her husband has just been beheaded on Tower Hill and the sheriffs now come to escort her to the scaffold. On the way it seems almost certain that she passed the headless corpse of her husband being brought back in a cart. She prays as she being led to the place of execution by Sir John Brydges, the Lieutenant of the Tower, although according to Foxe, she is continually interrupted by Feckenham who is trying to persuade her to renounce the Protestant faith and recant. Having come to the scaffold the executioner falls on his knees and begs her forgiveness, which she most willingly grants to him. Her resolve is not affected as she sees the block but she asks him to despatch her quickly. She herself ties the handkerchief over her eyes and guided by a bystander, she feels for the block, lays down her head upon it, and stretching forth her body, cries 'Lord, into thy hands I commend my spirit.' Immediately the axe falls – and the world closed forever on one of the most interesting women who ever adorned it.[5] This woman was none other than Lady Jane Grey, who died affirming that she was a true Christian woman who expected salvation only through the mercy of God in the merits of the blood of his Son Jesus Christ. She was a pattern of true 'Puritan' womanhood, a product of her age, singularly intellectual (reading the *Phaedo* of Plato in Greek in her room while others were out enjoying the hunt in the park), strictly brought up, submissive to her parents, and yet in adversity showing true perseverance and a costly attachment to the doctrine of the gospel she professed.

The doctrinal springs and influences that produced this kind of woman are to be found in Geneva. Under the influence of John Calvin, Geneva developed a surprising reputation as *le paradis des femmes*. The Consistory had even taken steps against the forced betrothal of grown men and under-age girls and had passed measures in support of ill-treated and deserted wives.[6] Calvin has left us a kind of résumé of what he believed was required in a good wife:

> Concerning the marriage I shall now speak more plainly . . . But always keep in mind what I seek to find in her [i.e. a good wife]; for I am none of those insane lovers who embrace also the vices of those they are in love with,

where they are smitten at first sight with a fine figure. This only is the beauty which allures me, if she is chaste, if not too nice or fastidious, if economical, if patient, if there is hope that she will be interested about my health . . .'[7]

However, even Calvin, as is frequently the case with other men, did not find the discovery of a suitable wife easy. Writing in March 1540 just under a year later he says:

We are as yet in a state of suspense as to the marriage, and this annoys me exceedingly, forasmuch as the relations of that young lady of rank are so urgent that I may take her unto myself, which, indeed, I would never think of doing, unless the Lord had altogether demented me![8]

Later he did in fact marry a widow by the name of Idelette de Bure by whom he had at least three children. Her early death left him desolate, as we see from a letter he wrote to Viret:

Although the death of my wife has been bitterly painful to me, yet I restrain my grief as well as I can . . . You know well enough how tender, or rather soft, my mind is. Had I not exercised a powerful self-control, therefore, I could not have borne up so long. And truly mine is no common grief. I have been bereaved of the best companion of my life, who, if any severe hardship had occurred, would have been my willing partner, not only in exile and poverty but even in death. As long as she lived she was the faithful helper of my ministry. From her I never felt even the slightest hindrance. During the whole course of her illness she was more anxious about her children than about herself. Since I was afraid that she might torment herself needlessly by repressing her worry, three days before her death I took occasion to mention that I would not neglect my duties (to her children). She spoke up at once, I have already committed them to God.[9]

The predominant view of women prior to the time of Calvin was that which was heavily influenced by Thomas Aquinas.

> From the writings of the Angelic Doctor, woman as a group and generality emerges as inferior to man in every aspect of her being. Psychologically she is inferior, since St Thomas perpetuates the Aristotelian concept of women as misshaped and half-formed men. The relative weakness of her reason is emphasised and from this weakness follows greater susceptibilities of her soul to the disorder of sin . . .[10]

These ideas about woman, together with the Catholic exaltation of celibacy over marriage, help us to appreciate something of the monumental changes which the Reformers and Puritans introduced to the world with their concept of the truly virtuous woman.

If Calvin's Geneva and Lady Jane Grey form our starting point where shall we make the terminus of our studies? We could hardly do better than to make it the life of Katherine Brown, whom Thomas Boston married on 17 July 1700. Writing after thirty years of married life, Boston describes her as:

> A woman of great worth, whom I therefore passionately loved, and inwardly honoured: a stately, beautiful, and comely personage, truly pious, and fearing the Lord; of an even temper, patient in our common tribulations, and under her personal distresses. A woman of bright natural parts, an uncommon stock of prudence; of a quick and lively apprehension, in things she applied herself to; great presence of mind in surprising incidents; sagacious and acute in discerning the qualities of persons, and therefore not easily imposed upon; modest and grave in her deportment, but naturally cheerful, wise and affable in conversation, having a good faculty at speaking, and expressing herself with assurance; endowed with a singular

dexterity in dictating letters; being a pattern of frugality, and wise management of household affairs, therefore entirely committed to her; well fitted for, and careful of, the virtuous education of her children . . . useful . . . through her skill in physic and surgery, which, in many instances, a peculiar blessing appeared to be commanded upon from heaven; and fully a crown to my public station and appearances.[11]

Boston then goes on to describe the terrible mental distresses his wife suffered, which only serve to increase the value of the foregoing testimony.

The life of Puritan women in the early years of the Reformation and Puritan period was one of potential danger and violent death. By 1700 times were changing, but right up until that date Puritan women often experienced a danger which, today, is only to be found in areas of war and revolution.

For example, in March 1696 Indians attacked Haverhill in New England, killing twenty-seven people, including thirteen children. The wife of Thomas Duston was in bed, still recovering from the birth of her twelfth child a few days earlier. The Indians dragged her from her bed and murdered her baby before her eyes. In Scotland, while many know of the martyrdom of the two Margarets, (Margaret McLachlan and Margaret Wilson, who was only about 18 years old), yet the hanging of Marion Harvey and Isabel Alison are not so well known. They were executed at the Grassmarket, Edinburgh, in January 1681 for no other reason than expressing opinions that were objectionable to the authorities.

Another less well-known execution was that of the godly Lady Lisle who was beheaded for giving hospitality to a man implicated in the Monmouth rebellion, although she thought the man in question was in trouble only for preaching the gospel. This godly Christian woman was beheaded on 2 September 1685 in Winchester market place. Elizabeth Gaunt was charged with a similar kind of offence and suffered death by burning at Tyburn, London, on 23 October 1685. Macaulay wrote of this:

> It was much noticed that while the foulest judicial murder which had disgraced even those times was perpetrating, a tempest burst forth which has not been known since that great hurricane which had raged round the death bed of Oliver . . . Since that day no woman has suffered death in England for any political offence.[12]

Puritan women lived in times of distress, war, persecution, danger, and great difficulty but remarkably displayed in their lives the grace of God and whole-hearted submission to his Word.

PRELIMINARY CONSIDERATIONS

Before going on to examine different aspects of the life of the Puritan woman it is necessary to deal with several preliminary matters.

First of all there is the issue of *sources*. Recent studies suggest that illiteracy among women was very high during the sixteenth and seventeenth centuries – as high as 80% in London around 1640 and nearly 100% in East Anglia around the same period. In other words, female illiteracy was as high as that among labourers and husbandmen. Puritan women aristocrats saw it as their duty to teach their maids to read so they could at least read the Bible and sing Psalms. 'A forlorn creature came to Elizabeth Walker's door who only knew her name was Mary Bun, "almost as eat up with scabs and vermin with scarce rags to cover her, and as ignorant of God and Christ as if she had been born and bred in Lapland or Japan." Elizabeth Walker decided to save her, not only by stripping her, washing her, and curing her of "The Itch", but also by teaching her to read, so that finally, a rich farmer took Mary Bun as his apprentice.'[13]

We do of course have Bunyan's description of 'typical' Puritan women in *The Pilgrim's Progress,* and he wrote as a minister of a relatively poor congregation. Nevertheless, it has to be said that many of our written records about Puritan women come from the pens of female members of the aristocracy or squirearchy.

This leads us to another significant issue: that of the importance of *class distinctions* in the Puritan era. Many Puritans belonged to aristocratic families of the landed gentry and in such matters as marriage this fact certainly affected the approach fathers took in the arrangement of their daughters' marriages. Distinctions of status in society were far more marked than they are today.

Thirdly, women have always been (and no doubt still are!) interested in *clothes.* The Puritan era was no exception to this. In late seventeenth-century New England we find that John Hutchin's wife was admonished for wearing a silk hood, while two daughters of Hannah Bosworth were fined ten shillings each for wearing silk. These sumptuary laws, imported from Europe, were intended primarily to maintain the outward distinctions between the social orders, not for religious purposes.[14]

More astonishing, but nevertheless probably arising partly from issues of social distinction, was the so-called 'Millinery War'. Francis Thompson, a leader of the separatist congregation associated with Henry Barrow, had married Thomasina Boys in 1594, the widow of a rich Fleet Street haberdasher who had died as a martyr. His imprisoned brother George was infuriated by Thomasina's outward adornment. She was a 'bouncing girl', really like the wife of the Bishop of London. She wore 'three, four or five gold rings at once'. George thought that she should take off her 'excessive deal of lace', 'exchange her showish hat for a sober tafety and felt', and 'stop wearing musk and fancy white ruffs' stiff with starch – 'the Devil's liquor'.[15] Thomasina bluntly told George to mind his own business, but the latter continued hurling Scripture texts and personal abuse at Pastor Francis Thompson and his wife. This singularly unedifying story shows that quarrelsomeness in Christian congregations is not a phenomenon from which the professed godly were immune in the sixteenth century!

THE LIFE OF THE PURITAN WOMAN

In order to understand the Puritan woman let us briefly look at different aspects of her life. The field is vast and the available material quite considerable. Nevertheless we must attempt to sketch the Puritan woman as a Christian, and having done this, to survey the different aspects of her life, such as childhood and education, courtship, marriage and motherhood. As we do so, we ought to bear in mind that the vast majority of women in the sixteenth and seventeenth centuries married, and in such places as New England, because of the high incidence of death through childbearing, women were often in very short supply.

Brilliana Conway married Sir Robert Harley as his third wife in July 1623. She kept a commonplace book which is dated 1622. It contains transcripts from her reading and contains mainly portions from the Bible, Calvin's *Institutes*, William Perkins' *Cases of Conscience* and his *Exposition of the Lord's Prayer*. The main themes of her Journal are the marks of the elect and the evidence of her religious beliefs. Her beliefs included 'predestination and her certainty that faith, good works and obedience to God's laws were not as the Catholics believed, the means of salvation but were instead the external signs of election'. She wrote, 'Man since his fall has his will so detained with such bondage to sin, that he cannot once move it to goodness, for moving is the beginning of turning to God, which the Scripture does wholly give to God. Man, since his fall, sins willingly by his own lusts and by foreign constraint. It is God that first turns our will to that which is good and we are converted by the power of God only; it is God that works all in us.'[16]

Naturally the religion of the Puritan woman, in terms of the covenant of grace, was the same as that of the Puritan man. She had similar exercises of heart and similar proneness to doubts about election; she sat under the same preachers, attended the same family worship, and sought to glorify the same God.

While, of course, some Puritan women were born into non-Puritan families and were converted during their early years, many Puritan women were born into Puritan families and grew up under the godly order which characterized these little commonwealths, for so the family was termed. In spite of the caricatures of Puritanism that are all too common in today's press, Puritan families were very loving. As we shall see, the married Puritan woman might expect to have a loving and devoted husband, and such husbands and wives were wise and discriminating parents.

From their earliest years, little Puritan girls were taught that life was serious and that diligence and work were pleasing to God. There is a touching illustration of this in Samuel Sewall's letters. On 28 March 1687, he wrote:

> I have two small daughters who begin to go to school; my wife would entreat your good lady to pleasure her so far as to buy for her whole Fustian drawn, enough for curtains, woollen counterpane for a bed and half a duz. chairs with four threaded green worsted to work it.

The little seamstresses were Elizabeth and Hannah Sewall, aged five and seven years respectively.[17]

The education which the Puritan young lady might receive would often depend upon the tutors who were employed to teach her brothers. She might benefit from their services, although the great emphasis was always on the education of the boys to fit them for their calling in life. The assumption was that the girls in the family would grow up to be wives and mothers.

However, within this context we come across a great diversity of accomplishments. Lady Russell, a noted Puritan woman, complained that her inability to spell properly in her letters was due to the inadequacies of her education. On the other hand we have a woman such as Lucy Hutchinson who was exceedingly bookish. In an account of her life she writes:

> By the time I was four years old I read English perfectly, and having a great memory I was carried to a sermon, and while I was very young could remember and repeat them exactly, and being caressed, the love of praise troubled me and made me attend more heedfully. When I was about seven years of age, I remember I had at one time eight tutors in several qualities; languages, music, dancing, writing and needlework . . . my father would have me learn Latin, and I was so apt I outstripped my brothers who were at school, although my father's chaplain that was my tutor was a pitiful dull fellow.

Lucy seems to have been a formidable character even when she was young, for she writes:

> Play among other children I despised, and when I was forced to entertain such as came to visit me, I tired them with more grave instruction than their mother, and plucked all their babies to pieces, and kept the children in such awe, that they were glad when I entertained myself with elder company.[18]

Courtship followed on from childhood and, interestingly enough, it was Lucy's academic inclination that, in the providence of God, led to her marriage to Colonel Hutchinson. The latter had resisted all previous attempts to lure him into matrimony. Lucy wrote:

> In the house with Mr Hutchinson there was a young gentlewoman of such admirable tempting beauty and such

excellent good nature, as would have thawed a rock of ice, yet she could never get an acquaintance with him.[19]

One day, however, while Mr Hutchinson was in Lucy's house during her absence, he saw some Latin books belonging to her and, learning to whom they belonged, he began to grow very interested in their owner, even though he had never met her.

Then he grew to love to hear mention of her, and then other gentlewomen who had been her companions used to talk to him of her, telling him how reserved and studious she was and other things which they esteemed no advantage. But it so much inflamed Mr Hutchinson's desire of seeing her, that he began to wonder at himself, that his heart, which had ever entertained so much indifference for the most excellent of womankind, should have such strong impulses towards a stranger he never saw.[20]

Needless to say a romance which began in such an unusual way resulted in a marriage of great blessedness and delight.

The Puritans had very definite ideas on courtship. Daniel Rogers wrote of 'poor green leaves who married purely for love; when a year or two had passed and they had skimmed the cream of their marriage, they would soon envy the good fortune of those whose union was built upon stronger foundations'. In *Matrimonial Honour*, Rogers even went so far as to argue that passionate marriages might actually result in contaminated offspring![21]

It is of course true that all kinds of considerations came into the choosing of a husband for a Puritan woman. We must remember that it was expected that she would marry into a family of a similar social standing. It is also true that consideration of dowry and marriage settlements would have their place, varying according to the spirituality of the two sets of parents. Yet the young would not normally be married against their own wishes, although parents would have had a vastly greater say in the marriage of their children than would be the case today.

Although marriage was not to be entered into lightly on the basis of passion, the Puritans were immensely loving husbands and wives, fathers and mothers. The evidence for this is so copious that one is continually amazed at how the perverted stereotype of the 'Puritan' view of conjugal love gained such ascendancy in the Western world. Cotton Mather called his second wife

> A most lovely creature and such a gift of Heaven to me and more than the sense thereof . . . dissolves me into tears of joy.

While Thomas Hooker wrote:

> The man whose heart is endeared to the woman he loves dreams of her in the night, hath her in his eye and apprehension when he awakes, museth on her as he sits at the table, walks with her when he travels . . . she lies in his bosom and his heart trusts in her, which forceth all to confess that the stream of his affection [is] like a mighty current with full tide and strength.[22]

Ryken argues that the Puritans exalted women, especially in their roles as wife and mother, and quotes Cotton Mather again:

> Women are creatures without which there is no comfortable living for man; they are a sort of blasphemer then who despise and decry them and call them a necessary evil, for they are a necessary good.[23]

The wives of the Puritans responded with the same devotion and affection, and one has only to read the letters of Brilliana Harley and Lady Russell to their husbands to see how they were devoted and affectionate lovers. Thus Betty Bowman who married Basil, Lord Fielding (later Earl of Denbigh) wrote:

My dear heart, my dear life, my sweet joy . . . p.s. a hundred thousand kisses I give thee as I might be so happy as
this paper; I long so much to see you . . .

She longs to see him, sends him presents of cakes, candied
flowers, borage, and marigolds. This is all summed up by another ecstatic postscript. 'Dear. How thy Betty loves thee.'[24]

Of course, marriage (although not in the case of the Countess
of Denbigh) often resulted in child-bearing. This was an occasion of great delight, but could also often tragically be the
occasion of the death of both mother and infant. Most women
approached childbirth knowing that it could lead to their rapid
departure from this world. They were thus frequently confronted
with their need to prepare for eternity. Death was a frequent
visitor to the Puritan home and the Puritan woman knew that
the excruciating pains of labour could signal the rapid approach
of death, even as they brought a new life into this world.

John Winthrop's wife May bore her husband six children
before she died in 1615. He married Thomasina Clapton six
months later. On Saturday 30 November 1616 she was delivered of a daughter who died the following Monday.

Next day a fever seized her and she haemorrhaged.
Thomasina asked that the bell of Groten Church should
be tolled for her so that her neighbours should know she
lay on her deathbed and would visit and pray for her. By
Saturday the fever had become strong. She prayed vehe-
mently to God to overcome the tempting Devil and not
to remove his lovingkindness from her, as we might see
by her setting her teeth and fixing her eyes, shaking her
head and whole body . . . she took farewell of her family
and household. John continued to pray by her bedside
and 'discoursed with her of the sweet love of Christ unto
her and of his glory that she was going into, and what
holy everlasting Sabbaths she would keep, and how she
should sup with Christ in Paradise that night . . .'

At five o'clock she died. Such scenes of anguish could be multiplied over and over again. Life for women, Puritan or otherwise, was often short and frequently painful.

In the Puritan home the wife was clearly in subjection to her husband: he was the head of this little commonwealth. However, Winthrop writes:

> A true wife accounts her subjection her honour and freedom and would not think her condition safe and free but in subjection to her husband's authority. Such is the liberty of the church under the authority of Christ, her king and husband, his yoke is so easy and sweet as a bride's ornament.[25]

As a wife under authority she herself had authority and a duty of care over her children. On a spiritual level she laboured and prayed for their salvation.

> The tender mother will own no other of all her numerous brood. But such as stand at Christ's right hand, acquitted through his blood.[26]

She not only travailed in body for their physical birth, she laboured in spirit for their spiritual birth. Yet the Puritan woman cared for her children's bodies also. When Edward Harley was at Oxford his mother sent him 'liquorice's for colds, "eye water" for sore eyes, and to preserve the sight an *aurium potable*, literally "drinkable gold", tiny slivers of gold to be drunk in water and believed to be a powerful restorative. In spite of her husband's protestations she also sent pies made from turkey, pigeon, and kid, presents of bacon and sweetmeats for Lent, a loin of veal, apples, and violet cakes'.[27]

Generally, Puritan women were outstandingly industrious. The question may be asked whether a study of Puritan women sheds any light on whether Christian wives should 'go out to work'. Conditions were so different in the centuries we are studying that it is extremely difficult to make a valid comparison. What is clear, however, is that the Puritan woman was immensely hard working. Thus Elizabeth Walker who married in 1650 began her day at four o'clock in the morning and sometimes as early as two or three, so that she had hours of solitary meditation. At six the servants were summoned for a reading from the Bible, and prayers with the day-labourers were held after breakfast. During the day she would engage in needlework and inspecting the dairy. During the afternoon she would visit the sick, distributing salves and medicines. Mrs Walker also visited women in childbirth, rising at any hour of the night. She seems to have been a prodigious cook who, for her last wedding anniversary, enveloped thirty-nine pies in one dish!

The Countess of Warwick who embraced Puritanism after a conversion, rose at six and visited sick servants and the village girls' school, administering medicines, which were mainly herbal remedies prepared at home.[28]

Although the Puritans emphasized a wife's submission to her husband, how this worked out in practice is somewhat of a rebuke to the more extreme and ignorant modern male neo-Puritans. Samuel Sewall, for instance, records that he delegated the family finances to his wife because she had 'better faculty than I at managing affairs'.[29] Mather wrote that 'particular exception to the husband's authority may have place if she exceed her husband in prudence and dexterity', whilst William Gouge said, 'There are many things in well governing a family more fit for one to meddle withal than for the other.'[30] Common sense should surely teach a rationally minded husband that in some areas of intellect and practice the competence of his wife is superior to his own. Even Calvin, commenting on 1 Peter 5:5 writes: 'The husband is the head of the wife, yet he is to be in some things subject to her.'[31] Unfortunately, or perhaps fortunately, Calvin fails to inform us what these things are!

Lest it should be thought that sin had disappeared from the Puritan era and that marriage among Puritans was always unalloyed happiness, it must be recorded that this was not the case. Adair, in *The Founding Fathers,* writes:

> The English characteristic of aggressiveness also surfaced in the home especially in the ill treatment of wives . . . the Plymouth magistrates punished a man for 'abusing his wife by kicking her from the stool to the fire'.

However, violence was not all one way, for in 1655 Joan Miller of Taunton appeared before a court charged with 'beating and reviling her husband and egging her children to help her, bidding them knock him on the head and wishing his victuals might choke him.'[32] The wife of Christopher Collins was presented for railing at her husband and calling him 'Gurley gutted devill'. Although, as she was discharged, Morgan supposed the court must have agreed with her estimation of him.[33] Even the most pious of husbands and wives could occasionally disagree. It is recorded of Oliver Heywood, the great Puritan preacher of Lancashire, that he

> unwarily invited a houseful of guests without consulting his wife and discovered she had other and quite different plans. Heywood quickly read the danger signals and offered to write at once and cancel the suggested visit. They spent a troubled day, followed by a restless night. After tossing and turning till 2 a.m. she rose; when he followed her, he found her with the Bible open before her. He suggested that they might pray; she demurred, but he ventured to begin, found right words and plenteous 'opening of heart' and they were reconciled. With gratitude he recorded in his diary that prayer was always his sovereign remedy, and that that never failed – but next morning he wrote to cancel the arrangements he had so rashly made.[34]

It may be well to conclude this section of our study by returning to the theme with which we began, namely the sheer courage and resolution that these women so often showed. In an age where neo-Puritan men seem so often to be womanish, it is immensely encouraging to find such resolute Christian women who retained their feminine beauty and yet manifested holy boldness. Today, if a Christian woman were molested and turned to a Christian man for help in the hope that some knight in shining armour would rush to help her, she might be deeply disappointed. I fear that those who call themselves men would, all too often, refuse to help her, hiding behind some specious pretence. They are cowards who shrink from the trouble that any such intervention might bring.

The feminine virtues of Lady Brilliana Harley are well documented. A loving wife and devoted mother, she was left to conduct the defence of Brampton Bryan against Royalist assault. The siege lasted seven weeks and a seven hundred-strong force of horse and foot soldiers surrounded her. Inside the castle there were fifty musketeers and fifty civilians – men, women, and children. Lady Harley resolutely defied all calls for surrender and 'taking full advantage of her position as a woman, she argued she could only act on Sir Robert's instructions, and since she did not know he would approve this plan, she could not take the decision herself because "I never will voluntarily betray the trust my husband reposes in me."'[35]

Just as moving is the account of Grisell Hume, later Lady Baillie of Jerviswood, who at the tender age of seventeen or eighteen, daily crept through the churchyard at midnight to take provisions to her father who was hiding in the family vault from the Stuart persecution of the Covenanters. She went in fear, trembling at every noise she supposed to be soldiers, searching for her father in the darkness. The first night the dogs of the nearby manse (who seemed to favour the Stuart cause!) barked with great violence. Her mother then hit on the scheme of persuading the minister that his dogs were mad and exceedingly dangerous. So skilful and persuasive was her case that the minister promptly hanged his 'mad dogs' the next day. So, night after night, Grisell went and sat with her father in the vault where the skeletons of his ancestors were interred. Through her help her father's life was sustained and he eventually escaped to Holland.[36]

CONCLUSIONS

It is now necessary to come to some conclusions and relate what has been said about the Puritan woman to our present situation.

Firstly, it is essential that we consider the Puritan woman *as she really was*. The subtitle of Leland Ryken's book entitled, *Worldly Saints* is *The Puritans as They Really Were*. For several centuries Puritanism has been subject to a campaign of negative propaganda. The Puritan woman was not some stereotypical Victorian matron (such a phrase is not meant to imply any derogatory evaluation of the Victorians!). She was both a godly and a sensitive, practical human being. As a woman she desired to be loved. Elizabeth Walker would smilingly ask her husband, 'Dost thou love me?' On one occasion, Dr Walker explained why he loved her and began by saying, 'First, for conscience.' She interrupted him immediately: 'I would have thee love me, not because thou must but because thou wilt, not as a duty but delight. For', she added, 'we are prone to reluctate against what is imposed but to take pleasure in what we choose.'[37] These Puritan women had husbands who really loved them. We see this in their lives and letters but we also learn about it by reading their husbands' lamentations over their deaths. Daniel Finch, later second Earl of Nottingham, on the death of his wife, wrote: 'for I have surely a better friend, a wife without her equal, and that I loved as myself, for she was willing even to die to wean me from this world . . . that we might meet in a better and live together eternally . . . I can say I once had the best woman in the world.' The Puritan minister Oliver Heywood on the death of his first wife, Elizabeth Augnier, wrote that she was, 'the mirror of patience and subjection in her relation as a child, as a wife, and of tenderness and care as a sister and as a mother. I want her at every times, everywhere, and in every work. Methinks I am but half myself without her.'[38]

Secondly, you will notice nothing has been said about the role of the Puritan woman *in the church*. This is mainly because her principal role was within the family as wife and mother and because, apart from the Quakers and exceptional circumstances such as that of Anne Hutchinson, there was no question of women teaching in the church. Perkins wrote: 'It is not warrantable for a woman by God's word to administer the sacrament of baptism . . . women are not allowed to preach, no, not in . . . case of necessity when men are wanting.' While Robinson declares, 'they are so debarred by their sex, as from ordinary prophesying, so from any other dealing (in the charge) wherein they take authority over the man . . . in a case extraordinary, namely where no man will, I see not but a woman may reprove the church rather than suffer it to go on in apparent wickedness and commensurate with it therein . . . Neither is there respect of person with God in the common duties of Christianity.'[39]

Thirdly, *these women were willing to take a line, in terms of personal holiness, that was totally contrary to the attitude of the world around them.* The Puritan woman would know well such texts as: 'The world cannot hate you; but me it hateth, because I testify of it that the works thereof are evil' (*John 7:7*) and 'They are of the world, therefore speak they of the world and the world heareth them' (*1 John 4:5*). We are not surprised, therefore, to find that the Puritan woman did not dress according to the fashion dictates of some seventeenth-century Mary Quant. She would never have dreamed of reasoning that if her dress stirred up lust in men, then that was their problem and they must deal with it; she was going to dress like her worldly friends so that she could witness effectively to them. Nor, for that matter, would she regard her children as 'kids' ('little goats'!), the upbringing of which was an inadequate sphere for her 'great talents and abilities'. The Puritan woman would have seen through such monstrous nonsense for what it is – a devaluing of the souls of her children. To say she would be content with her lot in life as a wife and a mother would be a grievous understatement; she gloried in her role as wife and mother. We must, of course, recognize here that because of the high incidence of death through childbirth women often tended to be in very short supply. Only very rarely did Puritan women face the painful problem of singleness faced by many evangelical women today.

Similarly, in education, the emphasis was on the education of the boys in the family. Yet many Puritan households were significantly ahead of their time. The Puritan family would not have consented to the comments of James I who, when it was suggested that his daughter Elizabeth should learn Latin, replied, 'to make women learned and foxes tame had the same effect: to make them more cunning'. Not surprisingly, he forbade it.[40]

Let us remember also that this period (1550–1700) was a very different age from our own, both nationally and spiritually. While we live in an age of national degeneration, indeed of disintegration, the Elizabethan age was one in which the very idea of what it was to be English came to be more clearly defined. (Certainly, there are parallels to be drawn between our own age and the moral degeneracy of Charles II coupled with James II's active promotion of the Roman Catholic cause within our nation; but even here the parallels are limited.) Let us remember that the Puritan era was one of intense spiritual activity, sometimes described in terms of a revival. In 1662, 2,000 ministers were ejected from their churches on grounds of conscience. The population at that time was approximately 4,750,000. That is comparable to finding 20,000 preachers today who would be willing to forsake their manses and stipends over matters of biblical principle.

We live in a very different age not only politically but also spiritually.

Let us also remember that our Puritan women often had Puritan fathers, brothers, husbands, and ministers, and like them had a great appetite for the preaching of the Word of God. Our much-admired Brilliana Harley would have happily attended a fast day, the character of which is described in the following:

> Upon such a day Mr Gower will go into the pulpit between eight and nine o'clock in the morning and there pray and preach extempore till past one of the clock following. They then sing a psalm but Mr Gower cometh not forth the pulpit by past five of the clock following, if daylight continues so long.[41]

Confused by the teachings of strident feminism there are those who are agitating for the exercise of more female power in the church. However, we maintain that what evangelicalism needs is not more feminine influence, but less! Of course, there may not be *de jure* female ministers, elders, and deacons in our churches but if *de facto* the minister, elders, and deacons are dominated by their wives, petticoat-government by proxy is the result. Once this begins to happen the church is in danger of being governed not on the basis of biblical principles but on the basis of sentiment. Mrs Mary Kassian draws our attention to this very issue:

> Ideas that were once considered radically bizarre are now considered conventional. Feminist wisdom is even being forwarded by officials in the highest level of the judicial system. For example, Canadian Supreme Court Justice Bertha Wilson, in a speech to the Osgoode Hall Law School in February of 1990 called for the transformation of the law along feminist principles and for the re-education of her male colleagues in 'summer schools on sexism'.

She endorsed the idea, proposed by second-phase feminist philosophers, that women are more caring and
inherently 'nicer than men', and that they are less concerned than men with abstract notions of justice, less
preoccupied with what is 'right' and 'wrong' and hence
less inclined to separate their feelings from their thinking.
She went on to chastise her fellow judges for relying too
much on the evidence of a case instead of entering 'into
the skin of the litigant and making his or her experience
part of your experience and only when you have done
that, to judge'. According to Wilson, a woman who had
suffered at the hands of a particular man could not read-
ily be judged as guilty in the murder of that man. The
implications of these feminist notions are radical and drastic to the traditional practice of law and justice, and yet
they hardly met a raised eyebrow. Little public debate
resulted, just a praising article in a leading national newspaper.[42]

It should be remembered that for Isaiah female rule among
the people of God was a sign of divine judgment. 'As for my
people, children are their oppressors and women rule over
them. O my people, they which lead thee cause thee to err and
destroy the way of thy paths' (*Isa.* 3:12.)

You may ask whether I am saying that feminism and undue
female influence is the cause of our present troubles in many
areas. I have no doubt it is *a* cause but not *the* cause. You
remember that when Adam sinned he blamed his wife: 'The
woman whom thou gavest to be with me she gave me of the
tree and I did eat' (*Gen.* 3:11). That God rejected Adam's
whingeing abdication of his responsibilities is evidenced by
the fact that God testifies, 'For since by man came death, by
man came also the resurrection of the dead. For as in Adam all
die even so in Christ shall all be made alive' (*1 Cor.* 15:22). It
does not say, 'as in Eve all died', nor does it say, 'For as by one

woman's disobedience many were made sinners', but 'by one man's disobedience many were made sinners' (*Rom.* 5:19).

Whilst Elizabeth I was not a Puritan, the statement she made at Tilbury on 19 August 1588 when addressing her troops during the Armada crisis, may be adapted here.

> I am come to live or die amongst you all, to lay down, for my God and for my kingdom and for my people, my hon-our and my blood even in the dust. I know I have the body of a weak feeble woman but I have the heart and stomach of a king and a King of England too – and think foul scorn that Parma of Spain or any Prince of Europe should dare to invade the border of my realm.[43]

Some of the neo-Puritan men whom I know would prob-ably say, 'I have the body of a strong and vigorous man, but I have a pusillanimous spirit, and if I see the church under attack and corrupted by evil, or someone – some man or some woman – being molested, I will at all costs avoid trouble and by administrative stratagems and pious platitudes, under a guise of spirituality, avoid doing anything to help such a woman or cleanse the church'!

'Ye that are men' must, on the one hand, not be like the male macho neo-Puritan who speaks great swelling words and alien-ates thinking women from this awful misrepresentation of true manhood. Christian men – and indeed Christian husbands – who are afraid to admit that women in general and wives in particular may be superior to them in intellect and ability do no good to the cause of Christ. It is indeed ironic that two English Queens, Elizabeth I and Victoria, witnessed the greatest periods in Britain's national fortunes, while under the libidinous and lecher-ous Charles II the nation was reduced to a kind of bondage. In the book of Judges we read of Deborah who was raised up by God as a reproach to Barak for his want of manhood.

We need real men in the church! The trouble is that in a church whose ethos is feminine and where women exercise undue control and influence any man worthy of the name is going to feel uncomfortable. There is here a vicious circle that needs to be broken. This is particularly worrying to many who do not believe that an effeminate evangelicalism will be able to stand before the energetic advance of a militant masculine Islam.

Some neo-Puritan men seem to think that crushing their wives is an evidence of their spirituality. This is, however, not a biblical way to think and behave at all: the wife is a help-meet to her husband, not some kind of doormat upon which he wipes his feet. Let us hear Gataker:

> It is no shame . . . for a woman to be house-wifely, be she never as well-born, be she never so wealthy. For it is the woman's trade to be; it is the end of her creation; it is that that she was made for. She was made for man and given to man, not to be a play-fellow or a bed-fellow, or a ta-ble-mate. Only with him (and yet to be all these too) but to be a yoke-fellow, a work-fellow, a fellow labourer with him, to be an assistant and an helper unto him, in the managing of such domestical and household affairs . . . Art thou to make any choice of a wife? Choose thee an housewife. It is no shame for thee, though thou beest wealthy, to seek her at the washhouse . . . Seek her at the needle, at the wheel, at the spindle. It is no disgrace for any to be found and taken at such employments.

Again, and in a fashion that serves well to climax and close this topic, Gataker proclaims the function of a wife as a help-meet:

> It is not good, saith God for man to be alone; I will make him an Help, or an Assistant; not a mate only, but an helper; not a companion only, but an assistant too. Man being a creature of the kind, not of those that love only to a flock . . . and live together . . . but of those that desire to combine and work and labour also together . . . Now

behold here a fit and a ready help . . . For who fitter to help man, than she whom God himself hath fitted for man and made for this very end to be a fit help for him? I will make him such an help, saith God, as shall be meet for him: one that shall be as his match . . . one that is in all parts and abilities in a manner as himself . . . and certainly, as there are offices not a few, that none can in many cases so fitly perform about a man as a wife may; so there is no help that he hath, or ordinarily can have, so ready at all times as this help . . .[44]

Let us raise our daughters in such a way that they will not only live in glad and loving submission to their husbands, but that they will also be real 'help-meets' for their husbands. May the wife's spiritual-mindedness bring great blessings both to her husband and to their children. As Proverbs says of the virtuous woman: 'She will do him good, and not evil all the days of her life . . . her children arise up and call her blessed, her husband also, and he praises her' (*Prov.* 31:28).

So let us learn from the example of the Puritan woman and let us pray that, in this degenerate age, God will raise up women of such eminent godliness, who are willing to suffer for the sake of Christ and unwilling to conform to the pattern of a rotting age. Let us pray that God will raise up Christian men worthy to be husbands of such virtuous women. Such women will be an honour to their parents and a blessing to their husbands, a true mother to their children and an ornament to the church. Above all, 'They shall be mine, saith the LORD of hosts, in that day when I make up my jewels' (*Mal.* 3:17).

[1] A paper given at the Westminster Conference in 1994.

[2] Antonia Fraser, *The Weaker Vessel: Woman's Lot in Seventeenth Century England* (Weidenfield and Nicolson, 1993), p. 45.

[3] Nicholas Harris Nicolas, *The Literary Remains of Lady Jane Grey*, (London: 1825), p. 42.   [4] Ibid., p. 49 f.   [5] Ibid., p. lxxxvii f.

[6] Menna Prestwich, (ed.), *International Calvinism 1541-1710* (Oxford: Clarendon Press), p. 49.

[7] Henry Beveridge & Jules Bonnet (eds.) *Calvin's Selected Works: Tracts and Letters*, Vol. 4, (Grand Rapids: Baker Book House), p. 141.

[8] Ibid., p. 175.

[9] William J. Bouwsma, *John Calvin* (Oxford University Press), p. 23.

[10] Charles H. and Katherine George, *The Protestant Mind of the English Reformation 1570–1640* (Princeton: 1961), p. 262 f.

[11] Thomas Boston, *Memoirs* (Edinburgh: Banner of Truth, 1988), p. 157.

[12] James Anderson, *Memorable Women of the Puritan Times*, vol. 2, (London: 1862), p. 371.

[13] Fraser, p. 143.

[14] John Adair, *Founding Fathers, The Puritans in England and America* (London: J. M. Dent, 1982), p. 261.

[15] G. F. Willison, *Saints and Strangers* (New York: 1945), p. 66–7.

[16] Jacqueline Eales, *Puritans and Roundheads, The Harleys of Brampton Bryan and the Outbreak of the English Civil War* (Cambridge University Press, 1990), p. 49.

[17] Edmund S. Morgan, *The Puritan Family* (New York: Harper Row, 1966), p. 67.

[18] Lucy Hutchinson, *Memoirs of the Life of Colonel Hutchinson* (London: George Beck, 1905), pp. 17–18.   [19] Ibid., p. 53.   [20] Ibid., p. 57.

[21] Fraser, p. 28.

[22] Leland Ryken, *Worldly Saints, The Puritans as They Really Were* (Grand Rapids: Zondervan, 1986), pp. 39–40.   [23] Ibid., p. 52.   [24] Fraser, p. 59.

[25] Martha Saxton, 'Bearing the Burden? Puritan Wives', *History Today*, October 1994, p. 28.   [26] Ibid., p. 31.

[27] Eales, p. 27.

[28] Fraser, p. 52–4.

[29] Ryken, p. 78.   [30] Ibid., p. 28.

[31] John Calvin, *Commentary on Hebrews; 1 &2 Peter* (Oliver & Boyd, 1963), p. 318.

[32] Adair, p. 255–6.

[33] Morgan, p. 40.

[34] Cragg, *Puritanism in the Period of the Great Persecution 1666-1688* (Cambridge University Press, 1957), p. 145–6.

[35] Eales, p. 169–71.

[36] Anderson, p. 552.

[37] Fraser, p. 54.   [38] Ibid., p. 38.

[39] George, p. 288–9.

[40] Fraser, p. 135.

[41] Eales, p. 58.

[42] Mary A. Kassian, *The Feminist Gospel* (Crossway Books), p. 252.

[43] Elizabeth Jenkins, *Elizabeth and Leicester* (Gollancz, 1961) p. 155–6.

[44] George, p. 287–8.

3

WALTER MARSHALL AND
SANCTIFICATION[1]

Walter Marshall was a Presbyterian minister whose book *The Gospel Mystery of Sanctification* was published in 1692. The word 'mystery' used in the title derives probably, although not certainly, from 1 Timothy 3:16: 'And without controversy, great is the mystery of godliness: God was manifest in the flesh, justified in the Spirit, seen of angels, preached unto the Gentiles, believed on in the world, received up into glory.' I say 'probably' because the words of Ephesians 5:32: 'This is a great mystery: but I speak concerning Christ and the church', could well have been in the forefront of his mind as he wrote this book.

We do not know very much about Walter Marshall: his fame rests on his book, not on the achievements of his life, of which little is recorded. He was born at Bishop's Wearmouth in Durham on 15 June 1628. His father was a Clerk in Holy Orders. In 1643 he went as a scholar to Winchester College and from there he proceeded to the sister foundation, New College, Oxford where he was Fellow from 1648–57. In 1654 he was approved to the living of Fawley and in 1656 became Vicar of Hursley in Hampshire. There he married and had two daughters, Rebeka and Ann. Being a Presbyterian, he was immediately in trouble at the Restoration and one 'N.N.' wrote: 'He was put under the Bartholomew Bushel with near two thousand more lights (a sin not yet repented of) whose illumination made the land a Goshen.' Fairly soon after this he was instituted Minister of a Presbyterian congregation at Gosport, Hampshire. His preaching was edifying and acceptable but he was not noted for his public gifts. He ministered over a wide area and there are records of his preaching in Winchester, Alton, Winton, Taunton, and Crewkerne. An unsympathetic Royalist described him as a 'violent Nonconformist'. He died at Gosport in 1680.

During his time at Gosport, Marshall seems to have come into great spiritual difficulties. He sought after holiness and peace but could not find them. He is said to have read Richard Baxter extensively, but when he spoke to Baxter the author complained that Marshall had taken him too legally. He went to Thomas Goodwin and spoke freely of his great troubles of heart and mind, and of the sins that weighed upon him. At the conclusion of the interview, Goodwin told him 'he had forgotten to mention the greatest sin of all, the sin of unbelief, in not believing on the Lord Jesus Christ for the remission of his sins and the sanctifying of his nature'.

In due course he came into an experience of deliverance from his bondage and realized that his trouble was that really, although unconsciously, he had been trying to make his own righteousness the basis of his dealings with God and the ground of his peace, and consequently had erred from the biblical way of submission to the righteousness of God in Jesus Christ. Henceforward, 'he set himself to studying and preaching Christ and attained to eminent holiness, great peace of conscience, and joy in the Holy Ghost'.

While the above account tells us about the man, it still really gives no indication why we are studying the one book he wrote. An answer is to be found, of course, in the contents of the book itself, but another answer is to be found in the many eminent divines who have borne testimony to the value of this book. It is true that just because a man praises a book it does not necessarily mean that he has read it or, even if he has read it, that he has understood it. Thus W. H. Griffith Thomas writing of the Keswick Movement with its distinctive holiness teaching, mentions Marshall, with a number of others, as being one from whom this teaching derived, as a note in an article by Dr J. I. Packer indicated:

> The roots of the distinctive teaching can easily be traced in the writings of Walter Marshall, William Law, John Wesley, Fletcher of Madeley, Thomas à Kempis, Brother Lawrence, Madame Guyon, the letters of Samuel Rutherford, and the memoirs of M'Cheyne. To this notable array of Calvinistic Puritans, Wesleyan Perfectionists, and Mystical Quietists, J. B. Figgis adds Francis de Sales, Molinos, and Jonathan Edwards, and Dr Barabas . . . adds Romaine.[2]

Seeing Marshall in such company might make the mind reel! However he has far more sober recommendation than these. Thus William Cowper testified of him,

> The book you mention lies now upon my table; Marshall is an old acquaintance of mine: I have both read him and heard him read with pleasure and edification. The doctrines he maintains are, under the influence of the divine Spirit, the very life of my soul, and the soul of all my happiness; that Jesus is a present Saviour from the guilt of sin by his most precious blood and from the power of it by his Spirit; that, corrupt and wretched in ourselves, in him and in him only are we complete.[3]

James Hervey, the author of Theron and Aspasio, is similarly laudatory:

> It is with great pleasure and without any diffidence that I refer my readers to Mr Marshall's treatise on sanctification, which I shall not recommend in the style of a critic

nor like a person of taste, but with all the simplicity of the weakest Christian: I mean, from my own experience. It has been made one of the most useful books to my own heart. I scarce ever fail to receive spiritual consolation and strength from the perusal of it, and were I to be banished on to some desolate island possessed of only two books beside my Bible, this should be one of the two, perhaps the first that I would choose.[4]

He comments elsewhere: 'Here the gospel diamond is set, not in gold but in steel.'[5]

THE CONTEXT

If we are to understand *The Gospel Mystery*, and also if we are to understand the reason why Marshall wrote it as he did, it is necessary to say something about the historical context. In point of fact the book is very controversial, although in a casual reading you might not realize this. This is partly because Marshall is subdued most of the time in the way he conducts his controversy. Nevertheless, all the way through the book he does refer explicitly or in more subtle ways to those from whom he differs.

Sometimes of course he is quite direct and speaks with some force. Two instances may be given simply to illustrate the kind of thing Marshall says. Thus, referring to the Neonomian reaction to Antinomian licentiousness he writes:

I hope to show that this, their imagined sure foundation of holiness, was never laid by the holy God; but that it is rather an error in the foundation, pernicious to the true faith and to holiness of life. I account it an error especially to be abhorred and detested because we are so prone to be seduced by it, and because it is an error whereby Satan, transforming himself into an angel of light and a patron of holiness, hath greatly withstood the gospel in the Apostles' time, and stirred up men to persecute out of zeal for the law: and hath since prevailed to set up and maintain Popery, whereby the mystery of iniquity worketh apace in these days to corrupt the purity of the gospel among Protestants and to heal the deadly wound that was given to Popery by preaching the doctrine of Justification by faith without works.[6]

This is pretty violent language, especially as one suspects it was directed to the teaching of Baxter, or, if not specifically at Baxter, at those who derived their views from him.

Marshall was pretty even-handed in his controversial passages. Later we find him delivering a broadside in a different direction.

Though all holiness be effectually attained by the life of faith in Christ, yet the use of any means appointed in the Word for attaining and promoting it is not hereby made void but rather established. This is needful to be observed against the pride and ignorance of some carnal gospellers who, being puffed up with the conceit of their feigned faith, imagine themselves to be in such a state of perfection that they are above all ordinances except singing hallelujahs . . .[7]

There is a real difficulty here, which constitutes the second great mystery concerning Walter Marshall. For while he frequently refers to the teaching of those with whom he disagrees, he does not identify them by name, nor does he cite chapter and verse of their teaching, unlike Samuel Rutherford who, in his *Survey of Spiritual Antichrist*, gives precise details of those against whom he is so forcefully contending. This means one has to try and identify, by a kind of detective work, whom Marshall was actually fighting, for fighting he certainly was.

On the one hand Marshall is fighting the Antinomians. Historically this refers to the sort of people and the kind of teaching which occurred in New England in the years 1634–36, and which has been associated with the figure of Ann Hutchinson. Cotton Mather heads one section of his account with the words '*Dux faemina facta*' ('woman made leader'), and then adds '*Nulla fere causa est, in qua non faemina litem moverit*' ('there are few controversies where a woman is not at the bottom of them')![8] There are easily available accounts of this controversy in Kenneth Campbell, 'The Antinomian Controversy', (*Westminster Conference, 1974*) and in the lengthy article by Iain H. Murray in the *The Banner of Truth* magazine, Issue 179–180. 'Ann Hutchinson made claims to special revelation, that most of the pastors in New England were under the law, that though she would be persecuted in New England yet God would deliver her and destroy those who opposed her.'[9] The controversy involved the relationship of the law and gospel, and was concerned with what constituted true gospel preaching which brought men to liberty in Christ, and what kind of preaching tended to bring them into bondage to the law.

In England the Antinomians varied from the near respectability of Tobias Crisp (1600–41), through such people as Eaton (1575–1641) and Saltmarsh (d. 1647), to the extreme position of the Ranters. One of their number, Thomas Clarkson, wrote: 'At this time my judgment was this, that there was no man could be freed from sin till he had acted that so-called sin as no sin.'[10] The Ranters seem to have created a stir out of all proportion to their numbers. They were characterized by a hostility to Scripture and they exalted the universal witness of the Spirit. Thus Rutherford lists fifty-three errors of the Antinomians using Saltmarsh as his principal source. Here are just a few:

'3. As Christ was God manifested in the flesh, so is he incarnate and made flesh in every saint . . .

'5. The whole letter of the Scriptures holdeth forth a covenant of works . . . by which believers under grace are not to hear or read the Scriptures, nor to search them . . .

'7. The due search and knowledge of Holy Scripture is not a safe way of searching and finding Christ . . .

'10. A Christian is not bound to the law as a rule of his Christian walking . . .

'20. The witness of the Spirit is merely immediate without respect to sanctification or acts thereof as signs in concurrence of the Word . . .

'22. To question assurance of a spiritually good estate upon the commission of a murder or adultery is a token of no true assurance.'[11]

On the other side to the Antinomians were men such as Baxter and it was upholders of his opinions who became engaged in a further outbreak of the Antinomian controversy towards the end of the seventeenth century. Baxter was both a bitter opponent of Antinomianism and one of the principal architects of Neonomianism. Dr J. I. Packer's thesis on Baxter,[12] a most valuable work which one wishes was more easily available, describes Baxter's violent reaction on reading Saltmarsh. In Baxter's view Antinomianism had arisen as 'a reaction against the "overdoing" of tears and terrors in a second-rate Puritanism – many godly Protestants' seldom and unskilful opening of the mystery of redemption . . . preaching all for humiliation and little of the wonderful love of God revealed in Jesus Christ.'[13] According to Baxter, 'Antinomianism comes from gross ignorance and leads to gross wickedness.' Packer speaks of some of the basic views of the 'Enthusiasts' who 'held that over and above what he [God] may do through the means, the Spirit works immediately, going beyond Scripture both in revelation of truth and in direct impulses to action. Man's duty therefore was to forego religious routine and to wait passively before God until the Spirit spoke. He must not tie himself to the means, for the Spirit was now working above and without means. To be tied to means is legal and carnal, the mark of spiritual religion is immediacy of communion with God.'[14]

Packer gives a masterly summary of the issues:

Baxter had no doubt that the impulse and the theology behind the Antinomian quest for 'comfort' at all costs came from the pit, for its outcome in practice was this; men went to the Antinomians troubled about their sins and all the advice they received was to be troubled about them no longer, for Christ had taken them away. Where the Puritan had said, Put sin out of your life, the Antinomian said, Put it out of your mind. Look at the law, consider your guilt, learn to hate sin and fear it and let it go, said the Puritan; Look away from the law and forget your sins and guilt, look away from yourself and stop worrying, said the Antinomian. The way to 'comfort', said the orthodox, is to come to Christ that he may justify you. The way to 'comfort', again retorted the Antinomian, is to believe here and now that Christ has already justified you so that nothing remains for you to do . . . In short, Antinomianism made repentance unnecessary for assurance and good works unnecessary for heaven. Its leaders proclaimed the paradox that sanctity would spontaneously appear in the lives of those who did not need it, but Baxter knowing human nature did not believe this. He consistently treated Antinomianism as an exotic and streamlined version of the happy-go-lucky religion of the pagan Englishman which the Puritan Pastor had fought so long, a religion equally notable for its liberal offers of 'comfort' to those who were not entitled to it.[15]

With Saltmarsh saying that 'many preachers are like some chirurgeon [surgeon] who keep their patient from healing too soon that they may make the cure more admired, do accordingly keep . . . souls with their wounds open'[16] and Baxter not only attacking the Antinomians but vigorously propagating his peculiar views on the atonement and justification, you should by now have got the idea that Marshall did not write in a time of theological calm. With a certain grace and an eye set upon the spiritual need of his hearers Marshall entered the fray. He attacks both the Neonomians and the Antinomians. In some things he is nearer to Baxter than to the Antinomians, while in others he is much nearer a man like Crisp than Baxter.

CONTENT

It is necessary to give some indication of what Marshall actually taught. It would not be profitable to enter into discussion without giving the main thrust of his argument. Bacon in his essay 'Of Studies' writes, 'Some books are to be tasted, others to be swallowed, and some few to be chewed or digested.'[17] *The Gospel Mystery* fits into the last category and since Marshall was not a man to waste words it is not easy to condense his writing.

Marshall gives fourteen directions concerning the subject he is dealing with.

DIRECTION 1

'That we may acceptably perform the Duties of Holiness and Righteousness required in the Law our first work is to learn the powerful and effectual Means by which we may attain to so great an End.'[18] You will immediately recognize that Marshall was not an Antinomian. Indeed to give such a prominence to the law in his first direction might lead to a misunderstanding concerning Marshall's grasp of the issues involved.

Marshall then begins to explain hastily, 'The scope of all is to teach you how you may attain to that practice and manner of life which we call holiness, righteousness or godliness, obedience, true religion, and which God requireth of us in the law, particularly the moral law, which is summed up in the Ten Commandments and more briefly in those two great commandments of love to God and our neighbour, Matthew

22:37–39.' This holiness he says, 'Consists not only in external works of piety and charity, but in the holy thoughts, imaginations, and affections of the soul, and chiefly in love; from whence all other works must flow or else they are not acceptable to God: not only in refraining the execution of sinful lusts, but in longing and delighting to do the will of God, and in a cheerful obedience to God, without repining, fretting, grudging at any duty, as if it were a grievous yoke and burden to you . . . The Lord is not at all loved with that love that is due to him as Lord of all, if he is not loved with all our heart, spirit, and might. We are to love everything in him, his justice, holiness, sovereign authority, all-seeing eye, and all his decrees, commands, judgments, and all his doings . . .'

Marshall goes on to magnify the excellency of the law and says our great need is to learn how we may attain to this keeping of the law. Many men and preachers are concerned with the practice of the law without considering how we may find the effectual means to practise it. He then teaches concerning man's complete inability, his position as a lawbreaker and therefore cursed of God. He argues, 'Sanctification, whereby our hearts and lives are conformed to the law, is a grace of God communicated to us by means as well as justification, by means of teaching and learning something we cannot see without the word (*Acts* 26:17–18). There is a form of doctrine made use of by God, to make people free from sin . . . the learning of it requireth double work; because we must unlearn many of our former deeply-rooted opinions and become fools that we may be wise.' He also lists the various false views of sanctification and their consequences.

DIRECTION 2

'Several Endowments and Qualifications are necessary to enable us for the immediate Practice of the Law.

1. 'An inclination and propensity of heart to the duties of the law is necessary to frame and enable us for the immediate

practice of them.' He attacks the view that the universal redemption of mankind has endowed all men with a kind of freedom of the will.

2. 'We must be well persuaded of our reconciliation with God . . . And herein I include the great benefit of justification as the means whereby we are reconciled to God which is described in Scripture either by forgiving our sins or by the imputation of righteousness to us.' This, he comments, is thought by some to be a great pillar of antinomianism and that the only way to establish sincere obedience is to make it rather a condition to be performed before our own actual justification and reconciliation with God. He goes on to assert 'That we cannot be beforehand with God in loving him before we apprehend his love to us. And consult your experience if you have any true love to God, whether it were not wrought in you by a sense of God's love first to you.'

He emphasizes the need for a conscience purged from dead works: 'This evil guilty conscience whereby we judge God is our enemy, and his justice is against us to our everlasting condemnation, by reason of our sins, doth strongly maintain and increase the dominion of sin and Satan in us, and worketh more mischievous effects in the soul against godliness, even to bring the soul to hate God, and to wish there were no God, no heaven, no hell, so that we might escape the punishment due to us . . . God hath abundantly discovered to us in his word, that his method in bringing men from sin to holiness of life, is, first to make them know that he loveth them, and that their sins are blotted out . . . And during all the time of the Old Testament, God was pleased to make the entrance into religion to be by circumcision; which was not only a sign, but also a seal of the righteousness that is by faith, whereby God justifieth people while they are considered ungodly (*Rom.* 4:11, 15). And this seal was administered to children of eight days old, before they could perform any condition of sincere obedience, for their justification, that their furniture for holy practice might be ready beforehand.'

3. '. . . that we be persuaded of our future enjoyment of the everlasting heavenly happiness . . . This assertion oft hath several sorts of adversaries to oppose it. Some account that a persuasion of our own future happiness before we have persevered in sincere obedience tendeth to licentiousness, and that the way to do good works, is rather to make them a condition necessary to procuring of this persuasion. Others condemn all works that we are allured or stirred up to by the future enjoyment of this heavenly happiness, as legal, mercenary, flowing from self-love and not from any pure love to God; and they figure out sincere godliness by a man bearing fire in one hand to burn up heaven, and water in the other to quench hell; intimating that the true service of God must not proceed at all from hope of reward, or fear of punishment, but only from love.'

4. The last endowment is that 'we be well-persuaded of sufficient strength both to will and perform our duty acceptably, until we come to the enjoyment of heavenly happiness'.

DIRECTION 3
'The way to get holy Endowments and Qualifications necessary to frame and enable us for the immediate Practice of the Law, is to receive them out of the Fulness of Christ, by a fellowship with him; and that we may have this Fellowship, we must be in Christ, and have Christ himself in us, by a mystical Union with him.'

Marshall explains this by saying, 'As we are justified by a righteousness wrought out in Christ, and imputed to us; so we are sanctified by such a holy frame and qualifications, as are first wrought out, and completed in Christ for us, and then imparted to us. And as our natural corruption was produced originally in the first Adam, and propagated from him to us; so our new nature and holiness is first produced in Christ, and derived from him to us, or as it were propagated. So that we

are not at all to work together with Christ, in making or producing that holy frame in us, but only to take it to ourselves,
and use it in our holy practice, as made ready to our hands.'
Many people go through great agonies in seeking to mortify
their sins and find the entrance into the Christian life, because
they do not realize that sanctification results from union and
communion with Christ. This mystical union between Christ
and the believer is one of three in Scripture, the other two
being 'the union of the Trinity of Persons in one Godhead, and
the union of the divine and human natures in one person,
Jesus Christ, God and man.'

This kind of statement may be why some of those propound-
ing Keswick doctrines felt that they had a friend in Marshall;
any proper reading of his works will show how far they were
mistaken in their view that he taught similar ideas to their
own.

Marshall is always anxious to avoid being misconstrued,
and so he adds that this does not mean that a believer is made
God, but only the temple of God. Nor does it mean that a
believer will be perfect in holiness or that Christ will be made
a sinner, for 'Christ knoweth how to dwell in believers by certain measures or degrees, and to make them holy so far only
as he dwelleth in them.' Presumably this comment is aimed at
very dangerous views held by Antinomians: thus Rutherford
summarized Saltmarsh: 'As Christ was God manifest in the
flesh, so is he made flesh in every saint.'[19]

This direction emphasizes the part the Holy Spirit has in the
work. 'Our sanctification is by the Holy Ghost, by whom we
live and walk holily (*Rom.* 15:16; *Gal.* 5:25). Now, the Holy
Ghost first rested on Christ in all fullness, that he might be
communicated from him to us . . . And when he sanctifies us,
he baptizes us into Christ, and joins us to Christ by himself, as
the present bond of union (*1 Cor.* 12:13).'

He further argues that in this way the saints of the Old Testament were sanctified, thus guarding against any unwarranted

division of the Covenant, such a division as the Antinomians were prone to make. 'Now, the Spirit was able and effectual to unite those saints to that flesh which Christ was to take to himself in the fullness of time, because he was the same in both, and to give out to them that grace with which Christ would afterwards fill his flesh, for their salvation, as well as ours. Therefore David accounted Christ's flesh to be his, and spake of Christ's death and resurrection as his own, beforehand, as fully as any of us can do since (*Psa.* 16:9–11).'

DIRECTION 4

'The Means or Instruments whereby the Spirit of God accomplishes our Union with Christ, and our Fellowship with him in all holiness, are the Gospel, whereby Christ enters into our hearts to work faith in us; and faith, whereby we actually receive Christ himself, with all his fullness, into our hearts. And this faith is a grace of the Spirit, whereby we heartily believe the gospel, and also believe on Christ, as he is revealed and freely promised to us therein, for all his salvation.'

Marshall then proceeds to explain what he means by faith. 'Saving faith must necessarily contain two acts, believing the truth of the gospel, and believing in Christ, as promised freely to us in the gospel, for all salvation . . . And both these acts must be performed heartily, with an unfeigned love to the truth, and a desire of Christ and his salvation *above all things.* We must desire earnestly that God would create in us a clean heart and right spirit, as well as hide his face from our sins (*Psa.* 51:9-10); not like many, that care for nothing in Christ but only deliverance from hell.'

Marshall then deals with difficulties and objections. Some Protestants consider this a dangerous doctrine and their correction to it is 'that sanctification is necessary to salvation as well as justification; and that though we be justified by faith; yet we are sanctified by our own performance of the law; and so they set up salvation by works and make the grace of

justification to be of none effect, and not at all comfortable.'
He further argues against those who would not have this faith
the principal saving act, but they had rather it should be
obedience to all Christ's laws, at least in resolution; or a consent that Christ should be their Lord, accepting of his terms of
salvation, as a resignation of themselves to his government in
all things.

However, he is very careful to guard against possible confusion here. 'By the very act of hearty trusting or believing on
Christ for all salvation and happiness, the soul casteth and
putteth away from itself, everything that keepeth it at a distance from Christ; as all confidence in our strength, endeavours,
works, privileges; or in any worldly pleasures; profits, honours; or in any human helps and succours for our happiness
and salvation: because such confidences are inconsistent with
our confidence in Christ for all salvation.' He then goes on to
show that faith is a grace worked by the exercise of God's
mighty new creating power. 'When saving faith is wrought in
us, the same Spirit giveth us fast hold of Christ by it. As he
openeth the mouth of faith to receive Christ, so he filleth it
with Christ . . Thus are we first passive and then active in this
great work of mystical union: we are first apprehended of
Christ, and then we apprehend Christ. Christ entereth first
into the soul to join himself to it, by giving it the spirit of faith:
and so the soul receiveth Christ and his Spirit by their own
power.'

DIRECTION 5

'We cannot attain to the Practice of true holiness, by any of
our endeavours, while we continue in our natural state, and
are not partakers of a new state, by union and fellowship with
Christ through faith.'

He first of all speaks of the error of the natural man who
seeks to reform his life according to the law without any
thought that his state must be changed before his life can be

changed from sin to righteousness. He then reminds us that 'we have no ground to trust on Christ to help us to will or to do that which is acceptable to him while we continue in our natural state; or to imagine that freedom of will to holiness is restored to us by the merits of his death'.

DIRECTION 6

'Those that endeavour to perform sincere obedience to all the commands of Christ, as the condition whereby they are to procure for themselves a right and title to salvation, and a good ground to trust on him for the same, do seek their salvation by the works of the law, and not by the Faith of Christ, as he is revealed in the gospel: and they shall never be able to perform any true holy obedience by all such endeavours.'

He writes, 'the persuasion of salvation, by the condition of sincere obedience, has its original from our corrupt natural reason, and is part of the wisdom of this world.' He obviously has in mind the teaching of Baxter and the Neonomians when he writes, 'they plead not for doing duties, as obliged thereto by the authority of the law given of God by Moses, but only in obedience to the commands of Christ in the gospel. Neither do they plead for salvation by sincere obedience without Christ, but only by Christ, and through his merits and righteousness. And they acknowledge, that both salvation itself, and sincere obedience are given to them freely by the grace of Christ: so that all is of grace. They acknowledge also, that their salvation is by faith, because sincere obedience is wrought in them by believing the gospel, and is included in the nature of that faith which is the entire condition for our salvation, calling it the resignating act of faith. But all their reasons are but a fallacious vizard upon a legal way of salvation, to make it look pure gospel.' He then shows this is but the Galatian heresy appearing again. He emphatically maintains that 'The difference between the law and the gospel does not at all consist in this, that the one consists in perfect doing; the other, only in sincere doing: but in this, that the one requires doing, the other no doing, but believing for life and salvation. Their terms are different not only in degree, but in their whole nature.'

He argues that though this idea of sincere obedience as acceptable to God may produce a kind of result, yet it never produced one act truly pleasing to God. 'Though they labour earnestly and pray fervently, fast frequently and oblige themselves to holiness by many vows, and press themselves to the practice of it by the most forcible motives, taken from the infinite power, justice, and knowledge of God, the equity and goodness of his commands, the salvation of Christ, everlasting happiness and misery, or any other motive improved by the most affectionate meditation; yet they shall never attain to the end which they aim at in such an erroneous way. They may restrain their corruptions, and bring themselves to many hypocritical slavish performances, by which they may be esteemed among men, as eminent saints; but they shall not be able to mortify one corruption, or to perform one duty in such a manner as God approveth . . . This is but a chip off the same block . . . It requires of us the performance of sincere obedience before we have the means necessary to produce it, by making it antecedent to our justification, and persuasion of eternal happiness, and our actual enjoyment of union and fellowship with Christ, and of that new nature which is to be had only in him by faith.'

The effect of this doctrine is but to stir up the corruption of the human heart and make sinners hate God and rebel against him, and to sink into unutterable despair. While supposedly upholding the law, in point of fact it frequently leads to a corrupting of the law in such a way as to make carnal men think they may keep it. Marshall concludes: 'Therefore the doctrine of salvation by sincere obedience, that was invented against Antinomianism, may well be ranked among the worst Antinomianian errors. For my part, I hate it with perfect hatred, and account it mine enemy, as I have found it to be.'

DIRECTION 7

'We are not to imagine that our Hearts and Lives must be changed from Sin to Holiness in any measure, before we may safely venture to trust on Christ for the sure enjoyment of himself, and his Salvation.'

Marshall here touches on the issue of preparation for faith. He argues that what people think of as preparation for faith is either faith itself or pertains to those things that are the result of faith. To try to make ourselves fit for Christ is to be led away from Christ by a satanic delusion. 'While we endeavour to prepare our way to Christ by holy qualifications, we do rather fill it with stumbling blocks, and deep pits, whereby our souls are hindered from ever attaining to the salvation of Christ.'

He then begins to deal with particular difficulties which arise in this field. First of all, some think it necessary to repent before they believe in Christ for their salvation because repentance is absolutely necessary for salvation (*Luke* 13:3). He writes: 'We are to know that Christ requires repentance first as the end to be aimed at, and faith in the next place, as the only means of attaining it; and though the end be first in intention, yet the means are first in practice and execution, though both be absolutely necessary to salvation.'

The second difficulty has to do with regeneration, for evidently regeneration is necessary to salvation (*John* 3:3). He says, 'But consider what regeneration is. It is a new begetting or creating us in Christ (*1 Cor.* 4:15; *Eph.* 2:10). Now faith is the uniting grace, whereby Christ dwelleth in us, and we in him, as hath been shown: and therefore it is the first grace wrought in our regeneration, as the means of all the rest; when you truly believe, you are regenerated, and not till then.' It must be said that Marshall's treatment of regeneration is a weak point in his argument, and while accepting that we are not to wait to believe until we are regenerated, yet he does not deal adequately with the issues that arise in this area.

The third issue is the thinking of some that 'it is necessary to receive Christ as Lord and lawgiver, by a resignation of themselves to his government and a resolution to obey his law, before they receive him as Saviour.' But he argues, 'He is a saving Lord; trust on him first to save you from the guilt and power of sin, the dominion of Satan, and to give you a new spiritual disposition; then, but not till then, the love of Christ will constrain you to resign yourself heartily to live to him that died for you.' It would of course be quite inappropriate to lump Marshall with the present-day preachers of 'easy believism', who forget about the Lordship of Christ altogether, which Marshall never does.

DIRECTION 8

'Be sure to seek for Holiness of Heart and Life only in its due order, where God has placed it, after Union with Christ, Justification, and the gift of the Holy Ghost; and, in that order, seek it earnestly by Faith, as a very necessary part of your salvation.'

First of all Marshall emphasizes the importance of getting things in their right order as God is a God of order. He then severely warns against Antinomianism. He heads off this particular delusion: 'The way to oppose this pernicious delusion is not to deny as some do that trusting on Christ for salvation is a saving act of faith, but rather to show that none do or can trust on Christ for true salvation, except they trust on him for holiness; neither do they heartily desire true salvation if they do not desire to be made truly righteous in their hearts and lives.' Salvation is not only salvation from hell but salvation from sin.

DIRECTION 9

'We must first receive the Comforts of the Gospel, that we may be able to perform sincerely the duties of the Law.' Men naturally think it is as unreasonable 'to expect comfort before duty as wages before work. Therefore some preachers will advise men not to be solicitous and hasty of getting comfort, but that they should rather exercise themselves diligently in the performance of their duty.' As usual he is careful to guard against misunderstanding. 'I acknowledge God comforteth his people on every side (*Psa.* 71:21) both before and after the performance of their duty, and that the greatest consolations do follow after duty; yet some comforts God giveth his people beforehand.'

He then reasons, 'Can we be persuaded of the love of God, of our everlasting happiness and our strength to serve God, and yet be without any comforts? Can the glad tidings of the gospel of peace be believed, and Christ and his Spirit actually received into the heart, without any relief to the soul from oppressing fear, grief, and despair? Can the salvation of Christ be comfortless, or the Bread and Water of life without sweet relish, to those that feed on him with hungering and thirsting appetites?' He then argues from the relative positions of the doctrinal and practical parts of the Epistles.

DIRECTION 10

'That we may be prepared by the Comforts of the Gospel to perform sincerely the Duties of the Law, we must get some Assurance of Salvation, in that very Faith whereby Christ himself is received into our Hearts: therefore we must endeavour to believe on Christ confidently, persuading and assuring ourselves, in the Act of believing, that God freely giveth to us an Interest in Christ and his Salvation, according to his gracious promise.'

Marshall asserts that assurance of salvation is necessary to holiness and then goes on to speak of the nature of assurance. The old Protestants taught 'that faith was a persuasion or confidence of our salvation by Christ; and that we must be sure to apply Christ and his salvation to ourselves in believing. This doctrine was one of the great engines whereby they prevailed to overthrow the Popish superstitions, whereof doubtfulness of salvation is one of the principal pillars.'

He then refers to the issue of assurance of salvation resulting from the reflex action of faith, and notes that some have objected to his doctrine of assurance because it destroys self-examination. He proceeds to make some very significant observations.

> First observe diligently, that the assurance directed unto, is not a persuasion that we have already received Christ and his salvation, or that we have been brought into a state of grace; but only that God is pleased graciously to give Christ and his salvation unto us, and bring us into a state of grace . . . I acknowledge that men may, yea, must be taught to doubt whether their present state be good; and that such assurance belongeth to that which they call the reflex act of faith . . . and is not of the essence of that faith whereby we are justified and saved; and that many precious saints are without it . . . But the question he deals with is not whether I am already in a state of grace or salvation. There is another great question that the soul must answer that it may get into a state of grace: Whether God be graciously pleased now to bestow Christ and his salvation upon me, though I have been hitherto a very wicked creature.

Secondly, 'The assurance directed unto, is not a persuasion of our salvation, whatever we do or however we live and walk, but only in a limited way, through mere free grace in Christ by partaking of holiness as well as forgiveness, and by walking in the way of holiness to the enjoyment of the glory of God.'

Thirdly, 'Beware of thinking so highly of this assurance, as if it were inconsistent with any doubting in the same soul.' He writes in detail about the character of this faith that carries with it some degree of assurance. He shows that believing in Christ is the same as resting, relying, leaning, staying ourselves on God through Christ for our salvation. He concludes: 'We may note that the doubtings we meet with in the saints of old, were commonly occasioned by some extraordinary affliction, or some heinous transgression, not by common failings or the common original deprivation of nature, or the uncertainty of their election, or any thought that it is humility to doubt, and that they were not bound to be confident of God's salvation, because then many might be bound to believe a lie.'

Marshall next proceeds to the direct witness of the Spirit and the place it has in assurance. Quoting first such verses as Romans 8:15–17 and Galatians 4:6 he writes: 'And the apostle tells the Ephesians, that, after they believed, "they were sealed with the Holy Spirit which was the earnest of their inheritance" (*Eph*. 1: 13–14); i.e. they were sealed from the same time that they believed; for the original words are in the same tense. If this witness, seal, and earnest of the Spirit had not been ordinary to believers, it would not have been sufficient to prove that they were the children of God; and such manner of arguing might have driven some to despair, that wanted this witness, seal, or earnest.'

He summarizes his views as follows: 'Therefore we may judge rather, that the Spirit worketh this in us by giving saving faith itself, by the direct act of which all true believers are enabled to trust assuredly on Christ for the enjoyment of the adoption of children, and all his salvation, according to the free promise of God; and to call God Father without reflecting on any good qualifications in themselves: for the Spirit is received by the direct act of faith (*Gal*. 3:2); and so he is the Spirit of adoption, and comfort, to all that received him. They that assert that the Spirit witnesseth our adoption, only by assuring us of the sincerity of our faith, love, and other gracious qualifications, or by the reflex act of faith, do teach also commonly that you must again try whether the Spirit thus witnessing be the spirit of truth, or of delusion, by searching narrowly, whether our inward grace be sincere or counterfeit: so that hereby the testimony of the Spirit is rendered so hard to be discerned, that it standeth us in no stead; but all our assurance is made at last to depend on our uncertain knowledge of our own sincerity.'

He speaks of the experience of his contemporaries. First, he says that we are not to trust the judgment of many concerning themselves who are true Christians but entertain serious doubts about their salvation: they do not understand that assurance may exist contemporaneously with doubts. Yet he also warns that 'The blind charity of some moveth them to take *all* for true believers who are full of doubts and troubles concerning their salvation, *though it may be* they are only convinced of sin, and brought to some zeal of God, that is not according to the knowledge of the way of salvation by Christ: and they think it their duty to comfort such ignorant persons, by persuading them that their state is good.' Such people, he adds, are then hardened in their unsaved state instead of being directed to true faith in Christ.

DIRECTION 11

'Endeavour diligently to perform the great Work of believing on Christ, in a right Manner, without any Delay; and then also continue and increase in your most holy Faith; that so your Enjoyment of Christ, Union and Fellowship with him, and all Holiness by him, may be begun, continued, and increased in you.'

He lays down the importance, the duty, and the urgency of faith. The purpose of the whole of Scripture is to bring men to faith. Yet faith is difficult; in itself it is very pleasant, but is difficult by reason of the opposition it meets with from our own inward corruptions and from Satan's temptations. He further speaks of the connection between election and the Holy Spirit's work in giving faith.

Marshall warns of the necessity of performing this duty in the right manner, for he says: 'There is a feigned faith, that doth not really receive Christ into the heart, and will not produce love, or any true obedience.' He then refers back to his original description of saving faith, when he said it contained two things: 'The one is believing the truth of the gospel; the other is believing in Christ as revealed and freely promised to us in the gospel.' He argues that, 'When any fail in the second act of faith, the reason of their failing is commonly some defect in the first act. There is some false imagination or other in them contrary to the belief of the truth of the gospel; which is a stronghold of sin and Satan that must be pulled down before they can receive Christ into their hearts by believing on him. If they knew the name of Christ as he is discovered in the gospel, and judged aright of the truth and excellency of it, they would not fail to put their trust in him.'

He then speaks of how, having received the truth of the gospel, we are to come to the Christ of the gospel. We are to come to him only, not trusting anything else for salvation, we are to receive him as a free gift, not seeking to perform any condition to procure a right to him. Not only this, but we are to come to him with ardent affection. Oh, how our cold-hearted evangelicals of today should note this carefully – those who deal with the great matters of salvation in a lukewarm way and who cannot bear any preaching that is fervent and heart-searching! Marshall says:

> You must also come to him with an ardent love and affection to him, and esteem him better than a thousand worlds and the only excellent portion, loathing and abhorring yourself as a vile, sinful and miserable creature, and accounting all things dung in comparison of his excellency.

Having pressed the urgency of faith, Marshall concludes by showing the importance of continuing and increasing in faith: 'We may, we must not think that when we have once attained to the grace of saving faith, and thereby are begotten anew in Christ, our names are up in heaven and therefore we may be careless.' He warns against trusting in faith itself as a work of righteousness, instead of trusting on Christ by faith.

DIRECTION 12

'Make diligent use of your most holy Faith, for the immediate performance of the duties of the law, by walking no longer according to your old natural state, or any principles or means of practice that belong unto it; but only according to that new state, which you receive by Faith, and the principles and means of practice that properly belong thereunto; and strive to continue and increase in such manner of practice. This is the only way to attain to an acceptable performance of these holy and righteous duties, as far as it is possible in this present life.'

The manner of practice to which the reader is directed consists in moving and guiding ourselves in the performance of works of law by gospel principles and means. This is 'the rare and excellent art of godliness, in which every Christian should strive to be skilful and expert.' He recommends the diligent and prayerful study of Scripture as necessary for a proper understanding of the way of holiness. Though we receive a perfect Christ by faith, yet he reminds us that the measure of our enjoying him is imperfect, and the blessings treasured up in Christ are not to be enjoyed in this life more than we receive Christ himself by faith.

He then proceeds to deal with the issue of the corruption that remains in believers, and which to a greater or lesser extent affects our enjoyment of spiritual blessings. 'What reason is there to question that the old state remaineth in believers to some degrees, seeing all sound Protestants acknowledge, that the sinful deprivation and pollution of our natures, commonly called original sin, which is one principal part of the old state, doth remain in all as long as they live in this world?' He considers objections to the views of a two-fold state in believers and emphasizes that God works all this for good to those who are his called ones.

He attacks perfectionism which, while appearing to be the friend of holiness of life, is in fact its enemy. 'The doctrine of perfectionism hardens people to allow themselves in sin and to call evil good. It also discourages those that labour to get holiness in the right way, by faith in Christ, and makes them to think that they labour in vain, because they find themselves still sinful and far from perfection when they have done their best to attain it. It hindereth our diligence in seeking holiness by those principles and means whereby only it can be found: for who will be diligent and watchful to avoid walking according to his own carnal principles, if he think that his own carnal state with its principles is quite abolished, and is out of him, so that at present he is in no danger of walking according to them? Whatsoever good works the doctrine of the perfectionists may serve to promote, I am sure it hindereth a great part of that work which Christ would have us to be employed in as long as they live in this world.'

We must be careful to remember that the flesh is irremediable and is never to be improved, but death is its destiny. The answer to the flesh is always the new nature that is in Christ. Furthermore, we must not look for any blessing by means of any works of the moral law. At all times we must go to Christ by faith as the fountain of holiness. Some people press God's power, knowledge, and his exact justice, the joy of heaven and the damnation of hell, as the great motives to holiness. But Marshall emphasizes again and again that we are to live upon Christ in all his excellencies and beauty and the fullness of his provision for us. While in no way diminishing the obligations of the law, Marshall teaches that believers should realize the kindness of Christ to our failures.

He concludes this section with some very wise words, reminding us that Christ will not overdrive his sheep. 'He shall gather the lambs with his arm, and carry them in his bosom, and shall gently lead those that are with young (*Isa.* 40:11). We are to beware of being too rigorous in exacting righteousness of ourselves and others beyond the measure of faith and grace. Overdoing commonly proveth undoing. Children that venture on their feet beyond their strength have many a fall; and so have babes in Christ, when they venture unnecessarily upon such duties as are beyond the strength of their faith. We should be content, at present, to do the best we can, according to the measure of the gift of Christ, though we know that others are enabled to do much better . . .'

DIRECTION 13

'Endeavour diligently to make the right use of all means appointed in the word of God, for the obtaining and practis- ing [of] Holiness only in this way of believing in Christ, and walking in him, according to our new state by faith.'

All that has been said previously does not make void the use of means. But while we use means, we must not abuse them by putting them in the place of Christ, and thus turn helps into hindrances.

DIRECTION 14

This is really an exhortation to go back over the ground already covered, and showing the excellency of the way that has been taught.

ISSUES ARISING

Having given some idea of what Marshall actually taught it is possible to turn now to comment on his views. A large number of issues arise out of his treatment of this subject. Comment has already been made about his treatment of *regeneration*. Another issue of importance is *the place of the Holy Spirit* in his scheme. While Marshall does speak of the Holy Spirit's work, his principal emphasis is on union with Christ. Never- theless, since it would be unwise to judge a preacher on what he did not say in one sermon, so it would be unjust to criticize Marshall for what he did not say in one book. While these and other subjects might justify further comment, time and space demands that we concentrate upon three issues. The first arises out of the necessity of giving a fair picture of the historical situation. In the introduction to this paper I listed a number of well-known Christians who approved of Marshall's work. It must be said that it did not receive unqualified praise. In fact Joseph Bellamy of Connecticut in New England (1719–90) wrote a fairly lengthy attack on Marshall and on Hervey the author of *Theron and Aspasio*, who spoke most highly of *The Gospel Mystery.*

There is only time to glance at the kind of criticisms which Bellamy makes. First he objects to Marshall's definition of faith.[20] He then gives eleven particulars in which he disagrees with Marshall and Hervey:

'1) Regeneration is necessarily previous to the first act of true faith but your faith may exist in an unregenerate heart. 2) True faith supposes that law and gospel are rightly understood and beheld in their glory, the law approved with all the heart as holy, just, and good; the gospel believed and complied with with all the heart. But your faith is consistent with a reigning enmity against both law and gospel, etc.'

He then asserts:

'Sanctification, taking the word in a large and comprehensive sense, is the evidence, the only Scripture evidence, of a good estate.' Finally we may note he attacks the notion of the direct witness of the Spirit: 'This immediate witness of the Spirit which you plead for is certainly contrary to Scripture, for it will tell a man his state is good, when according to God's Word it is bad, and, which is directly to the case in hand, it leads men to build their assurance not on the rock our Saviour points out as the only safe foundation, but on something entirely different. And I am sorry to say, it tempts me to compare what our Saviour calls a rock to the stalk of a tulip. This spirit therefore, being contrary to Scripture, is not the Spirit of God but the spirit of delusion.'[21]

I give these criticisms, not because I think Bellamy succeeds in making his case against Marshall, but to indicate the kinds of criticisms that were made against him. It should also be noted that Bellamy also concedes that there is much good in Marshall's book.[22]

Having given some account of the historical objections to Marshall, I want to concentrate upon two further issues.

First, Do we need to *think* in order to be holy? Putting it in this rather bald way may come as something of a shock; the fact is, however, that if you read Marshall you will have to think. So I ask again, do you need to think to be holy? I do not say do we need to be educated to be holy. In point of fact, in asking this question I am raising an issue of great present concern. One of the characteristics of the world today is a tendency to irrationalism. The emphasis on entertainment in the media, the appeal of some kinds of contemporary music primarily to the senses, and much else also should alert us to this situation. Of course the world frequently affects the church; here some of the true worldliness of the church is manifested, for it simply capitulates without much resistance. It gives way to the demands of many to have comfort without thought, and surrenders to those who consider that the kind of entertainment they are used to in the world should be found in the church, with a slight religious gloss, of course. It was not an inspired writer but a shrewd observer of human nature who wrote, 'There is no expedient to which a man will not go to avoid the real labour of thinking' (Edison).

It is a matter of surprise when we find some of those who claim particular experiences of the Holy Spirit attacking the practice of teaching doctrine, even though the Holy Spirit himself bids us give attention to doctrine (*1 Tim.* 4:13) and says that we are to be transformed by the renewing of our minds (*Rom.* 12:2), which he relates to the renewing of God's image in us (*Eph.* 4:23). Pascal was right when he remarked, 'Man is but a reed, the weakest thing in nature, but he is a thinking reed.'[23]

This is not a new issue. Baxter often tells the story of 'one Dishforth' who went 'for novelty to a meeting of the followers of Hacket and Coppinger called Grundletonians . . . They breathed on him and he came home so transported that he left his former ways of praying in his Family . . . and did all by Ecstasy . . . and so continued about a fortnight and then returned to Humility and repented.' Baxter asserts that this was satanic delusion.[24] Gataker disputes with Saltmarsh about the same kind of issue. 'Did not our Saviour himself make use of logic, when from Moses by way of syllogism against the Sadducees he confirmed the doctrine of the resurrection?'[25]

This was one of the issues in the Antinomian attack upon the Puritans, and one would not wish to deny that in the seventeenth century there were instances of an arid scholasticism that did not engage the heart and emotions. But the issue was much deeper than this, and the attack upon the use of reason among the Puritans was much wider than was justified by such aberrations as have been mentioned. Thus a follower of Mrs Hutchinson says:

> I'll bring ye to a woman that preaches better gospel than any of your black coats that have been at University . . . and for my part . . . I would rather have such a one that speaks from the mere motions of the Spirit without any study at all, than any of your learned scholars, although they may be fuller of Scriptures.

Campbell who quotes this adds: 'In England the orthodox complain "self appointed preachers were proclaiming . . . [that] the arts, sciences, languages etc. are idols, anti-Christian, the smoke of the bottomless Pit, filth, froth, dung, needless, and useless for the right understanding of the Scripture." The Spirit alone (they say) is sufficient without these human helps.'[26]

Packer summarizes the issues in this way:

> Sin and Satan are out to smother and suppress reason, but not God. Baxter was therefore the diligent foe of

'enthusiasm'. He rejected its axioms that sometimes Christ's Spirit works in believers independently of, even in defiance of, their reason and impels them to action by quasi-physical impulses. Quakers, Ranters, Antinomians as we shall see, and a hundred and one other sects of the Commonwealth period were all 'enthusiasts' in this sense, all sure that sometimes Christ spoke and moved them apart from his written Word and in a way that bypassed the intellect altogether. They claimed that revelation thus given was more certain than the conclusion of rational exegesis; their action, thus prompted by imperious inner constraints, was more certainly God's will than that done according to the dictates of rational conscience. Its very immediacy proved that it was wholly and purely divine. Baxter rejected this claim entirely. Such experience, he held, was less than rational and could not therefore originate with God whose whole aim is to restore man's rationality to him. God reveals his will by causing man to understand the law which he published in his written Word and he evokes action by giving men reason for it. To do otherwise would be an insult to his own image.[27]

Marshall was insistent on the engagement of the affections and no one could accuse him of a cold intellectualism or lack of emphasis on experimental religion. Holiness is to be promoted by addressing the mind, and instructing believers thoroughly in the biblical teaching concerning their union with Christ. So in this insistence he is nearer to Baxter than he is to the enthusiast. Beware of those who in the supposed interests of spirituality ignore, indeed deny, the place the mind has in man as created in God's image, the place the mind has in the Man Christ Jesus, and the place the mind has in the teaching of Scripture generally.

A second issue concerning which Marshall is extraordinarily relevant is that of the 'second blessing' teaching. Second blessing teaching is often associated with, at best, an inadequate view of the law and, at worst, with a scornful hostility to it which never seems to have read Paul's saying, 'the law is holy, just and good'. This inadequate view of the law is manifested both in a reluctance to preach it to sinners to humble them and also in a failure to set it forth as a rule of life for believers. Marshall is very clear here. 'The manner of the practice here directed to consists in moving and guiding ourselves in the performance of the works of the law by gospel principles and means. This is the rare and excellent art of godliness, in which every Christian should strive to be skilful and expert.'[28]

Secondly, second blessing teaching thrives in a situation of inadequate and grossly deficient preaching of the gospel. In an age when men hear woefully inadequate gospel preaching large numbers of people are brought to some kind of decision and some kind of experience which falls far short of true faith and repentance. Sincerely but misguidedly thinking they have become Christians when they have merely been moved or convicted of sin, and therefore having no true saving knowledge of Christ, such people find a great inward emptiness; their experience does not seem to correspond with the picture of the believer painted in the Scriptures. Instead of telling such poor creatures that they need to be converted, those who have preached this inadequate gospel then say that what these 'converts' lack is some further experience which will remedy their present deficiencies. Marshall recognizes 'that when any fail in the second act of faith, the reason is commonly some defect in the first act. If they knew the name of Christ as he is discovered in the gospel, and judged aright of the truth and excellency of it, they would not fail to put their trust in him.'[29]

Thirdly, second blessing teaching is sometimes associated with an intense dislike of the teaching that insists on the need for self-examination. Marshall writes: 'I acknowledge that we may, yea many must be taught to doubt whether their state be good, and that it is humility to do so; and that we must find out the certainty and sincerity of our faith and obedience by self-examination before we can have a well-grounded assurance that we are in a state of grace and salvation already.'[30]

Fourthly, second blessing teaching thrives among those who are troubled about assurance and the lack of the experimental comforts that Scripture associates with believing. Marshall deals with this issue in two ways. First of all, by his repeated teaching concerning the relationship of faith to assurance he promotes the strengthening of assurance. Since assurance is an integral part of faith it should be the normal experience of those who believe. Secondly, by his affirmation of the doctrine of the direct witness of the Spirit, Marshall effectively answers those who maintain that the Puritans and the doctrines they promoted lead to a cold and unfelt religion. While there were differences of emphasis among the Puritans, it is nevertheless clear that Marshall believed in a felt and experiential religion. Marshall held that a sound assurance is an essential help in the pursuit of holiness.

We should also mark well that Romans 8:16, 'The Spirit bears witness with our spirit that we are the children of God', comes in one of the most mind-stretching books in the Bible and such a verse must never be wrenched from its context and somehow made to teach that doctrine and experience, the mind and the heart are at loggerheads one with the other.

Furthermore, it is worth listening to what other notable writers have said about this matter. Gataker says: 'Nor is it denied that God's Spirit in a more immediate way may not sometimes insinuate itself into the soul by sweet and terrible raptures and soul-ravishing comforts in times especially of tribulation and extremities of distress.'[31] He qualifies and explains what he means, but evidently Gataker believed in the Spirit's direct testimony to the soul in the way of believing. As you might expect, Rutherford is strong here and is anxious to repudiate the arrogant claim of the Antinomians that they were the only ones who really knew about God's direct dealings with the soul.

> Now this revelation is a clear evidence in the conscience by the Testimony of the Spirit that I am a child of God (Rom. 8:16) whether it be immediate or from speaking signs and marks of sanctification (1 *John* 3:14, 18, 19, 20). It is the knowledge of no new Article which is not contained in the Word in general; and is not proper and incommunicable to none but Antinomians, but in the mystery of the Spirit revealing these things that are graciously given to us of God (1 *Cor.* 2:12), even to all believers. The particular actings of the Spirit of grace cannot be written in Scriptures yet they are not to be thought unlawful revelations and destitute of the Word.[32]

Finally Witsius, an eminent Dutch theologian, wrote in his book on the covenant:

> There are some special acts of divine love which God vouchsafes only to his own children. Hence it is that while they are sometimes ravished on high by his Spirit, he surrounds them with the beams of his super-celestial light, gives them a view of his face shining with the brightest love, kisses them with the kisses of his mouth, admits them to the most endearing mutual intercourse of mystical love with himself, and while he plentifully sheds abroad his love in their hearts, he gives them to drink of rivers of honey and butter, and that often in the greatest drought of the parched soul when expecting no such thing. There are many more mysteries in this secret intercourse with our Heavenly Father which believers sometimes see, taste and feel, and which no pen of the learned can represent as they deserve. And it is not fit that the spirit of man should be unacquainted with these things since it is admitted as a witness of his state, for though this is not

the lot of all the children of God, nor the case at all times nor indeed frequently, yet they whose lot it has at any time been are certainly children of God.[33]

Fifthly, Marshall is the great antidote to the implications of much second blessing teaching, namely that Christ is insufficient. The Galatians were told that Christ and circumcision were necessary, the Colossians that Christ and angels and asceticism were necessary. Paul's answer was that everything that the sinner needs is to be found in Christ; in him are hidden all the treasures of the wisdom and the knowledge of God, in him dwells all the fullness of the Godhead bodily. Second blessing teaching says that though you may be justified by faith, regenerated by the Spirit, adopted, forgiven, indwelt by the Holy Spirit, and though you may be united with Christ Jesus in an unbreakable union as a branch to a vine, or as a bride to her husband, yet you still lack that without which you can never lead a victorious life, never know true deliverance from sin, never have a full assurance, and so you will live all your life in a deficient and stunted manner, unless you come to receive this new essential experience. And so it sets men on a course of gross dissatisfaction with what they have in Christ, and a looking for something extra. Now, of course we are to press toward the mark; of course we are to long for an ever-increasing knowledge of our Saviour; of course we are never to be satisfied with that which we have attained to, yet as Marshall so repeatedly emphasizes, you are united with Christ, God's appointed Saviour. It is not a matter of seeking a new experience, but of drawing by faith out of him to whom you are already joined. Doubtless this will lead to fuller experiences, but nevertheless, the emphasis in his writing is always upon understanding and living by that which God has already so gloriously given the believer in the Lord Jesus Christ. Marshall, then, does not proceed by promoting dissatisfaction but satisfaction – satisfaction with Christ and satisfaction in Christ.

We probably would not wish to hand Marshall's book to a new convert, although we would wish to teach such a person the substance of the book. But we would unreservedly hand the book to anyone wanting to know how to be holy and who wishes to avoid the manifold pitfalls and errors into which earnest Christians are often led by misguided teachers and by the delusions of the carnal mind.

We may close by quoting a letter from Hervey to Whitefield:

> Your journals, dear Sir, and sermons, especially the sweet sermon on the text 'What Think Ye of Christ?' were a means of bringing me to the knowledge of the truth. Another piece has been also like precious eye salve to my dim and clouded understanding. I mean Marshall's *Gospel Mystery of Sanctification.* These, blessed be he who is a light to them that sit in darkness, have in some degree convinced me of my former errors. I now begin to see I have been labouring in the fire and wearying myself for very vanity while I have attempted to establish my own righteousness. I trusted I knew not what, while I trusted in some imaginary deeds of my own, these are no hiding place from the storm, they are a refuge of lies. If I had the meekness of Moses and the patience of Job, the zeal of Paul and the love of John, I durst not advance the least plea to eternal life on this footing. As for my own beggarly performances, wretched righteousness, gracious Emmanuel! I am ashamed, I am grieved, that I should thrust them into the place of thy divine, thy inconceivably precious obedience. My schemes are altered, I now desire to work in my blessed Master's service, not for life, but from life and salvation. I would study to please him in righteousness and holiness all the days of my life.[34]

[1] This paper was given at the Westminster Conference in 1981. Information of a biographical character was derived from three sources a) *Dictionary of National Biography*; b) Walter Marshall, *The Gospel Mystery of Sanctification*, (Haddington: 1817); c) Rev. A. Skevington Wood – Article in the *Evangelical Quarterly*, vol. 30, no. 1, Jan–March 1958.

[2] J. I. Packer, *'Keswick' and the Reformed Doctrine of Sanctification*, *Evangelical Quarterly*, vol. 27, no. 3, July 1955 p. 154n.

[3] Marshall, p. vii.

[4] Marshall, p. xx.

[5] James Hervey, *Works*, vol. 4, (Edinburgh: 1769), p. 437.

[6] Marshall, pp. 123–4.

[7] Ibid., p. 307–8.

[8] Cotton Mather, *Magnalia Christi Americana* (Edinburgh: Banner of Truth, 1979), p. 516.

[9] K. Campbell, 'Living the Christian Life', Westminster Conference, 1974, p. 69.

[10] J. F. McGregor, *The Ranters, 1649–1660*. B.Litt. Thesis, Bodleian Library, Oxford, p. 71.

[11] Rutherford, p. 171f.

[12] J. I. Packer, *The Redemption and Restoration of Man in the Thought of Richard Baxter*. PhD.Thesis, Bodleian Library, Oxford.

[13] Ibid., p. 405.

[14] Ibid., p. 391.

[15] Ibid., p. 425.

[16] John Saltmarsh, *Free Grace* (1649, 6th Edition) p. 37.

[17] Bacon's *Essays*, (Macmillan 1868), p. 205.

[18] Marshall. As the quotations from Marshall in this section are easily traceable by reference to the *Direction* number, exact page numbers are not given.

[19] Rutherford, p. 172.

[20] Joseph Bellamy, *Works*, vol. II, (New York: 1871), p. 236n.

[21] Ibid., p. 270f.

[22] Ibid., p. 291.

[23] Pascal, *Pensées*, Pt 1, Article 4, No. 6.

[24] Op. cit., Packer, p. 34, ln.2.

[25] Thomas Gataker, *Shadowes Without Substance – Pretended New Light* (1640), p. 19. This was a reply to Saltmarsh's *Shadowes Flying Away*.

[26] Campbell, p. 78.

[27] Packer, p. 371.

[28] Marshall, p. 269.

[29] Ibid., p. 243.

[30] Ibid., p. 196.

[31] Gataker, p. 83.

[32] Rutherford, pp. 41–2.

[33] Herman Witsius, *On the Covenants*, vol. 2, (London: 1762), p. 623.

[34] J. C. Ryle, *Christian Leaders of the Eighteenth Century* (Edinburgh: Banner of Truth, 1978), p. 337.

4

THOMAS SCOTT AND *THE FORCE OF TRUTH*[1]

In the past Thomas Scott was principally known for his *Commentary on the Whole Bible*, a work which involved him in massive labour and trouble and which in its day enjoyed an enormous circulation both in Great Britain and abroad. By the time of Scott's death copies to the value of £199,000 had been sold, £67,000 of English copies and £132,300 of American. These are of course enormous sums in equivalent modern currency. Unfortunately Thomas Scott's other important work, *The Force of Truth*, has fallen into obscurity in recent years. This is a great pity for it ranks among the best of short spiritual autobiographies.

The Force of Truth is valuable for three reasons. First of all, it is *instructive*. God says: 'I will bring the blind by a way that they knew not; I will lead them in paths that they have not known: I will make darkness light before them and crooked things straight. These things will I do unto them and not forsake them' (*Isa.* 42:16). God's works in the lives of those he is determined to save are always instructive, and *The Force of Truth* is a particularly remarkable account of such a work. It is also interesting to note how slowly God's work in Scott's soul proceeded, with a gradual removal of erroneous principles and a slow emergence into the light of truth.

173

Secondly, the book has a *warning* for us. We are often prone to write off people as beyond hope of salvation. Saul of Tarsus before his conversion was held in the grip of false doctrine, a slave of sin and a vicious persecutor of God's people, yet God saved him. We profess that salvation is by grace, and so it is, but this means that the most depraved of sinners may be saved. Even professed ministers of the gospel who have entered the ministry upon false grounds and hold to false teaching and are negligent of their duty may be saved by grace. The case of Thomas Scott supplies the reader with a warning not to limit the grace of God.

Thirdly, this account is immensely *encouraging*. There is force, there is power in the truth. The truth may be working in a man and yet we may know nothing about this. Certainly John Newton who was a great help to Scott recognized the power of the truth and was content to let Scott's spiritual development proceed unimpeded by human meddling.

Thomas Scott was born on 16 February 1747. His place of birth was a small farmhouse at Braytoft in Lincolnshire about six miles from the present town of Skegness. His father was a grazier (cattle farmer), and Scott was the tenth of thirteen children. At the age of ten he was sent to a boarding school at Scorton in Yorkshire where he remained for five years without returning home. Scott's eldest brother had been a surgeon's mate in the Royal Navy and would undoubtedly have become a surgeon had he not died of some disease at the age of twenty-four. His father wished Scott to follow in his brother's footsteps and thus in 1762 he was apprenticed to a surgeon and apothecary at Alford, about eight miles from Braytoft. After two months, however, he was dismissed by his employer and due to a dispute over the payment of various fees, his employer refused to return his indentures. In consequence it became impossible for Scott to obtain employment with another surgeon and so his father's purposes were frustrated and the course of his own life was changed.

It is worth commenting at this juncture that Scott never lost his interest in medicine. When he became a curate in Buckinghamshire ten years later this interest manifested itself in a very practical way.

> About this time I began with great caution to administer medical assistance to a few of my poor neighbours and Mr (now Dr) Kerr of Northampton bestowed some pains in directing my proceedings, for he felt, as I have always done, that the poor in country villages are under great and pitiable disadvantages in this respect, which no humanity of their neighbours without medical skill, can prevent.

A few years later we learn of him labouring, at great risk to himself, to help those affected by smallpox and gaol fever in his parishes. We read: 'He had little confidence in the neighbouring apothecaries and none in the nurses . . . he called in Dr Kerr and "under him", he says, "I was physician, apothecary, and almost nurse. I inoculated none, but some inoculated their neighbours, and I subsequently directed their proceedings."' Dr Kerr was so impressed with Scott's medical talent that 'he frequently expressed a wish that he could change his profession, and would never himself give his directions to any other person when he was present.'

But we must return to Scott's earlier life. His dismissal by his employer necessarily meant that he had to work for his father as a grazier. In this situation he met with great hardship and incessant labour. Though he worked with immense diligence and considerable success he became increasingly embittered and thoroughly disgruntled with his lot. He began to study what books he had available and in April 1772 avowed his intention to his father of seeking ordination in the Church of England. His motives for seeking entry into the ministry were of a most worldly kind. He tells us that the first of these was the desire for a less laborious way of getting his living

than working upon a grazing farm. The next was the expect-
ation that the clerical life would afford him more leisure for
reading, which was the passion of his life. And lastly, he hoped
that in due time he would distinguish himself as a literary man,
as he felt within himself the capacity for success.

The spirit in which Scott entered upon the Christian ministry figures largely in the pages of *The Force of Truth* but we
must repeat here his memorable words on his ordination:

> As far as I understand such controversies, I was nearly a
> Socinian and Pelagian and wholly an Arminian: yet, to my
> shame be it spoken, I sought to obtain admission into the
> ministry, in a Church whose doctrines are diametrically
> opposed to all three . . . While I was preparing for this
> solemn office, I lived as before in known sin, and in utter
> neglect of prayer . . . Thus with a heart full of pride and
> wickedness, my life polluted with many unrepented,
> unforsaken sins; without one cry for mercy, one prayer for
> direction or assistance, or a blessing upon what I was about
> to do, after having concealed my real sentiments under the
> mask of general expressions, after having subscribed Arti-
> cles directly contrary to what I believed, and after having
> blasphemously declared in the presence of God and of the
> congregation, in the most solemn manner, sealing it with
> the Lord's Supper, that I judged myself to be 'inwardly
> moved by the Holy Ghost to take that office upon me' (not
> knowing or believing that there was a Holy Ghost), on
> 20th September, 1772, I was ordained a Deacon.

In another place he writes of the same event:

> It suffices here to say, that, considered in all respects, I
> deliberately judge this whole transaction to have been the
> most atrocious wickedness of my life. But I did not, at
> that time, in any degree regard it in this light; nor did I,
> till long after, feel any remorse of conscience for my pre-

varicating, if not directly lying subscriptions and declarations, and all the evil of my motives and actions in the whole concern.

In order to balance this comment we must add what he writes further:

> For ever blessed be the God of all long-suffering and mercy, who had patience with such a rebel and blasphemer, such an irreverent trifler with his majesty, and such a presumptuous intruder into his sacred ministry! I never think of this daring wickedness, without being filled with amazement that I am out of hell; without admiring that gracious God who permitted such an atrocious sinner to live, yea to serve him, and with acceptance, I trust, to call him Father, and as his minister to speak in his name.

On his ordination Scott did not remain in Lincolnshire but became curate of two villages in Buckinghamshire, Stoke Goldington and Weston Underwood. It was whilst here that the great change recorded in *The Force of Truth* took place, and it was here that he first met John Newton, then minister in Olney. It was Newton's visit to two of Scott's dying parishioners which had a profound effect upon him.

> In January 1774 two of my parishioners, a man and his wife, lay at the point of death. I had heard of the circumstances, but according to my general custom, not being sent for, I took no notice of it; till one evening, the woman being now dead, and the man dying, I heard that my neighbour Mr Newton had been several times to visit them. Immediately my conscience reproached me with being shamefully negligent, in sitting at home within a few doors of dying persons, my general hearers, and never going to visit them . . . This reflection affected me so much, that without delay, and very earnestly, yea, with tears, I besought the Lord to forgive my past neglect.

Scott had in fact already heard Newton preach and a remarkably disturbing experience it had proved to be. At the request of a friend he attended a Thursday evening meeting at Olney where Newton was the preacher.

> I sat fronting the pulpit and verily thought Mr Newton looked full on me when he came into the desk; and when he named his text, to my great astonishment it was this, 'Then Saul (who also is called Paul) filled with the Holy Ghost, set his eyes on him, and said, O full of all subtlety and all mischief, thou child of the devil, thou enemy of all righteousness, wilt thou not cease to pervert the right ways of the Lord?' (*Acts* 13:9–10). As I knew that he preached *extempore*, I took it for granted that he had chosen the text purposely on my account . . . I thought his doctrine abstruse, imaginative, and irrational; and his manner un-couth; and the impression that, though Elymas was named, I was intended, abode with me for a long time: nor was it wholly effaced till I discovered some years afterwards that he was regularly expounding the Acts of the Apostles, and that this passage came in course that evening; and that, in fact, he neither saw nor thought of me.

Another event of note during these years was his meeting with the lady who subsequently became his first wife. Scott relates that he first met with Mrs Jane Kell – obviously a widow – 'at a christening and won her money at cards'. It is recorded that the perfect composure and good temper with which she bore her loss was what deeply impressed Scott. Scott was blessed with an excellent wife and wrote to his sister of his wife that she

> seems to me to possess whatever can render woman amiable – beauty excepted: whom nature has blessed with a variety of her choicest gifts – sense, prudence, sensibil-ity . . . who has many advantages of education, has read

much, and is fit to appear with credit in any company, who has a heart fraught with most virtuous and generous sentiments . . . No woman in the world is better adapted for the management of a family.

Scott was a man of great force of character, inflexible, and of a somewhat fiery temper. His wife's good influence on him may be seen in two areas.

She would say, 'Only act according to the dictates of your conscience; we shall doubtless be provided for': yet, when she saw as she frequently did that my eager spirit and violent temper were hurrying me into wrong measures, she uniformly checked me, and though often not till after much opposition on my part, she always carried her point with me; to my unspeakable benefit. After I had written my sermons for the Sunday, I, for a long time, constantly read them to her before they were preached and, at her instance I altered many things, especially in exchanging words unintelligible to labourers and lace-makers, for simpler language.

When John Newton left Olney for St Mary Woolnoth, London, in 1779, it was proposed that Scott should succeed him. This proposal excited violent opposition among the parishioners of Olney, which led to the proposal being dropped. But the curate chosen to replace Newton turned out to be a veritable Tartar. Cowper says, 'He even quarrelled with his auctioneer in the midst of the sale of his goods and would not permit him to proceed, finishing that matter himself.' He is reported to have left his parishioners with the words, 'Now let us pray for your wicked vicar.' By that time those who had opposed Scott's coming to Olney had a change of heart and asked him to accept the now vacant situation. Scott in the end acceded to the request but his period at Olney was not to be a happy one. Writing about his situation at Olney in 1784 he says to a Scottish minister in the north of England:

I am a moderate episcopalian and a paedobaptist; but I am entirely willing my brethren should be, some presbyterians, and some independents, and not extremely unwilling that some should be Baptists . . . There are above two thousand inhabitants in this town, almost all Calvinists, even the most debauched of them; the gospel having been preached among them for a number of years by a variety of preachers, statedly and occasionally, sound and unsound, in church and meeting. The inhabitants are become like David, wiser than their teachers; that is, they think themselves so, and in an awful manner have learned to abuse gospel notions to stupify their consciences, vindicate their sloth and wickedness, and shield off conviction.

In 1785 Scott removed from Olney to London, to become chaplain to the Lock Hospital, or to give it its full title, 'The Lock Hospital for Persons Afflicted with the Venereal Disease'. His experiences at the Lock, his troubles and distresses, constitute a story in themselves. It is not possible to give a balanced view of his labours there in a short space. His ministry among the inmates of the hospital, his preaching of Christ to them, and his attempts to help them to a better way of life through judicious practical measures, reveal Scott at his best.

The reports drawn up by him, detailed many instances of those who were not only reclaimed and restored to society, but evidently converted to God by the means thus used; and who showed this by a long course of consistent conduct, terminating, in several cases, in a Christian and happy death.

Scott's troubles originated with the aristocratic Board of Governors who controlled the Hospital and who were all divided by party spirit before Scott came. Also the aristocratic congregation, connected with the Hospital, did not take kindly to Scott's blunt preaching and close application of the truth.

Their high views of divine sovereignty made them suspicious of exhortations to practical obedience.

We find him grappling with his difficulties as he lectured on Ephesians at his Wednesday night meetings:

> At first I was very well attended, my congregation gener-
> ally consisting of more than three hundred persons. This
> continued while I was going through the more doctrinal
> part of the Epistle . . . When I arrived at the latter part of
> the fourth chapter, the alarm was spread, though I stamped
> every exhortation strongly with an evangelical seal. But
> at length, when I preached from the fifth chapter, on the
> words 'See that ye walk circumspectly' etc, the charge
> was everywhere circulated that I had changed my princi-
> ples and become an Arminian: and at once I irrecoverably
> lost much above half my audience.

It must be remembered that Scott was an avowed Calvinist. He had become settled in his mind concerning the issues of the Arminian-Calvinist controversy years before. However the Governors of the Lock Hospital became very much troubled over Scott's emphasis on a Christian's *duties*, they being very zealous for what they considered as 'Calvinism'. Scott preached a sermon on Election and Perseverance in order to vindicate his position. Furthermore at a large gathering of the Gover-nors of the Lock, at which discussion was expected, he proposed a question concerning the precise boundaries between Calvinism and Arminianism. He writes of this discussion: 'But in conference they added nothing unto me: and, two dissent-ers excepted, no one offered anything sufficient to show that he understood the subject. So that, when I concluded my own remarks, it was allowed that I was more decidedly Calvinistic than the rest of the company!' Some of the Governors adopted an authoritarian attitude in telling Scott what he ought to preach, but he replied by saying, 'Gentlemen, you possess authority sufficient to change me *for* another preacher whenever you please but you have no power to change me *into* another preacher.' He became very discouraged and resolved to leave. But sharing this determination with his wife he received the reply, 'Take heed what you do; if you leave your station in this spirit, you will perhaps soon be with Jonah in the whale's belly.' As has already been noted, he seemed to take much notice of what his wife said, and so he retained his chaplaincy at the Lock Hospital.

Scott stayed at the Lock until 1801, undertaking many and varied labours, including service as the first Secretary of the Church Missionary Society. In September 1790 his wife died, which was the occasion of the profoundest anguish to him. In 1791 he married again; this second marriage lasted for thirty years and 'was an unspeakable blessing to him'.

We conclude this account of Scott's life in London with a record of his Sunday labours, as recorded by a contemporary.

At four o'clock in the morning of every alternate Sunday, winter as well as summer, the watchman gave one heavy knock at the door and Mr Scott and an old maid servant arose – for he could not go out without his breakfast. He then set forth to meet a congregation at a Church in Lothbury, about three miles and a half off; I rather think the only church in London attended so early as six o'clock in the morning. I think he had from two to three hundred auditors, and administered the sacrament each time . . . From the City he returned home and about ten o'clock assembled his family to prayers: immediately after which he proceeded to the Chapel . . . His sermons were most ingeniously brought into an exact hour, just about the same time (as I have heard him say) being spent in composing them. I well remember accompanying him to the afternoon Church in Bread Street (nearly as far as Lothbury), after taking his dinner without sitting down . . . I have calculated that he could not go much less than fourteen miles in the day, frequently the whole of it on

foot, besides the three services and at times a fourth sermon at Longacre Chapel, or elsewhere, on his way home
in the evening; and then he concluded the whole with
family prayer, and that not a very short one. Considering
his bilious and asthmatic habit this was immense labour!
And all this I knew him to do very soon after he had
broken a rib by falling down the cabin stairs of a Margate
packet; and it seemed to me as if he passed few weeks
without taking an emetic! But his heart was in his work
and I never saw a more devoted Christian.

Here we must leave this outline of Scott's life. He left
London shortly after the nineteenth century opened and
laboured at Aston Sandford in Buckinghamshire until his death
in 1821. His first interests in the service of Christ remained
with him till the last.

The Force of Truth by no means deals with the whole of
Scott's Life. His Preface to the first edition was dated 26 February 1779, that is to say, shortly after his thirty-second
birthday, while he was still curate at Ravenstone and Weston
Underwood. Apart from the opening pages it covers only the
first five years of his ministerial life. But these were the
decisive years of his inner history for reasons which the
author himself makes abundantly clear.

The year 1779, when this book first appeared, was also the
year, it is interesting to note, when the youthful William Carey
first met Scott. Years later in India Carey was to write of their
friendship: 'If there be anything of the work of God in my
soul, I owe much of it to his preaching, when I first set out in
the ways of the Lord.'

Thomas Scott's *The Force of Truth* is reprinted with the
prayer that it will encourage many others both to love the
truth and to serve the Lord Jesus Christ.

[1] The Introduction to the Banner of Truth edition of *The Force of Truth*
(Edinburgh, 1984).

5

'RABBI' DUNCAN AND THE PROBLEM OF ASSURANCE[1]

The Book of Proverbs tells us that 'The memory of the just is blessed' (*Prov.* 10.7). There can be no doubt therefore that great benefit can flow to us from a consideration of the lives of godly men of previous generations. Some Christians have left behind them a mass of writings and it is because of this we pay attention to them. Yet other Christians who have not left much in the way of literature, are studied because they have had a profound influence upon the church and their own generation. 'Rabbi' Duncan certainly would not come into the first category for he left very little in the way of written work. Indeed the absence of such work raises certain problems in any study of him. All we have are two books of sermons, the recollections of his friends, and a record of a few of his addresses.

It is also questionable whether Duncan comes into the second category. His influence in the sphere of Jewish Missions should not be underestimated, yet it could not be said of him that he had deeply influenced his generation. Nevertheless, it is the universal testimony of men of discernment who knew him that he was one of the godliest men of his time. He is certainly one from whom, in spite of his idiosyncrasies, we may learn much and through whose own experience and thought we may find some light on the issue of Christian assurance.

John Duncan, to give him his proper name, earned his nick-name 'Rabbi' because of his encyclopaedic knowledge of Hebrew and of Jewish literature, and because of his passionate espousal of the cause of the Jews. His learning was such that Jewish Rabbis delighted to converse with him and his love for the Jews was one of the controlling influences of his life.

To many 'Rabbi' Duncan is known principally for his eccentricities. It would be quite wrong to give undue prominence to these, yet at the same time to ignore them would be a failure to give an adequate picture of the man. Early on in his ministerial career efforts were made to bring John Duncan forward as a possible minister of St Andrew's Chapel, Dundee. Various testimonials were given concerning his suitability. However one Ross-shire minister, after giving particulars of his many excellencies, concluded with the following statement of his defects: 'He is a perfect child as to the things of this world, and shows a lamentable, if not sinful, absence of mind about his person, dress, etc; indeed, so much is the case, that he would require the frequent attention of a prudent careful friend to take care of his worldly concerns, to put him in mind of those parts of his duty which he is apt to forget, and to rouse him from the indolence to which he seems constitutionally liable.'

That he was eccentric no one would wish to deny. Nor for that matter would any deny the immense power and activity of his brain. His particular interest was languages and when making application on one occasion for the Chair of Oriental Languages in the University of Glasgow, after giving an account of his extensive knowledge of Hebrew literature (so extensive apparently that there was no one who was in a position to examine him in it!) he goes on to refer to his reading in other languages. The list includes Syriac, Arabic, Persian, Sanskrit, Bengali, Hindustani, and Mahrati. To this of course should be added Latin in which he had the ability to express himself with amazing elegance and lucidity. Perhaps his powers may best be summed up in the words of a German student:

> The Germans study one thing and know it thoroughly; the Scotch have a smattering of everything, and know nothing well; but there is one man in Scotland, John Duncan, who knows everything, and he knows them all better than we know any one.

But it is not primarily as a scholar that we are interested in John Duncan; indeed at the end of his life he uttered a solemn warning: 'One thing I must tell you, "Abuse not reliefs; grieve not the Holy Ghost. It's that I have done. Linguistic studies have occupied more of my life and more of my heart than they should have done."' It is with John Duncan as a Christian that we are concerned, and especially John Duncan as a Christian who knew many trials and testings in the realm of assurance. Dr John Kennedy of Dingwall was a great man, a great preacher and a man of shrewd discernment, nor, let it be added, was he one who would give glib or easy praise. Knowing that Duncan was preaching in a certain church he determined to hear him. 'When I estimated that Dr Duncan had got under way with the service, I stole quietly into the church, and heard a sermon that did not seem to be prepared on earth, but felt as if one of the old Prophets had come from within the veil to tell us what was going on there. Nothing more heavenly did I ever hear from human lips.'

HIS LIFE

John Duncan was born in 1796 in Aberdeen. His father was a shoemaker and John was the only surviving child of the marriage between his father and Ann Mutch who also came from near Aberdeen. His mother died when he was still young, but his father married again; his stepmother was a great blessing to him and he regarded her with affection till the end of her life. Both John's parents were members of the Secession Church.

One of Duncan's biographers describes his father as 'a detached boulder of granite, hard and solitary . . . an upright man, walking in the fear of God, strict in his Secession principles, rugged and stern, in family discipline inexorable'.

John was sent to Grammar School and then to the University in Aberdeen. While at University, in spite of the strictness of his upbringing and in spite, no doubt, of the excellent teaching he received in the Secession Church, he lapsed into complete atheism, denying the existence of God, of angelic spirits and of the human soul. Strange though it may seem, we know that in 1813 Duncan offered himself for examination and was accepted as a student of Divinity in the Constitutional Associate Presbytery of the Secession Church. In 1816, however, he left the Secession and joined the Established Church of Scotland.

Duncan himself gave very little information about the reasons for this change and, therefore, the reasons for it and the thinking that led to it are shrouded in a certain mystery. What we do have is his testimony to his condition at the time when he entered the Divinity Hall of the Established Church: 'I was an Atheist when I entered Dr Mearns' Class. I had a godly upbringing, but I broke off from it. I had three years of dreary Atheism and during that time I made a doctrinal atheist of a pupil of mine who died.' This atheism could not fail to affect his life and there is no doubt that it was associated with an inevitable bondage to sin and with a fearful sense of intellectual desolation. In describing his condition at this time he frequently repeated in later years the words from the dream of a man called John Paul: 'I wandered to the furthest verge of Creation, and there I saw a Socket where an Eye should have been and I heard the shriek of a Fatherless World.'

But God had purposes of grace and mercy for this poor deluded sinner. His recovery from error was not to be rapid; indeed while, as we shall see, his conversion was sudden and drastic yet the processes that led up to it were slow. It was through the teaching of one of his tutors, Dr Mearns, that he was led out of his atheism into an intellectual acceptance of the existence of God. Duncan himself described what happened to him: 'I first saw clearly the existence of God in walking along the bridge at Aberdeen; it was a great discovery to me; I stopped and stood in an ecstasy of joy at seeing the existence of God. When I was convinced that there was a God, I danced on the Brig o' Dee with delight.'

Yet his recovery from error was, as we have said, a lengthy process. While now relinquishing his atheism, he became a Sabellian, that is to say, he held the view of Sabellius that the Father, Son and Holy Ghost are not three distinct personal subsistences in the one Godhead, but only three modes or manifestations of the one personality in the Godhead.

His condition at this time is well described by Dr David Brown, one of his biographers:

Henceforward for a period of nine years, Mr Duncan was little troubled with theological difficulties, and concerned himself but little about his spiritual state – indeed, scarcely about his moral reputation. In theism he was now so established as never to have his belief again shaken; and having soon after become convinced of the truth of Divine revelation, he was never again seriously disturbed on that head. Yet so unsubdued was his intellectual pride, as long afterwards he confessed to myself, that he resolved to 'stand out against all doctrines'. [He was] . . . untroubled by any questions about the Divinity of Christ, the Atonement and other peculiar doctrines of the Gospel. In this generalized Christianity he found little to trouble his conscience, and nothing to control his wayward will, while the fear of damnation – strong at first as a feeling – got so reduced by habitual disregard of its voice, as to amount to nothing beyond the mere intellectual result of a readjusted theology.

He was at this time, according to his own confession, living without prayer and in habitual sin.

In such a condition he took licence to preach in 1825, having held back from this step for a long time. Speaking of this many years later he said, 'I took licence in unbelief, in ungodliness and doctrinal unbelief and heresy.' On being asked how the authorities allowed him to pass when his views were such he replied, 'Because I was a hypocrite, not willingly, for I kept back for long; but at last the people were upon me, and out of very shame I acted the hypocrite; I did not choose to tell them why I was not taking licence.' One cannot help being reminded of the similar testimony of Thomas Scott the commentator and a leading Calvinistic preacher in England at the end of the eighteenth century (*The Force of Truth*, p. 4).

We should admire the glorious longsuffering of our Saviour that instead of leaving these men to perish in their deceit and hypocrisy, he gloriously magnified his grace by bringing them to a true trust in himself and then using them as instruments in the establishment of his kingdom. The time for John Duncan's deliverance was not far distant. A man called César Malan came to Aberdeen in 1826 and was to be the instrument used by God to bring John Duncan into light. It is significant to see how God prepared the way in the events which preceded his conversion. His friend and biographer David Brown yearned over John Duncan; he knew something of his state and prayerfully sought opportunity to speak to him about his soul. When the opportunity at length occurred it was seized upon and a lengthy conversation took place. Pacing the streets of Aberdeen together until the early hours of the morning Brown pressed home the truth upon his friend. In response Duncan professed his belief in a personal God but stated quite emphatically 'the doctrines I can't and won't believe, I mean the Divinity and Atonement of Christ . . . To tell you the truth, the words "heaven" and "hell" sound in my ears with as little effect as the words "tables" and "chairs". And yet I do sometimes feel a little.' To which Brown replied, 'What you feel is not the question. What I want you to tell me is, Are you holy?' The result of this conversation was that a great softening took place in Duncan's hard and proud heart.

Duncan went in that state to Dr Malan and as a result was converted. We shall have to look back to this event in more detail later, but at the moment it will suffice to say that a vast and permanent change took place in Duncan. He soon began to preach the high and immediate assurance which he himself experienced and which was one of the salient characteristics of Malan's own teaching. This assurance was not associated with any carelessness of life, for his biographer writes of him: 'I never knew of a more tender conscience on every point of duty, a more quick sensibility to whatever he thought morally or religiously wrong, and a deeper sense of compunction and distress at any deviation from duty whether patent to the eye of men or not.' In this state he little knew the doubts and difficulties which would soon beset him although he perhaps had a warning. Talking to Dr Kidd, a minister in Aberdeen who greatly influenced him, he expressed wonder that sincere believers in the Lord Jesus should doubt their own accept-ance, to which Dr Kidd replied, 'Young man, the Holy Ghost has wrought so powerfully in you that you cannot understand the difficulties of others.'

For about two years this high assurance lasted. He was full of zeal and love, but gradually things went wrong. Moody-Stuart, another of Duncan's biographers, describes what happened:

Through want of watchfulness and self-scrutiny, of humiliation, repentance, tenderness, through a latent antinomian tendency to adhere only to promise and privi-lege and joy, through the magnifying of faith and the practical disparagement of a good conscience, the fruits of the Spirit withered, the love, joy, peace, lost their beauty and freshness. But the words were the same as before; the doctrinal assurance remained but without the reality; and the profession of faith was as high as ever, while there lived no longer in its strength the faith which 'endures as seeing him who is invisible'. The lips and heart were not one. John Duncan could not long endure this hollowness; the Lord who had called him brought home to his conscience the warning, 'First of all beware of the leaven of the Pharisees which is hypocrisy.' The inflated air vessel was pierced and fell in with a terrible collapse. He fell into darkness, doubt, fear, all but absolute despair. He lost utterly all confidence in the past, had not one spark of light for the present and only a ray of hope for the future. 'You had a bright and true assurance of salvation after your conversion', I said to him, 'How did you lose that assurance?' 'Because I could keep it no longer without becoming a hypocrite, and whatever I am, I'm not a hypocrite and won't be one.' He saw that he was retaining the shadow without the substance and he cast the shadow away that he might recover the substance.

In 1830 Duncan removed to his first pastorate at Persie, a country parish in Perthshire. His stay there was brief but he showed a great love for the people and afterwards spoke highly of their capacity to listen to well-argued sermons. It was while he was there that an incident occurred which illustrates another side of Duncan's character. You may have thought of him so far as a highly intellectual man, almost a prototype of the absent-minded academic. However there was in him a decided pugnacity and when he chose he could speak with considerable force against what he thought was wrong.

In the parish of Kirkmichael it had been customary for many years for the church officer to 'cry the roups', that is, to proclaim all the forthcoming public sales and auctions in the parish, and this was done immediately after the service. Attempts had been made to stop this, but all had failed. One Sunday Duncan, having preached and left the congregation standing in close proximity to the church, was on his way home when he heard the loud proclamation of the church officer. 'There's the devil begun the moment I have closed my mouth.' But as he proceeded on towards home, with this thought uppermost, a change of mind occurred and he strode back to where the beadle, surrounded by the people, was making his announcements. At the first pause Mr Duncan immediately began, 'Is the devil over with his roups? If he is, then I a servant of the Lord Jesus will intimate a roup also: "Remember the Sabbath day to keep it holy."' He repeated these words with 'awful solemnity' and then added, 'My friends, there's the roup of a holy Sabbath to you. Sanctify it to God or to the devil as you please. I have done my duty!' No one said anything, and it was recorded, 'the poor beadle went off the ground uttering curses not loud but deep; but not another roup was from that day cried in the parish.'

In 1831 Duncan was called to Glasgow, first of all to a lectureship in Duke Street Gaelic Chapel, and then to the ministry at Milton Chapel. Whilst he was there he married a Miss Janet Tower of Aberdeen. She was a choice character of eminent godliness and his marriage was very happy. Perhaps it was characteristic of the man that during their courtship, which of course had to be carried on largely by letter, he set himself to teach her Greek. 'He covers his paper with Greek inflexions in bold characters, illustrates this by a comparison with the structure of Latin, crosses his writing, and fills with compact sentences every quarter of an inch of space in the margins and corners of the quarto pages.' He worries whether he is trying her too much and so breaks off into French! She obviously was a woman of great ability and perhaps of tact as well for she replies, 'As for Greek, I find your notes very interesting and very helpful to me. You make the thing appear simpler to me and more easy to be attained than I at first supposed.'

In 1838 they had a daughter Anne. Early in 1839 Mrs Duncan gave birth to another child, but shatteringly for Duncan the child only survived a few minutes and Mrs Duncan for a few days. Later Duncan remarried, this second wife being a widow, was also a woman of great worth. After her decease in 1852 Duncan had two excellent housekeepers, women of sterling character and piety who were a great boon to a man who really was quite incapable of looking after himself.

WORK AMONG THE JEWS

It was at this time that there was a reviving of interest in work among the Jews. A group of men was sent out to survey the situation, among them Robert Murray M'Cheyne. They travelled extensively in Europe and the near East and returned to give a report to the Church. At the same time Duncan had applied for the Chair of Oriental Languages in Glasgow but was unsuccessful. In July 1840 he was appointed first missionary to the Jews from the Church of Scotland. In June 1841 he left Scotland for his chosen field of labour which was Budapest. His labours there really warrant quite separate treatment. This was one of the happier periods of his life. It is a wonderful story to read of the way in which God had prepared the way for the Mission; how its coming was an answer to the prayers of the Archduchess Maria Dorothea, wife of Archduke Ferdinand of Austria who was the effective governor of Hungary, which country was then part of the Austro-Hungarian Empire. This lady was a devout Christian and was able to protect the Mission from the hostility of the Austro-Hungarian State. Duncan by his encyclopaedic knowledge of Hebrew and Jewish literature and his eminent personal piety gained ready access to the Jews. In due time many Jews were converted, among them some who would attain to eminence as Christians. These were times of a great working by the Spirit. Duncan's coming was instrumental in much blessing to the Hungarian Reformed Church and a new flowering of spiritual life among the Protestant churches in Hungary. Adolph Saphir (a Jewish convert) wrote thus to Dr Keith of the fruit of Dr Duncan's influence: 'The first time you were here there was not a village in all Hungary in which they knew there was such a thing as Evangelical religion. The second time you were here [in 1844] there was not a village in all Hungary in which they did not know; and now there is not a presbytery in Hungary in which the Gospel is not preached.'

At one time Duncan had to go to Leghorn in Italy for his health. Whilst he was there, there occurred a moving of the Spirit in Budapest. The date was 1 January 1843, and one of Duncan's co-workers described what happened on the Lord's Day:

We met in an upper room at night and in secret – for fear of the Jews and to escape the eyes of an intolerant Government. From the moment that the service began the place where we were assembled seemed to be filled with a mysterious presence. Indeed the risen Lord had entered by the closed door and stood, as at Jerusalem, in the midst of his disciples. Deep silence fell on the little company and they realized his nearness, a silence interrupted at intervals by the deep-drawn sigh of some bursting heart. The dividing wall which separated heaven and earth seemed for the time removed, and that fellowship between both was experienced which is the fullest blessedness of earth and anticipates the glory of heaven. Our hands now became so full of work that frequently we had not time so much as to eat bread; from early morning till late at night we were occupied in guiding, counselling, and instructing those who were enquiring earnestly what they must do to be saved, and from time to time we had the unspeakable happiness of seeing one and another, amidst manifest tokens of Divine power, enter the kingdom of God. A spirit of prayer was poured out in a remarkable

degree. Some of the younger brethren without any suggestion from us, and indeed without our knowledge at
the time, frequently spent whole nights as watchers
before the throne. Indeed, all of them from the moment
of their spiritual birth may be said to have lived and
breathed in an atmosphere of prayer. For a time the whole
Jewish community was deeply moved, wondering
whereunto these things would grow. Nor was the interest
confined to Pesth. It reached the highest point of intensity when, about the middle of May, Mr Saphir, universally
known and respected by the Jews throughout Hungary,
was baptized, along with his numerous family, each member of which had given evidence of a distinct work of
grace in the heart.

This movement, let it be remembered, was in connection
with the work of which Dr Duncan was the leader. Here then
was revival blessing sovereignly poured out by God upon the
work of a man who would be described by many today as
having a 'legal spirit' and who, by his own confession, was for
much of his spiritual pilgrimage plagued with doubts about
the character of his own relationship with God.

It is possible to speculate that Dr Duncan might have been
happier had he continued in this work for which he was so
eminently suited. In 1843 there took place the Disruption in
the Church of Scotland and, with his fellow missionaries, Dr
Duncan threw in his lot with the Free Church. He then
received a unanimous call to the Chair of Hebrew in the Free
Church of Scotland College in Edinburgh which he accepted
and it was in this work that he continued until his death on 26
February 1870.

While Dr Duncan's academic abilities were of the highest
order and his spirituality unquestioned, yet in some ways he
was not well suited to the task to which he was called in Edinburgh. As we have already noticed, he was somewhat irregular

in his habits and found the burden of a regular teaching routine a terrible trouble to him. A man with one of the finest minds of his age was not really suited to the teaching of elementary Hebrew to students, some of whom were not always very bright. Indeed the disorder of his teaching methods not only troubled Duncan but also some of his students. In later years he had assistants who were able to take the responsibility for a lot of this more basic work. Sad to say, the man who took on this work in 1863, the Rev. A. B. Davidson, became one of the exponents of a rationalism which eventually poisoned the life of much of the Church. Duncan tried with the help of Smeaton to reclaim Davidson but was unsuccessful and Davidson's influence subsequently affected Robertson Smith who spread the plague of scepticism very widely.

Nonetheless Duncan's value was recognized by many and in particular those interested in Hebrew received a stimulus and help from him of incomparable worth. His studies on the Old Testament itself were original and stimulating and of the highest order. Where Duncan excelled, however, was in personal conversation with his students. They found him to be a man of great sympathy and one who was deeply concerned with their spiritual state and welfare. One of his students wrote of him: 'The spiritual character of Dr Duncan was most impressive. The child-like simplicity of the man, his profound reverence, his sense of personal unworthiness, the absoluteness of his reliance on Christ, his devotedness to the Saviour appearing in all that he said and did . . . His prayers were very remarkable . . . On one occasion the prayer that should have preceded the lesson prolonged itself for an entire hour and it was only the ringing of the bell at the end of the hour that awoke him to a remembrance of the actual circumstances of the case and terminated the reverie. But many who listened to this prayer were unspeakably moved by it, were awestruck and had their hearts melted . . .'

It is necessary now to go into the particular issue of Duncan's conversion and those experiences subsequent to it which are relevant to the question of assurance.

CONVERSION

We must first of all glance at the character and teachings of César Malan, through whom Duncan was converted. César Malan was born in Geneva in 1787, became a schoolmaster, and later was ordained to the ministry in that city. His family originated in the Piedmontese valleys of the Waldenses. He was a man of a most moral and devout life, yet at the time of his ordination he had no living knowledge of Christ. 'His character explains why the gospel always presented itself to him as the proclamation of a salvation wrought for him and without him, rather than as the means God had put into his hands to dissipate doubts by which he had never been distracted and to alleviate convictions by which he had never been afflicted.' Malan wrote of his conversion: 'I have stated, on some occasions, that my conversion to the Lord Jesus might, with propriety, be compared to a mother rousing an infant with a kiss – a simile answering exactly to my experience in recalling it. Nor can I look back to that blessed epoch in my life without magnifying his tender loving kindness who spared me the doubts, terrors and perplexities through which so many souls have passed ere they tasted "joy and peace in believing".'

Malan, being converted, began to preach with great power and unction and ultimately was put out of the ministry by the church in Geneva, which was a great grief to him. This was, of course, as a result of his evangelical zeal. He preached in many places and his ministry was greatly blessed. In doctrine he was thoroughly Calvinistic, embracing that summary of doctrine contained in the Confession of Faith of the Reformed Churches of Holland, and he preached divine sovereignty, election and predestination. At the same time he dogmatically affirmed that he 'never deemed it possible for a work of grace to commence in any soul – that soul remaining unconscious of its operation'. When preaching in London on one occasion he was stopped on leaving the pulpit by an old man entirely unknown to him. 'I bless God that I have this day heard Romaine and White-field', said the stranger. On being asked who it was that addressed him, he replied, 'My name is Rowland Hill!'

Malan's method of dealing with people was very direct and very simple. He proceeded on the basis of syllogistic reason-ing. We have an account of Duncan's meetings with him from Duncan's own lips. Let us then hear Duncan himself.

> In this softened state of mind I went next day to meet Mr Malan . . . He was then here and everywhere working his syllogism, 'Whosoever believeth that Jesus is the Christ is born of God'; by which I believe he did much good and some harm. But for him I have to thank God. Malan that day greatly attracted me; his face beamed with happiness and love. You know he is overstrained but his dogmatism did me good . . . We talked, going away from the com-pany, till late into the night and going over many things . . . I fought against his syllogism. 'I believe Jesus is the Christ, but I don't believe I am born of God.' At last in our talk I happened to be quoting a text. He started for-ward and said, 'See! you have the Word of God in your mouth!' It passed through me like electricity – the great thought that God meant man to know his mind: God – his Word – in my very mouth. It was, I believe, the seed of perhaps all I have, if I have anything, to this hour. Seminally it was perhaps all there though I cannot even now unfold it, much less then.
>
> I went home and wrote a prayer which I wish I had preserved. 'O God, my God (my old Seceder training made me turn to appropriation of God), my God, because thou hast made me, teach me what is the meaning of being the Christ the Son of God, that I may believe on him.' It was

defective, but it was not false, it was true so far. Then I sat down and wrote out a series of syllogisms. Thus –

Major – He that believeth that Jesus is the Christ is born of God.
Minor – But I believe that Jesus is the Christ.
Therefore I am born of God.

There is much more, of course, in this account but we must hear the conclusion.

Well, next day, as I sat down to study and took my pen in my hand, I became suddenly the passive recipient of all the truths which I had heard and been taught in my child-hood. I sat there unmoving for hours and they came and preached themselves to me. There was here no investiga-tion such as I had desired: but presentation of the truth to me passive. And I felt sitting there as if in that hour I had got matter for sermons for a lifetime.

Now the temptation to daily sin was gone. I had not even to fight with it. And I was in an almost infantile state of mind, so that when I mislaid a paper in my study, I would kneel down and pray to find it, and then go and seek for it.

This trusting state of mind showed itself further, in that night after night he laid himself down to sleep with the infant's prayer on his lips:
> This night when I lie down to sleep
> I give my soul to Christ to keep;
> If I should die before I wake
> I pray the Lord my soul to take.

The consequences of this experience were numerous. First of all his attitude to Scripture was radically changed. From then on, the Scriptures were God's voice to his soul. With this went a fundamental rejection of error. Speaking of specula-tion about issues of man's existence prior to Adam, Duncan said, 'I never did enter into that discussion: for when I gave up my sceptical opinions I did not pick them out one by one, but I gave a vomit and vomited them all up. I might have attended more to the Apologetic had I picked them out bit by bit, but I threw up my speculations, and admitted the Bible just at once.' With this new faith in Scripture went the shattering of that pride of intellect which had previously been such a great hindrance to him.

Secondly, Duncan became very zealous in preaching the gospel and went everywhere compelling people to come in. He knew great inward joy, preached high and immediate assurance to large numbers of willing hearers. He delighted in spiritual conversation with his fellow Christians and showed a great breadth of sympathy, for while delighting in the company of Christians who could discuss with him on the level of his own intellect, he delighted also in the company of the humble and obscure of this world who served the same Saviour. His biographer David Brown, in seeking to understand what happened to Duncan, quotes a passage from Olshausen on Romans 8:16: 'The Spirit itself beareth witness with our spirit that we are the children of God.' The passage concludes, ' . . . This witness of the Spirit is not to be placed merely in the feeling (*1 John* 3:19) but his whole inward and outward efficacy must be taken together – his comfort, his incitement to prayer, his rebuke of sin, his impulse to works of love, to witness before the world and such like. Upon the formation of this immediate testimony of the Holy Spirit, all the regenerate man's conviction of Christ and his work fully rests. For the faith in the Scriptures itself has its basis upon this experience of the Divinity of the principle which it promises and which flows into the believer while he is occupied with it.'

'SECOND CONVERSION'
As we have seen, this joyful experience lasted for about two years and was followed by a time of terrible darkness. If

Duncan's first conversion was glorious, what he sometimes described as his 'second conversion' involved him in experiences of the most shattering kind. He began to doubt his salvation, that is, his own interest in Christ. Again Duncan left a quite full account of what happened and we can only quote from it briefly.

> Christ was now telling me of a cure for depravity, as he had before told me of a cure for guilt. As I was praying for a purpose, namely, to believe, I essayed the thing. After I had prayed for the Holy Ghost, I tried to believe on Christ, but was conscious of no manner of effect. So I then quarrelled with God for not giving his Spirit, and then quarrelled with myself for doing so. Then I thought, perhaps I am a reprobate, and I quarrelled with God for this, and then I quarrelled with myself for it.

A little later he tells how he ran away into some brick-kilns and went down on his knees.

> I prayed thus, 'O Lord, I have broken thy law, and I have not believed on thy Son, and I have refused thy Holy Spirit; and if thou shouldest now cast me into hell, all holy beings would say, Righteous art thou, o Lord, when thou judgest. But, Lord, for thy mercy's sake give me thy Holy Spirit that I may believe on thy Son.'

And he added, 'It is a prayer in which I see nothing yet to retract.'

We have seen that before Duncan's conversion he did not know any prolonged period of deep conviction. It was some time subsequent to his conversion that he began to experience this 'law work'. Only then did he know the exposing of his deep inward corruption and unbelief. How necessary is an understanding of the 7th chapter of Romans is vital in this context!

When Duncan wrote this record of events he left instructions that it was not to be published until after his death. It concludes in this way:

I can't put a negative upon my regeneration. I don't say I can put a positive. Sometimes hope abounds, and at the worst I have never been able dogmatically to pronounce myself unregenerate. I have the awful fear of being so, though you know the strong feeling we often have just to begin again, all over again, as sinners; and the perfect certainty that Christ can save me - can regenerate me - is essential to my ongoing, so that I should not be hopeless even were I proved to be unregenerate.

Sometimes I have strongly thought that that is formed between Christ and me which shall last for ever. At other times I fear I may be in hell yet. But if I can't affirm my regeneration, I can't deny it; my self-examination can go no further. And when self-examination terminates so, I must just leave my case in His hands who can make it good if it is bad, and, if it is good, clear it up to me. But whether I have received the truth in the love of it or not – and this is the only evidence of regeneration – I surely think that it is the Spirit of God who has made known to me this truth.

As might be expected, Duncan's views of his own condition fluctuated, so that at certain times he was more settled than at others. Perhaps his state at its most heartbreaking is revealed in the recollection of one of his students:

'His very darkness and distress, often so mysterious and humiliating and which he could not keep to himself, was, I believe, for our benefit, and I have known instances in which it produced the deepest impression and led to con-version. One memorable instance of this, of which I have a vivid recollection, occurred at the prayer meeting of the Professors and students, when Duncan, who was presid-ing, broke down, and in the presence of Principal, Professors and students wept and sobbed and said that God had forsaken him. It was one of the most solemn

scenes I ever witnessed, and long afterwards I learned that
God had a gracious purpose to serve by it.

Of course, Duncan did not lack people who tried to help,
nor did he sit down in his troubles and give up. What he felt
most feelingly was the want of that conscious sense of the presence of God as his own in Christ which before had made him
dance for joy. Frequently he would have upon his lips the cry
of Job, 'O that I knew where I might find him!' He sought
people's prayers and their advice but he was not an easy man
to help. Indeed it has been suggested that the sceptical frame
of mind which so characterized him before conversion, after
conversion became directed towards his own relationship with
Christ, as we find exemplified in a conversation he once held
with Dr Kidd of Aberdeen: 'I was pouring out my complaint
to him – I had a Socinian heart, and a Pelagian heart, and an
Arminian heart, and all kinds of hearts. As we were parting,
the Doctor says, "Lord, I have a Socinian heart, and a Pelagian
heart, and an Arminian heart, and every kind of bad heart;
but the Son of God loved me and gave himself for me. Good-
bye." I went away saying, "Ha! that's an easy way of getting
over it" [taking for granted just what he doubted, whether
Christ died for him]. I had two miles to go after I parted from
him, and I walked the first mile saying, "That is an easy way";
but the second I walked saying, "If that be an easy way, what
is the hard and right way?" And I could not find it. But
I would have disputed the matter with him if I had the
opportunity.'

Duncan also wrote to Malan about his problem and it is
interesting to read part of Malan's reply.

But beloved, what are those clouds of which you speak,
and which you say, like the mists upon the Alps rise and
vanish alternately in your faith? . . . It is nothing else than
unbelief under the appearance of humility; and that thus,
you make God a liar while professing to tremble at his

Word . . . you say, and here is your error, If I bring not forth fruit I am not elected. Answer: The fruits are produced by the Spirit of adoption; this is to say, we must first be sure that we are the children of God before obeying as children . . . so Duncan will, by the spirit of filial assurance or adoption, bring forth celestial fruits after he is assured he has life, that he is a child of God . . .

But Duncan remained unconvinced and his struggles remained with him till his deathbed, indeed were renewed with a terrifying intensity then.

I was in terrible agony last night at the thought of a Christless state, and that I might be in it. The fear of it exhausted my faculties. I had a flickering hope. Oh, what are we to deal with the great God, either in the greatness of his wrath or in the greatness of his love? or with that great transaction wherein is displayed the terribleness of his punitive justice and the riches of his grace?

Perhaps the clue to certain aspects of Duncan's trouble is to be found in his hatred of a shallow religion; he feared an antinomian spirit and feared it most in himself. He dreaded the 'gentle conviction of sin, the calm coldish admiration of Christ, the gentlemanly, scholarlike, prudent gratitude, the obedience of a freezing but not absolutely frozen state.' In his dread of shallowness there is much that is redolent of Samuel Rutherford in his attitude to Christ.

'What is man's chief end?' I pass over the first part mainly with an intellectual approbation of its moral rectitude as a requirement, 'Man's chief end is to glorify God', while every fibre of my soul winds itself round the latter part ('to enjoy him for ever') with unutterable, sickening, fainting desire. But I pray the Lord my God to circumcise my heart to love the Lord my God, to love him for his own essential, revealed excellencies with devoted love; that the

Beloved (O my soul, O Spirit of the Lord, is he or is he not my Beloved?) may be mine, and I his, and I his, and I his . . . Ohone! Ohone! [Alas, alas!] I wish I had a little more personal faith. I think with the Psalmist that these things are more precious than gold, yea, than much fine gold; but I cannot go so well with him in that 'they are sweeter also than honey and the honeycomb'. I stick at that; that has been often a plague with me; the precious things were more as casketed jewels than as meat and drink. They delight the intellect; but oh, I wish I had a loving heart! I go mourning all the day for want of it.

Do we not hear in these statements and laments the breathings of a gracious spirit? Do we, who may have more assurance than John Duncan, have the *same* longings after Christ, the same desire to love him? Would we not see rather more of this spirit in our churches than the brash antinomian spirit which professes to know Christ but is really unconscious of and unconcerned about its lack of love for him?

In saying this it is not asserted that these are the only two alternatives which face us. Nor for a moment are we implying that there is not a deep and real assurance which is also associated with deep longings after and love for Christ. It is to be remarked, however, that we live in an age which regards the questioning of one's assurance as legalism and a discouragement to Christians and yet this age is characterized by a significant absence of love to Christ. Moody Stuart writes most perceptively of Duncan that

He was peculiarly alive to the danger of a semi-antinomian resting on privilege and promise apart from the present activity of gracious affections and a daily progress in sanctification . . . The pity which many good people felt for his spiritual distress was often in so far misplaced that he was not unacquainted with their state of mind and preferred his own darkness to their light. An assurance of salvation founded on the fact of conversion, or on a present faith in the Word of God, but not accompanied or followed by corresponding spiritual affection and the present exercise of grace, would have yielded no comfort to him.

Interestingly enough, to ministers Duncan observed, 'My preaching was never more evangelical than when I myself was in the most legal state.' But in Duncan's sermons there is very little evidence of his own inward torments. He is a good example to us of rising above his own troubles in the zeal he had to commend his Saviour.

We have looked at what Duncan said of himself: let us hear the testimony of one of his students who closely observed him:

There we were – many of us fresh from discussions in philosophy which had engrossed and fascinated us, some groping their way through difficulties in the Evidences, and some through difficulties in systematic theology, while others, perchance, were passing through deep spiritual struggles as to the reality of grace in their own souls and their call to the work of the ministry; but whatever was the character of our difficulties, when we looked at 'the Rabbi' we all felt and were wont to say, 'There is the best evidence of Christianity, and especially the best evidence that there is such a thing as living personal godliness; there is a man who walks closely with God, who actually knows what it is to enjoy the light of God's countenance, and at the same time what it is to be without it, even for a day; there is a man who, while brimful of all knowledges, ancient and modern, evidently prizes most the knowledge of the only true God and Jesus Christ whom he has sent.'

VIEWS OF ASSURANCE

The Westminster Confession deals with the issue of assurance in chapter 18. Section 1 of that chapter reads:

Although hypocrites and other unregenerate men may vainly deceive themselves with false hopes and carnal presumptions of being in the favour of God and estate of salvation; which hope of theirs shall perish; yet such as truly believe in the Lord Jesus, and love him in sincerity, endeavouring to walk in all good conscience before him, may in this life be certainly assured that they are in a state of grace and may rejoice in the hope of the glory of God; which hope shall never make them ashamed.

It is perfectly clear from the New Testament that on a number of occasions conversion was immediately followed by assurance. Thus we read of the Ethiopian eunuch that after his conversion 'he went on his way rejoicing' (*Acts* 8.39). It was exactly the same with the Philippian jailer: 'And when he had brought them into his house he set meat before them, and rejoiced, believing in God with all his house' (*Acts* 16.34). Furthermore we are not confronted in the New Testament with large numbers of people who doubt their salvation, but with Christians, addressed as Christians who, while they may need strengthening, are nevertheless accepted as true believers and upon this basis taught truth. It must, of course, be recognized that 1 John was written (among other things) to strengthen assurance, as we find it stated in verse 10 of chapter 5: 'These things have I written unto you that believe on the name of the Son of God; that ye may know that ye have eternal life and that ye may believe on the name of the Son of God.' Duncan's comment on this verse is illuminating.

> This text implies three things: 1. That they who believe on the name of the Son of God have eternal life; 2. That they may be brought to the knowledge that they have eternal life; and 3. That this knowledge is not to supersede their living by direct faith on the Son of God; in saying 'And that ye may believe', etc., it is as if he had said, 'Now ye see what good ye have got by believing;

therefore keep believing; yea, grow in grace, and in the knowledge of the Son of God; for ye see what good comes by believing.' This correlation then between the Gospel and the Epistle seems very much to intimate that a man may believe on the Son of God and have life by his name, yet need somewhat to help him to know that he has eternal life. The whole Epistle presupposes faith in the Son of God and possession of life thereby, and then seems to bring believers to the knowledge of their having eternal life by what are commonly called marks of grace.

The New Testament also speaks of 'full assurance'. Thus we have 'full assurance of understanding' (Col. 2:2], 'full assurance of hope' (*Heb.* 6:11) and 'full assurance of faith' (*Heb.* 10:22). These verses imply that there are degrees of assurance, and that Christians should never be satisfied with little assurance but should always be striving for greater degrees of grace, so that in 2 Peter we are exhorted, 'Wherefore the rather, brethren, give diligence to make your calling and election sure: for if ye do these things ye shall never fall: for so an entrance shall be ministered unto you abundantly into the everlasting kingdom of our Lord and Saviour Jesus Christ' (2 *Pet.* 1:10–11). Finally, on the positive side we are confronted with such verses as Romans 8:16: 'The Spirit itself beareth witness with our spirit, that we are the children of God' and with those verses which speak of the sealing of the Spirit, e.g. *Eph.* 1:13; 2 *Cor.* 1:22. Many have argued rightly that an understanding of such verses is basic to a proper understanding of the true doctrine of assurance.

We note, then, that the New Testament age was characterized by a high degree of assurance in believers, yet there are passages that point to the fact that the issue of assurance may confront believers with real difficulties. When Jesus was baptized of John in Jordan we read, 'And lo, a voice from heaven, saying, This is my beloved Son, in whom I am well pleased'

(*Matt.* 3:17). Immediately after this Jesus was led of the Spirit into the wilderness to be tempted of the devil. Two of the devil's three temptations began with, 'If thou be the Son of God', and, clearly, Satan's design was to shed doubt upon that which God the Father had so recently and powerfully affirmed. He therefore sought to throw doubts upon Christ's divine Sonship. If that was the experience of our Saviour it should hardly surprise us if one of Satan's great activities is to stir up doubts and darkness concerning our assurance. A man who can speak as Paul did in the heavenly tones of Romans 8 is a great menace to Satan's kingdom.

Nor is it only the activity of Satan that will cause difficulty, but the fact that there is such a thing as spiritual self-delusion. The words of Jesus have an awful solemnity as he reveals to us the happenings of the last day. 'Many will say to me in that day, Lord, Lord, have we not prophesied in thy name? and in thy name cast out devils? and in thy name done many wonderful works? And then will I profess unto them, I never knew you: depart from me, ye that work iniquity' (*Matt.* 7:22, 23). The parable of the sower (*Matt.* 13:3ff), with its stony ground hearers and its unfruitful professors, and the account of the fate of the foolish virgins (Matt. 25) are just two passages which will lead any serious believer to ask himself whether there is in him a true work of grace or whether he is suffering from self-deception. Hebrews 6 and 1 Corinthians 13, with their account of the high and exalted experiences a man may have and yet have no real work of grace in his heart, will again make the serious-minded tremble. Paul tells the Corinthians, 'Examine your own selves, whether ye be in the faith; prove your own selves. Know ye not your own selves, how that Jesus Christ is in you except ye be reprobates?' (2 *Cor.* 13:5). Such words as these, together with the apostasy of Judas and the questioning of the apostles when Christ warned of what was about to happen - 'And they were exceeding sorrowful, and began every one of them to say unto him, Lord is it I?' (*Matt.* 26:22) -

should show the error of those professed evangelicals who teach that self-examination is unhealthy and unscriptural. We should regard such people with the same suspicion as we would a silversmith who objected when we desired to examine the hall-mark upon a piece of silver he was trying to sell us.

Finally, let it be remembered that the New Testament gives a full picture of the fruits of a work of grace in the soul. Those most tender of conscience and aware of their own failings may find a comparison between themselves and this picture most disturbing. An assurance derived from a low view of what it is to be a Christian is of little worth. As we shall see, some of 'Rabbi' Duncan's difficulties arose from the fact that he had a very high view of what it was to be a Christian and a very low view of what he himself was.

In the history of the church controversy has focused around three aspects of the doctrine of assurance. First of all is the question whether assurance is of the essence of saving faith. William Cunningham writes:

> There was not among the Reformers, and there has not been among modern Protestants, unanimity, as to what is involved in the *fiducia* which is included in justifying faith. The generality of modern divines and some of the Reformers held that this *fiducia* was just trust or confidence in Christ's person, as distinguished from mere belief of the truth concerning him, and as involving some special application or appropriation to ourselves of the discoveries and promises of the gospel, but not, directly and immediately, any opinion or conviction as to our actual personal condition; while the generality of the Reformers, and some modern divines, especially those known in Scotland as Marrow men, have regarded it as comprehending this last element also, and have thus come to maintain that personal assurance is necessarily and directly included in the exercise of saving faith, or

belongs to its essence.[2]

Thus we find Thomas Goodwin writing:

Even as in the first age of reformation, when they taught
that all faith was assurance that a man's sins were forgiven (which is as great an error as can be, it condemns
the generation of many of the righteous) and yet God did
apply himself unto this error in the experience of the most
of that age, and came upon them accordingly.[3]

Thomas Boston, in his notes on *The Marrow of Modern
Divinity*, writes:

Now saving faith being a persuasion that we shall have
life and salvation by Christ on a receiving and resting in
him for salvation, includes in it a knowledge of our
being beloved of God: the former cannot be without the
latter. In the meantime, such as the strength or weakness
of that persuasion is, the steadiness or unsteadiness of
that receiving and resting, just so is this knowledge clear
or unclear, free of or accompanied with doubtings', and
in *The Marrow* itself we read, 'You have perceived a willingness in Christ to receive you and to embrace you as his
beloved spouse; and you have thereupon felt a secret persuasion in your heart, that God in Christ doth bear a love
to you; and answerably your heart hath been inflamed
towards him in love again, manifesting itself in an unfeigned desire to be obedient and subject to his will in all
things and never to displease him in anything.[4]

It would be wrong to make too much of these differences,
however, and in a recent book a modern writer argues:

Nevertheless, the difference was always one of emphasis
rather than of principle. On the one hand, while Calvin
maintained that saving faith had within itself confidence
and certitude (*Inst.* Book 3, Chap. 2, sections 15–16), he

also recognized that Christians did often lack assurance and might begin with various and varying degrees in it (sections 17–20). On the other hand, those who differed from him in emphasis and expression – and this included the English Puritans generally – were yet quite prepared to accept that faith had within itself an essential, germinal assurance that might simply pass unrecognized by the holder of it in his reflections upon his state; for as they all held, at regeneration the Spirit communicates himself with all his powers and graces, and therefore the newborn Christian has within himself the root or seed or germ of all the graces – including of course, assurance! Thus a bridge always existed uniting the two views. A man may have assurance and not know that he has it.[5]

We shall be returning to Dr Duncan's views on this, but it is worth quoting two of his comments at this juncture: 'Of the doctrine that will allow none to be true believers who want full assurance of their own salvation, Andrew Gray of Glasgow (if I remember right) says, "It is more discouraging than the dark and doubtsome faith of the Papists." I have much sympathy with doubts which arise from a high estimate of Christian character as set forth in scriptural delineation of what all true believers (regenerate men) are, and, in contrast therewith, from a low view of their own attainments, that stimulates while it humbles.'[6]

He also makes the shrewd historical observation:

When the doctrine of assurance being necessarily contained in faith (so as to be essential to it) gets into a church, in the second generation it gets habituated to the use of highest appropriating language by dead carnal men.[7]

It is impossible at this point to do more than glance at the place evidences have in the history of the doctrine of assurance. But since Duncan was brought up in Scotland and would be well aware of some of the characteristics of what is termed

'Highland Religion'. It is worth quoting the following from the Days of the Fathers in Ross-Shire:

The Christians in the Highlands had been taught to distinguish between doubting the safety of their state and doubting the truth of the Word. They were accustomed to hear that one may be trusting in Christ while continuing to feel that he is a sinner. It was not the same kind of evidence they required to satisfy them as to the trustworthiness of Christ as they needed to assure them of being partakers of his grace. They had learned to be content with the Word as the evidence of the former, but they sought in their 'life and conversation' for the evidence of the latter. They could quite understand why Christ, who so often reproved his disciples for their unbelief, should yet excite them to self-jealousy when he said 'One of you is a devil' and 'One of you shall betray me', and why Peter, to whom a special message of comfort had previously been sent, should thrice be asked, 'Lovest thou me?' If some others understood this as well, the case of the Highland Christian would not be such a puzzle to them as it seems to be. There are some who, once obtaining somehow a hope of safety, banish all fears as to their interest in Christ from their hearts. A hope of being safe is all they desire, and having this they seek not for evidence of being holy.[8]

THE WITNESS OF THE SPIRIT

The third area of controversy surrounded the issue of the direct witness of the Spirit. To a large degree this controversy has centred on the interpretation of Romans 8:16: 'The Spirit itself beareth witness with our spirit, that we are the children of God.' Robert Shaw in *The Reformed Faith* illustrates the different opinions held concerning this.

There are different opinions however in regard to the manner in which the Spirit gives this testimony. Some have thought that the Spirit witnesses the believer's adoption by inward revelation, or by way of immediate suggestion. 'The Spirit', says one (Ralph Erskine), 'by himself witnesses in a distinct way from that which is by water and blood, by shedding abroad the love of God upon the heart in a soul ravishing way.' This is evident from the experiences of the saints. Many of them have been brought to assurance in this immediate way; and not merely by reflection upon marks and signs and qualifications within, which is the Spirit's witnessing by water or sanctification. The greater part of divines, however, concur in the opinion that the Spirit witnesses by means of his operation, or by the effects produced by him in hearts of believers. They reject the idea of an immediate testimony, and hold that the work of the Spirit is the testimony which he gives, assuring believers of their adoption and consequent safety. President Edwards speaks very decidedly and strongly against the opinion that the Spirit witnesses by way of immediate suggestion in revelation and declares that many mischiefs have arisen from this false and delusive notion.[9]

Weighty authorities may be cited on both sides, for while Edwards and many of the New England theologians of his age spoke in that way, Thornwell, an American Presbyterian of a later age, speaking with equal vigour for the opposite point of view, writes of Romans 8:16:

How can there be a testimony of the Spirit separate and distinct from the testimony of our own hearts if, after all, we know the presence of the Spirit only from the effects which he impresses upon us? How can a witness assure us of a fact when we do not *know* that the witness is speaking? If Paul does not proceed on the assumption that we are conscious of the *personal* presence of the Holy Ghost, language may cease to be employed as a vehicle of thought.[10]

Thornwell returns to the subject with even greater force and flashing eloquence in a later volume.

So important an element of personal religion is the direct witness of the Spirit that where it is cordially embraced it will infuse vitality into a dead system; it is a green spot in the desert, a refreshing brook in the wilderness. Wherever it penetrates the heart it engenders a spirit of dependence upon God, a practical conviction of human imbecility, and an earnest desire for supernatural expressions of Divine favour. It maintains a constant communion with the Father of lights, an habitual anxiety to walk with God, which, whatever may be the theory of grace, keeps the soul in a posture of prayer and cherishes a temper congenial with devotion and holiness. He that seeks for the witness of the Spirit must wait upon God; and he that obtains it has learned from the fruitlessness of his own efforts, his hours of darkness and desertion, his long agony and conflicts, that it is a boon bestowed in sovereignty, the gift of unmerited grace.[11]

For another point of view those interested should read the chapter on Assurance in R. L. Dabney's *Systematic Theology*. His comments on one particular aspect of the controversy in *Discussions: Evangelical and Theological* (vol. 1, p 169f) are penetrating. J. C. Ryle in his book *Holiness* also has a helpful chapter on Assurance.

Before we conclude this section it is necessary for us to consider two other issues. First of all, great care is needed in dealing with these issues. Dr Duncan himself warns of this when he says: 'There must be always great delicacy in dealing with these theological relations in respect of living men, inasmuch as there may be morbid states of soul even in true Christians.'[12] It is essential we always remember that these issues are closely bound up with the eternal welfare of men and there is no place for the barren pursuit of controversy for its own sake without regard to the needs of those to whom we are speaking. Paul warns us: 'Him that is weak in the faith receive ye, but not to doubtful disputations' (*Rom.* 14:1). There are probably many of us who have met with those who, when they have talked of their views of assurance, have promoted confusion and darkness among their hearers. We must be tender towards men and real care is needed here.

Secondly, while we have looked at past discussions, we may ask what are the prevailing needs of our age. Our age is an age of theological and spiritual confusion and it is impossible to do more than isolate a few issues that we ought to bear in mind as we come to look more closely at the relevance of Dr Duncan's views on assurance.

First of all we live in an age of superficiality, not least in spiritual experience. We are often confronted with those who, professing to be Christian, lack even basic evidence of regeneration. Such people point back to some experience they have had as the basis of their assurance and are most reluctant to engage in self-examination. Indeed there are those who would accuse us of spreading alarm and despondency because we hold to the quite clear biblical teaching that we are not saved by experience and that there is such a thing as a spurious conversion. With this there is much antinomianism; sometimes this is explicit, sometimes it is implicit. But there is teaching which, by a horrid confusion and misunderstanding of the doctrine of the perseverance of the saints coupled with a kind of easy believism, almost encourages professed believers to live in a careless manner in disregard of the law of God. At the same time it promises the blessedness of heaven to such unholiness.

Related to this is a confounding of intellectual assent to gospel truth with true saving faith. Some who have given intellectual assent to prepositional truth without exercising faith in a crucified and risen Redeemer then find a desperate inward emptiness and unreality. These people, then, become the happy hunting ground for various types of second blessing teaching which professes to remedy the recognized absence of experience. Those who have never been truly converted are encouraged to seek some kind of remedy for their leanness in experiences of doubtful value and origin. Paul tells us we can speak with the tongues of men and angels, perform miracles and yet be without that love which is one of the cardinal evidences of the Spirit's work. To direct people to seek for experiences when what they need is faith and repentance is to lead them into greater error and delusion.

Finally, we are today confronted, even among those who have true faith, with a coldness and a lifelessness which is extremely sad. What is even sadder is that people seem to be content to remain in this low state. Does such a condition arise because of a lack of understanding of what assurance brings? Dr John Love, a man whom Dr Duncan greatly admired, made this comment about spiritual desertion:

'The more sweet the Lord's presence has been to the soul, the more bitter, painful, and distressing must his withdrawing be. Then the soul will be in a special manner pained, being especially tender.'[13]

It may be that Dr Duncan can be of great help to us here because he was never satisfied with an assurance that was not related to fervent affection. Let us repeat,

'An assurance of salvation founded either in the fact of conversion or on a present faith in the word of God, but not accompanied or followed by corresponding spiritual affection and the present exercise of grace, would have yielded no comfort to him.'

His comment is also timely when he says, 'A "perhaps" of salvation works more in some souls than all the fullness of the Gospel in others.' Such a statement needs careful qualification and explanation lest it should be misunderstood. Nevertheless it is worth recording in the light of our present situation in England.

DUNCAN'S CONTRIBUTION

Having looked briefly at some of the issues raised in connection with assurance, we proceed to examine in particular Dr Duncan's own contribution to this subject, both in terms of his own words and in connection with his own experience. In some ways Duncan is a paradox. It has often been argued that assurance is related to usefulness, that if we are to serve God effectively then assurance is essential to such effectiveness.

'It was a saying of Bishop Latimer to Ridley, "When I live in a settled and steadfast assurance about the state of my soul, methinks then I am as bold as a lion. I can laugh at all trouble: no affliction daunts me. But when I am eclipsed in my comforts, I am of so fearful a spirit that I could run into a very mouse hole."'[14]

We have already learnt something of Dr Duncan's troubles and doubts. Yet his great usefulness to others can never be questioned. He was a man who by his preaching strengthened many and whose very presence could be a blessing.

Moody Stuart, one of his biographers and his minister in later years, tells of a very remarkable incident.

> In church one Sabbath, in the progress of the morning prayer, I became gradually, but at length clearly and definitely, conscious that my thoughts and words were flowing in a channel that was not indeed alien to my intentions, but was distinctly different from any previous conception of my own. The impulse of a sensible force seemed increasingly to move me onward, but after a time one petition after another filled me with wonder. As they came up in succession I thought at last, 'How is it that I am praying today in this manner? These thoughts are not my own thoughts, and the words that clothe them are words I have never used before, nor thought of using. They are Dr John Duncan's; it seems as if he were praying in me, for both the ideas and the language are his and not mine.

He must be here, yet he never comes to this church; and he cannot be here for he is in Hungary.' Bewildered how it could be, but confident that he was in the church, I bent over the pulpit as soon as I had finished the prayer, and saw him close under me in the session seat. The mystery was solved clearly to me, although remaining mysterious for those who doubt all mystery. Dr Duncan had entered the church after the commencement of the service, and in the exercise of his spirit there had surely been more than a merely passive following of the supplications that were pouring through my lips.[15]

Dr Duncan was ever suspicious of his own heart and was hard on himself. However this was not associated with any lack of charity towards others; indeed towards others he showed a breadth of spirit and great tenderness. Yet his charity was not of that sentimental kind that lacks any discernment or recognition that there may be faults in others.

I have said that there is great delicacy in applying these relations to the cases of living men who may be in a morbid state, or in whom some of the elements may as yet be merely seminal. I am not suspicious, therefore, of professing Christians merely because they want assurance of their own salvation; neither on the other hand, am I suspicious of the assurance of young converts: for I believe God may give assurance as soon as he gives faith. But I am suspicious of the profession of assurance and high joy, when it is without any indication of brokenness and contriteness of heart; when it is without the solemnizing of character which a view of God's tremendous wrath and great salvation must give; and when it is without docility when young converts set up to be teachers . . .[16]

David Brown quotes Duncan:

I have not much sympathy with those who have great suspiciousness about false religion. I have not much

sympathy with strong positive (condemnatory) affirmation about people's religion, when there is nothing
decidedly bad. I have not much sympathy with those who
are not disposed to admit and to hope that there may be
reality, where there is the appearance of some little good
thing toward the Lord God of Israel.[17]

However, this statement must be viewed in the light of what
Dr Duncan himself said concerning such errors as
Antinomianism, and his clearly stated view that he would never
allow an Arminian into his pulpit.

Brown also tells a story which not only illustrates this
aspect of Duncan but also his quick wit. It relates to a conversation Duncan had with Rev W. Tasker (Territorial Free
Church, Edinburgh):

Mr T.: 'I admitted a man of whom I thought if ever there
was a converted man it was he. But he went wrong upon my
hands. Now I have another case of which I think quite as well
as the other – but no better and I'm afraid to admit him, in
case he should turn out like the other. What say you?'

Dr Duncan: 'Oh, I have no difficulty there. You see there
was once a man called Simon Magus, and he took in Philip the
Evangelist, and when he was no doubt mortified about this he
was sent away from Samaria to a desert spot, and there he fell
in with an Ethiopian nobleman reading his Bible, as he drove
from keeping Pentecost at Jerusalem. The nobleman asked him
up to take his seat in the chariot, and they got into conversation about the passage in Isaiah that the gentleman had been
reading; when Philip threw such a flood of light upon it, that
he longed to be baptized, and on coming to a pool of water he
asked what was to hinder it there and then. Oh a great deal,
Sir, for you see I'm a Scotsman and I was taken in the other
day by a man they call Simon Magus and maybe you'll take
me in too; but if you'll come back next year, and I find you of
the same mind, I'll admit you.'[18]

Duncan's own experience and his reflections on it led him to emphasize two particular truths that need emphasizing to-day.

First of all, he recognized that the work of conversion was no easy work and was deeply exercised that men should not be satisfied with only a partial work in the heart.

> Gentlemen, let me tell you to beware in that in which I have failed and offended; beware of resting short of giving the whole heart unto God. Conversion is a great work of God, and of man under the mighty power of the Holy Ghost: a divine work upon a rational being having an understanding, will, and affection. Hence 'Turn ye, turn ye', and also the souls' cry, 'Turn us and we shall be turned.' Yea, that very command, 'Make you a new heart', must be obeyed. 'Ye have purified your hearts, keep yourselves in the love of God'; all these things must be done. Make not slim work of conversion. Give the whole heart as it is; we must give God the wicked heart.[19]

He was suspicious of mere comfort. 'Unmixed joy, that is not for earth; that hath never been on earth since Adam fell, unless perhaps in the Man of Sorrows, after his resurrection when the load was off. Purifying work is sorrowful work: sorrow at the thought of being impure, yet joy at the thought of coming purity.'[20] This belief in the need for a thorough work is of course in accord with the approach of such men as Thomas Halyburton and Dr John Love of whom Dr Duncan was a great admirer. Duncan refers to the three best biographies for Christians to read as Augustine's *Confessions*, Bunyan's *Grace Abounding* and Thomas Halyburton's *Memoirs*. These and men like them believed in the necessity for rigorous self-examination and a trying of the work of God in the soul to test its reality, and with these views Dr Duncan was in accord.

John Duncan had, of course, a very high view of what it meant to be a Christian, and this together with his own suspicion of himself was undoubtedly at the root of some of his difficulties. Yet, as we have seen, he was charitable to others and full of consolation, for he saw the dangers of an over-rigorous approach to the question of what constitutes a true Christian.

> Notwithstanding the sternness of his earlier doctrine and his lifelong severity against himself, his preaching was full of consolation; and during the long period of his latter years he was both large-hearted in his views of what constitutes a child of God, and most free in the offer of the Gospel. After an address on the tokens of regeneration, he said to me with a quiet smile, 'A man may want the marks you have given us, and be a true believer after all'; and of Thomas Shepard, a severe sifter of sincerity, he said, 'Shepard's books are fine books for basketing the fish (*Matt.* 13:47–48); but, mind, you must catch them before you basket them – Shepard is fine, but I wish I were as good as one of his hypocrites.'[21]

Incidentally, what is highly significant is that Duncan loved to hear evangelistic preaching.

> Night after night and one year after another, he sat with delighted interest to hear evangelists addressing crowds and preaching chiefly the judgment to come and a present acceptance of Christ with immediate joy of salvation. With such preaching he found no fault, provided it did not deny human inability, the Divine sovereignty, and the warrant and duty of prayer on the part of all men.[22]

This delight in hearing the gospel preached points us to one of the most universally admired of Duncan's characteristics, namely, his humility. That Duncan was conscious of his immense intellectual power and vast knowledge is no contradiction of this. But what pervaded his whole life was a childlike simplicity and lowliness. Moody-Stuart writes:

Its root lay in his sense of the majesty of God, which was far more profound than in other men, and humbled him lower in the dust; in his perception and his love of holiness and the consciousness of his own defect; in his sense of ingratitude for the unparalleled love of the Lord Jesus Christ, and his abiding conviction of past sin and present sinfulness. This habitual humbling was deepened by the wounding of his very tender conscience, through yielding himself to be carried away by what chanced to take hold of his mind.[23]

What Duncan really hated and opposed by every means was Antinomianism. While Antinomianism adopts many forms and manifests itself in many ways the definition of it given in *The Marrow of Modern Divinity* is adequate to give some true indication of its character.

And are there not others, though I hope but few, who being enlightened to see their misery, by reason of the guilt of sin, though not by reason of the filth of sin, and hearing of justification freely by grace, through the redemption which is in Jesus Christ, do applaud and magnify that doctrine, following them that do most preach and press the same, seeming to be, as it were, ravished with the hearing thereof, out of a conceit that they are by Christ freely justified from the guilt of sin, though still they retain the filth of sin! These are they that content themselves with a gospel knowledge, with mere notions in the head, but not in the heart; glorying and rejoicing in free grace and justification by faith alone; professing faith in Christ, and yet are not possessed of Christ; these are they that can talk like believers, and yet do not walk like believers; these are they that have language like saints, and yet have conversation like devils: these are they that are not obedient to the law of Christ, and therefore are justly called Antinomians.[24]

To this may be added Thomas Boston's comment of which Duncan would have thoroughly approved:

Mark here the spring of Antinomianism; namely, the want of a sound conviction of the odiousness and filthiness of sin, rendering the soul loathsome and abominable in the sight of a holy God. Hence, as the sinner sees not his need of, so neither will he receive and rest on Christ for all his salvation, but will go about to halve it, grasping at his justifying blood, neglecting his sanctifying Spirit . . .[25]

It was no doubt Duncan's love of holiness and of the law of God that lay at the root of his hatred of Antinomianism. 'Antinomianism was the object of his dread, loathing and hatred; he marked its subtle approaches with a wakeful jealousy and he met it with intense enmity when he discovered it seducing himself, or stealing upon his friends unsuspected by themselves or others.' It was this that made him suspicious of an assurance that was not associated with warm affection towards God and zeal against sin. He knew the treacherous character of the human heart: 'There's nobody perfect: that's the believer's bed of thorns: that's the hypocrite's couch of ease.'[26]

In understanding Dr Duncan at this point it is necessary to refer back to what has been termed his 'second conversion', and in particular to that tremendous apprehension of the nature of sin which was associated with it. Duncan himself describes it thus:

'A great change, a crisis in the soul's history takes place. The law is brought home to the conscience with power – the law, in its spirituality; the law in its exceeding breadth; the law, in its curse. Receiving the curse into the soul is scarcely anything short of actual damning.'[27]

David Brown, quoting this and speaking of those who might find some of Duncan's experiences repelling, says that perhaps they may see in all this:

only the lifelong effects of those scorching experiences through which he passed at the period of his 'second conversion', that they may perceive in it the exceeding tenderness of a conscience which once trifled with sin but now felt it as hell, and that they may haply be led to ask whether they themselves would not be better for some touches of that same mighty hand.[28]

But at the same time he also warns against thinking that any teaching which does not approach Duncan's in this area is shallow.

Brown also quotes a passage from John Owen of a somewhat similar character as illustrating that he had gone through a similar experience.

Indeed, when the recollection of that most melancholy period comes into my mind, when God was pleased by his Spirit to convince the heart of me a poor sinner of sin, and when the whole of God's controversy with me for sin is again presented to my view, I cannot sufficiently wonder what thoughts could possess those men who have treated of the remission of sins in so very slight, I had almost said contemptuous manner.[29]

Fortunately, Dr Duncan has left on record a summary of his views on those three issues associated with assurance to which we referred earlier. It is possible to abstract from this summary the results of his thought and experience over many years.

For convenience sake let us call assurance by direct faith No. 1; assurance by evidences of regeneration or marks of grace No. 2; and assurance by the witness of the Spirit No. 3. Undoubtedly the danger of No. 1 held exclusively, is antinomianism; that of No. 2 held exclusively is legalism; while if a man pretends to have the third without the first and second, it is either hypocrisy or the deepest self-delusion . . . Yet I do not think they are three independent ways of assurance, nor so much three steps of a ladder to assurance, as three elements found by analysis to be contained in all true assurance. In fact, they constitute a living organism - No. 1 being analogous to the root and No. 3 to the matured fruit of the tree.[30]

He then writes more fully on each of the elements of Assurance. On No. 1, Direct Faith, he writes:

Assurance by direct faith has, when held *ultra*, an element of truth and also one of falsehood. Its element of truth is the plenitude and freedom of the Gospel – Christ and his unsearchable riches offered to mankind – sinners as such. Its element of falsehood appears when the necessity of regeneration with faith is not exhibited, and we are represented as receiving Christ with the fallen hand of Adam; or where it is so held as to obstruct the way to No. 2 by putting aside such texts as these, 'If ye live after the flesh ye shall die; but if ye through the Spirit do mortify the deeds of the body ye shall live' (*Rom.* 8:13) . . . 'They that are Christ's have crucified the flesh, with the affections and lusts' (*Gal.* 5:24); or such as this, 'We must all appear before the judgment seat of Christ that every one may receive the things done in his body according to that he hath done, whether it be good or bad' (2 *Cor.* 5:10). It is a bad faith that has not room for these texts. Faith has room for them; and if it is really faith, they will set us to self-examination.[31]

To this we might add this further comment, 'Faith receives Christ lovingly; faith, not love; yet not without love too, lovingly.'[32]

In dealing with '2. Marks of Grace on Reflection – the second element of Assurance', there is an emphasis on 1 John, in particular on 1 John 5:13, and Duncan writes:

Believing and receiving life is direct (No. 1); the knowledge that we believe and have life must have in it reflection upon ourselves. And this reflection will embrace not only the actings of our faith but its fruits; for the Spirit who works faith works all the concomitant graces (in such a way as always glorifies Christ); and these are cognoscible things.[33]

Duncan deals with '3. The Witness of the Spirit - the third element of Assurance' particularly in connection with Romans 8:16: 'The Spirit itself beareth witness with our spirit that we are the children of God'. He says:

It seems to some to be enthusiastic and horrible; yet considered doctrinally, it is the apex of this question; and experimentally it goes into the very essence of religion.

What is meant in the above-quoted verse by 'our spirit'? Is it merely our intelligent minds? It is this, but it is the spirit born of the Spirit. 'The Holy Spirit', says one of the fathers, 'makes us holy and spiritual.' The testimony of God's Spirit, then, is only with the spirit of a regenerate man; it is the witness of the regenerating with the regenerated spirit.

Not only does the Spirit of God bring out his own graces into vivid exercise (No. 1); and not only is he pleased, especially at times to shine upon these - without which the believer's perception of them (No. 2) is dark and indistinct - this testimony is something more. It is the Father and the Son communicating with the souls of believers by the Holy Ghost, by means of the truth, and in this lies mainly the secret of experimental religion . . .

He then illustrates this in relation to prayer:

If there be as much reality in God's speaking to man as there is in man's speaking to God – then as certainly as the believer has access by the Spirit through Christ unto the Father in presenting his supplications, so certainly the Father has access through the Son by the Spirit that dwells in this man to convey the answer. Is this strange? Given a spiritual world – given a living God and (by regeneration) a living soul, is it incredible that there should be such intercourse between them; that the soul should speak to a hearing God and hear a speaking God? This indeed is the very kernel of experimental religion . . . For faith has an ear, as certainly as God hath a mouth; though if we be asked, 'How do you know that God speaks to you?' we could only answer 'Because I hear Him.' It is like asking a man 'Why do you believe your senses?'

Now then, to full assurance, we need a particular saying of God to our individual souls ('*Say* unto my soul', was David's prayer, 'I am thy salvation'); and this to a man without faith and without fruits of faith, he will never say. But wherever faith (No. 1) is – implying as it does, regeneration or good seed in good ground – it will be certainly followed by discernible fruits (No. 2) and by the witness of the Spirit (No. 3). Faith is seminal of all.[34]

CONTEMPORARY SITUATION

In seeking to evaluate the experience and teaching of 'Rabbi' Duncan, with a particular regard to our contemporary situation, it is necessary to concentrate upon a few major issues.

First, let it be remembered that Rabbi Duncan was a sinner. He never forgot this, and while rejoicing in the glory of Christ and ever seeking to point men to the Redeemer he loved so much, he was ever conscious of his own failures. He explained some of his difficulties in terms of his inordinate pursuit of his intellectual interests, and what could be termed his nearly idolatrous interest in foreign languages. 'My great temptation', he said on one occasion, 'is the inordinate study of languages, as if I would learn all the languages under the sun, and fit myself to be an interpreter at the Tower of Babel.' At times he would neglect prayer and study of Scripture whilst he gave himself to the intellectual delights that so fascinated him. This, combined with notoriously undisciplined habits, no doubt lay at the root of many of his difficulties. The man who would be left sitting in a chair reading a book when the household retired to bed, and be found at six a.m. the next morning in the same posture, or who would argue with his guest until five a.m., was always in danger of losing those blessings which may flow from an ordered and more regular style of life. Dr Duncan's own deep troubles of heart gave him an understanding of the inward difficulties that perplex Christians. This in turn was one of the reasons why he was able to be such a help to others. Those whose ministries are used in this way are often led into great trials themselves. It may be that a realization of this explains some of God's dealings with Duncan. We would do well to remember Luther's dictum that 'Bible study and meditation, prayer and temptation, make a minister.'

What needs emphasis is the warmth of Duncan's affection and the depth of his experience. That there are professing Calvinists whose Calvinism has got no further than their heads and whose hearts are cold is certainly true. But observe Duncan, a truly humble man, a truly loving man, to whom Jesus Christ was his delight, whose desire was to behold by faith the face of his Saviour and whose grief was to have that face hidden. What a truly warm-hearted man he was, what an example to this age with all its superficiality, frequent profession of high assurance, and yet lukewarm affection! As he wrote in a letter,

'Set no limit to the Holy Spirit of power. If sinners at all, we need Christ. A bitten Israelite would not have acted wisely to say, "When I am more severely bitten, when the poison has wrought more deeply, and I feel the agony more intensely, and I am nearly dead as such a one, then I will look." Who would not look till the moment he was about to expire? Convictions are not needed to make us welcome to Christ, but to make him welcome to us . . . Convictions are not lost by coming to Christ. The deepest convictions (I do not say terrors of wrath, oh no, but) convictions of sin and sinfulness are obtained after coming. The more progress in the divine life, the deeper the conviction of abounding sin, as well as the sweeter experiences of the grace which much more abounds. Come as you are, dear child, but suspect that comfort which does not maintain and tend at least to deepen conviction.'[35]

Next we should observe his balance. Maybe he was not so balanced in his experience, but he was in his thinking. Thus his comment: 'I would say, though it is an exaggeration, I would like to sit at Jonathan Edwards' feet to learn what is true religion, and at Thomas Boston's, to learn how to get it.'[36] He was balanced in his view of faith and quotes with approval Riccalton of Hobkirk who says,

'We divines, when we speak of faith, define it in the idea of perfection thereof. But I as well believe that there is more faith in some soul struggling with its own corruptions and manifold doubts than in another who may also be a believer, and whose faith, finding less opposition, may be more productive of joy and external fruits. For the strength of any principle is to be estimated not merely by the other effects it produces, but also by the resistance it has to overcome.'[37]

Furthermore Duncan was balanced in his view of the place of the intellect in relation to faith and affections. He was perplexed one day by the issue of the meagreness of the theology in the writings of those who succeeded the apostles and of the lack of bone or muscle in their theology as compared with that of Augustine, Luther, and Calvin. Duncan's answer was,

'Though then some were but poor theologians, they were burning and shining lights; though they could but poorly write for Christ they could fearlessly burn for Christ; and in their day Christ had more need of men who could burn in defence of his cause, than for men who could only write in defence of it.'[38] He said later, 'I don't think Polycarp could have stood a theological examination by John Owen; but he was a famous man to burn.'[39]

We live in an age of dreadful superficiality. Listen to a modern account of a Christian Union in one of the country's leading universities and then compare it with what we have read of John Duncan.

'On the first night of term, having written to and invited the new chaps, we put on an evening of music, drama, etc. in my room. — was a star on his sax, — slightly more subdued on the organ. We also had the star from the — Productions who was as usual very funny . . .'.

In the light of that we can see the extraordinary relevance of Duncan's comment about Reformation times:

'Then God raised up Luther. These were rough times; and there were awakened consciences, when God sent Luther, that were similarly tried. It was the awakened consciences that the Pope saw made a good market for Indulgences (They would not sell now – try them).'

Men are unlikely to have their consciences awakened by the sound of the saxophone, nor are those with wounded consciences likely to find much help from the so-called 'Christian Comedians'. Duncan saw only too clearly that in his age the awakened consciences of Luther's day were very much a thing of the past. He cried out against a superficial work, against superficial affections, against a superficial appreciation of Jesus Christ, indeed against all such surface religion. If this was necessary in his age, how much more is it necessary now!

As we read Duncan's sermons we meet a man striving to honour Christ. As we read his life we meet a man ever pressing on to love Christ more, and yet we meet a man who lacked the comforts of a deep assurance. May God give us grace so to minister the Word that the bruised reed is not broken, but also, so to minister it that those at ease in Zion are blasted out of their complacency and moved ever to seek a heart more filled with love to God the Father, God and Son, and God the Holy Ghost. In our own lives let us thank God for the assurance we have, let us ever seek a fuller assurance, but let us never be satisfied with an assurance not accompanied with a similar love to that which we see in Scripture and long to see in our people.

We would do well to remember Jonathan Edwards' statement in *The Religious Affections*: 'The Christians that are really the most eminent saints . . . are astonished at and ashamed of the low degrees of their love and their thankfulness, and their little knowledge of God . . . Eminently humble saints that will shine brightest in heaven are not at all apt to profess high' (Quoted in *Diary of Kenneth MacRae*, pp xi–xii fn.).

Let us conclude with two quotations from Moody-Stuart:

At this time of his life his great desire was to break up surface religion both of self-called and of sincere Christians. The 'hypocrisy' of the name to live, even the stagnation and all but corruption of death, which had been so terribly disclosed to him in Aberdeen two years after his conversion, and 'the coldish admiration of Christ' which he felt creeping over him in Glasgow, he also saw prevailing in the Church. This complacent security he denounced as Antinomian; not that it rested on a doctrine verbally Antinomian or resulted in a walk openly sinful: but it coincided with a conscience very partially alive to the holiness of God, the sinfulness of sin, and the unchangeable demands of the Law, 'Thou shalt love thy God with all thy heart and thy neighbour as thyself.' There was no depth or duration of doubt that he did not prefer to this carnal confidence, which he set himself most resolutely to dash in pieces; intent only to break down the pretentious evil, and leaving it to the Lord to rebuild the purified truth in the hearts and lives of his people.[40]

Jesus Christ, in his person, his character, his life and his death, was the central subject of his thoughts, and increasingly year by year till the end. It was not theology but Christ that filled both his mind and his heart; the whole stress of his theology sprang from him as its source and flowed to him as its ocean. The holy Lord God of his earlier years was his fear and delight to the last, and it was ever true of him that 'he feared God above many', but in the latter portion of his life Jesus Christ was peculiarly the one object of his desires and the constant subject of his meditation . . . This interest in Christ rose above every passing interest of earth. In the questions of the day he took a lively concern; not in party politics, on which I never heard him utter a word in the midst of all his talk, but in all subjects of national welfare. A friend met him in the street at a time of some public interest, and not in mere fun asked him, 'Is there any news today?' 'O yes', he replied, 'this is always news, the blood of Jesus Christ cleanseth us from all sin.'[41]

[1] Two addresses given at the Leicester Ministers' Conference, 1980, and published in three parts in *The Banner of Truth* magazine, nos. 201, 202, and 206.

[2] William Cunningham, *The Reformers and Theology of the Reformation*, (London: Banner of Truth, 1967), pp. 122–3.

[3] Thomas Goodwin, *The Objects and Acts of Justifying Faith*, p. 579.

[4] Edward Fisher, *The Marrow of Modern Divinity*, with notes by Thomas Boston, Reiner Publications, U.S.A.

[5] Peter Lewis, quoted in Erroll Hulse, *The Believer's Experience*, Carey Publications, 1977, pp. 128–9.

[6] Duncan, *Pulpit and Communion Table*, Edinburgh, 1874, p 60. [7] Ibid, p. 63.

[8] John Kennedy, *The Days of the Fathers in Ross-shire*, Inverness, 1927, p 119.

[9] Robert Shaw, *The Reformed Faith*, Christian Focus Publications, p. 186.

[10] *Collected Writings of J. H. Thornwell*, Banner of Truth, vol. 2, p. 355.

[11] Ibid, vol. 3, pp. 407–8.   [12] *Pulpit and Communion Table*, p. 53.

[13] *Memorials of Dr John Love*, Glasgow, 1858, vol 2, p. 318.

[14] Cited in J. C. Ryle, *Holiness*, James Clarke, 1956, p. 111 (note).

[15] Moody Stuart, *Life of Duncan*, pp. 92–3.

[16] *Pulpit and Communion Table*, pp. 58–9.

[17] Brown, *Life of Duncan*, Edinburgh, 1872, p. 425.   [18] Ibid, p 431.

[19] Moody Stuart, p. 196. [20] Ibid., p. 172. [21] Ibid., p. 95. [22] Ibid. [23] Ibid, p. 176.

[24] Fisher, p. 18. [25] Ibid, p. 18 (note). [26] Moody Stuart, p. 166.

[27] Brown, p. 220. [28] Ibid, p. 221. [29] Ibid, p. 223.

[30] *Pulpit and Communion Table*, p. 52. [31] Ibid, p. 53. [32] Ibid, p. 64.

[33] Ibid, p. 56. [34] Ibid pp.57. [35] Ibid., p 138. [36] Ibid, p 63. [37] Ibid, p 62.

[38] Brown, pp. 260-1. [39] Ibid, p 474.

[40] Moody Stuart, p. 94. [41] Ibid, pp. 166–8.

6

THE CHRISTIAN AND
MENTAL ILLNESS¹

From some points of view the structure of such an address as this is self-evident. First of all, there will be a section on the recognition of mental illness, in order that we may learn how to know it when we see it, and know when to recommend people to see a psychiatrist. Secondly, there will be a section on giving support to the patient and his family whilst he is undergoing psychiatric treatment. Thirdly, there will come a section on the provision of support for those who have undergone such treatment and are seeking to return to a more normal life. However, it is the purpose of this address to suggest that such an approach is quite inadequate, indeed misguided, and to outline an approach that is more truly biblical.

That the subject is relevant scarcely needs proof. The *Daily Telegraph* (17 October 1975) commenting on the report, *Better Services for the Mentally Ill,* writes: 'Mental illness is probably the major health problem of our time, affecting five million people a year in England alone and creating a demand for psychiatric help that is "virtually unlimited" . . . there were about two hundred and fifty thousand adult inpatients a year. In addition there were one and a half million outpatient attendances.' Possibly a number of you will have had experience of this matter either personally or in your family, probably most of you will have had some experience in your churches, whilst it is virtually certain that all of you will have met with cases of mental illness in the world around.

Nor for that matter will you need convincing of the serious-ness of the problem. One non-Christian writer with vast experience in this field informs us, that whilst he might not believe in a literal hell, he had certainly seen people experienc-ing hell upon earth. Mental illness is associated with great anguish both in the individual concerned and in those associ-ated with him. A quick survey of recent reports in a local paper reveals two people who had burnt themselves to death, a young man dying through a double dose of morphine, another young man blowing his brains out, whilst an older woman asphyxi-ated herself.

The problem, however, is ancient as well as modern. Christ-ian writers for many centuries have dealt with the issue of melancholia. John Cassian (c. 360–435 AD), John of Damas-cus (c. 675–750 AD), Hugh of St. Victor (c. 1096–1141) to name but a few, have written about it, while there is extant an Anglo-Saxon work on *Remorse of Conscience*. Among more recent writers has been Richard Baxter (1615–91) who included a section to the issue of melancholia in his *Christian Directory*. He writes:

> By melancholy I mean this diseased craziness, hurt, or error of the imagination and consequently of the under-standing (this is not the same as rational conviction of sin) and their thoughts are all about themselves, they think they are possessed of devils – yet they refuse to admit they are melancholy and reject any cure for their body. When this disease is gone very far, directions to the per-sons themselves are vain, because they have not reason and free will to practise them . . . It is your thinking faculty or imagination which is the broken pained part . . . you must not use it . . . I have seen abundance cured by physic, and till the body be cured, the mind will hardly

ever be cured, but the clearest reasons will be all in vain (*Christian Directory*, p. 314 f).

You will notice certain significant points in this quotation. First Baxter distinguishes this condition from 'rational conviction of sin'. Secondly, he asserts that people in this state are incapable of benefiting from directions because their reason is so affected. Thirdly, he believes that the condition has some physical basis in origin.

Another writer who deals with the matter is John Colquhoun (1748–1821). He writes:

By this distemper, the mind is so disordered, that, like an inflamed eye, it becomes disqualified for discerning its objects, clearly and justly . . . However great a believer's grief for sin and his dread of divine anger may be, he ought not to be called melancholy, so long as these appear to be rational and his imagination to be sound. But, on the other hand, however small his measure of sadness and of fear may be, yet if his imagination and mind be so distempered or impaired that he cannot assign a proper reason for his sadness and fear, nor express them in a rational manner, he is to be counted melancholy (*Treatise on Spiritual Comfort*, cited in *The Banner of Truth*, September 1971, p. 33).

It is, however, not simply that Christians have written about this subject; they have been confronted with it in their own lives or in the lives of members of their families. We are all familiar with the sadness that afflicted the life of William Cowper (see 'William Cowper and His Affliction', *The Banner of Truth*, September 1971). Another example is to be found in the experience of Thomas Boston of Ettrick (1676–1732). Boston was a man of eminent piety and exemplary godliness. He was married on 17 July 1700 to Katharine Brown of whom he writes: 'A woman of great worth, whom I therefore passionately loved, and inwardly honoured; a stately, beautiful, and comely personage; truly pious and fearing the Lord' (*A General Account of My Life* by Thomas Boston, p. 134). However, a dark shadow came over their lives. Writing in his journal on 10th May 1720 he says:

> Being that wherein my wife was seized with that heavy trouble, which hath kept her all along since that time unto this day in extreme distress, her imagination being vitiated in a particular point; and that improved upon and wrought upon by the great adversary to her great disquietment; the which has been still accompanied with bodily infirmities and maladies, exceeding great and numerous. Nevertheless, in the complications of trials, the Lord hath been pleased, not only to make his mighty power appear in preserving her life, as a spark of fire in an ocean, but to make his grace in her shine forth more bright than before (p. 390).

Boston was a man of prayer, and on a number of occasions he set aside times when he interceded especially for his wife. However there was no real improvement in her condition, and about seven years later we find him writing (11 July 1727): For several of these years she hath been free among the dead, like the slain that lie in the grave, remembered no more; being overwhelmed with bodily maladies, her spirits drunk up with terror by means of her imagination vitiated in a particular point, and harassed with Satan's temptations plied against her at that disadvantage . . . so the Lord has at times given her remarkable visits in her prison and manifested his love to her soul.

He entertained hopes of her deliverance but these were disappointed and she remained, as far as is known, like this until she died. William Carey, the great missionary to India, was beset with similar trouble.

In 1794 he (Carey) was prostrated with fever and his life was in danger. He recovered, but his son Peter, five years old, died after an illness of a few hours. Mrs Carey was so deeply affected that she gradually became deprived of her reason and had to be kept under restraint. It was part of the price William Carey and Dorothy paid for winning India for Christ (*William Carey* – Oussoren, p. 62).

Finally, in this introductory survey it is worth turning to William Shakespeare. The following quotation is taken from *Macbeth*, Act v, Scene 1. You will recollect the situation. Lady Macbeth has been responsible for the death of the king, who has been murdered to make way for her husband. Now she is deeply troubled in her mind and has taken to wandering about in her sleep and talking to herself of her crimes. Her lady-in-waiting has summoned the doctor, who sees and hears Lady Macbeth as she comes talking and wringing her hands as if to wash off the blood. The doctor then speaks :

> *This disease is beyond my practice . . .*
> *Foul whisperings are abroad; unnatural deeds*
> *Do breed unnatural troubles; infected minds*
> *To their deaf pillows will discharge their secrets.*
> *More needs she the divine than the physician.*
> *God, God forgive us all!*

What is peculiarly significant is that the doctor, confronted with this situation, this obsessive hand-washing and evidence of the troubled conscience, immediately recognizes that the issue is spiritual. This is the sphere of the minister, of the physician of souls, not of the body. How different is the situation today, when such behaviour is thought of as being the province of the medical profession and not to be dealt with by the minister! Indeed, many ministers confronted with such behaviour today would immediately send for the doctor and not attempt to deal with the situation themselves.

WHAT IS MENTAL ILLNESS?

There are clearly cases of mental illness; that is to say, the mind and therefore the conduct is affected by clearly recognizable pathological conditions, e.g. as shown in Alzheimer's disease and schizophrenia. It will be necessary for us to provide spiritual help and counsel to such as are affected in this way, but it will be the doctor who has to treat these conditions.

It must be said, however, that the many cases of so-called 'mental illness' do not come into any of the above categories. What we are principally concerned with are those cases of mental illness that have no apparent pathological or physiological causes. By calling conditions 'Mental Illness' a whole range of implications ensue. Illness is of course the sphere of the doctor. Ministers do not usually deal with physical illness; they will generally leave such matters to doctors. Plainly, to intrude into the doctor's sphere at this point would be most unwise if the term 'illness' is rightly used. Furthermore, illnesses are usually treated by some form of medication and if they become too acute must be dealt with in hospitals by nurses. By the use of the term 'illness', therefore, all the immense prestige of the medical profession is arrayed against the minister - who is so unwise as to intrude his opinions and activities into this sphere.

There are of course many Christians who are quite happy to accept a Freudian Model . Thus a Lutheran Symposium on the subject says: 'The psychoses and most fully developed neuroses are to be considered illness. To a substantial degree there is no difference between these syndromes and the more physical ones. The same organism is involved in both, weakened by sin and prone to disability, with the same physico-chemical structure operating in both physical and mental abnormalities.' 'Mental and emotional illnesses and their symptoms are beyond the control of the patient, just as are the causes of most physical illness' (*What Then Is Man?* Concordia, pp. 264, 271). A Christian psychiatrist writes: 'Cain slew Abel, the supreme act of selfishness, the end result of mental illness.' 'An unsound mind is just as much a sickness as a broken leg or an acute appendicitis' (*The Christian Handbook of Psychiatry*, Hyder, pp. 1, 5, 14). The mind simply reels at the first statement. Plainly, ministers have no real work to do! All sin is now the province of the psychiatrist. If Cain's sin is indeed 'mental illness', then the psychiatrists, some of whom are atheists and very few of whom are Christian, are to be given the task of putting right man's rebellion against God. Szasz, speaking of Benjamin Rush, 'The Father of American Psychiatry', says, 'Rush maintained that crimes were diseases . . . Murder and theft are symptoms of this disease complex' (*The Manufacture of Madness*, p. 142).

The recent researches of a psychiatrist interested in the relation of Christianity to Mental Illness are significant here. He has produced two charts. On the first there is a description of Anxiety, Depression, Involutional Melancholia, Accidie; according to modern psychiatric techniques, he gives their symptomatology, disposed in relation to the psychodynamics that give rise to them. On the other chart there is a description of Accidie or Melancholy as described by clinical theologians of the past centuries, and an attempt is made to show this is exactly the same as Depression. There are quotations from nearly twenty theologians, from John Cassian, John of Damascus and Gregory the Great, up to Charles Simeon and Archbishop Trench. Plainly in earlier centuries these symptoms were thought to be spiritual in origin and were to be treated by spiritual means (see Lake, *Clinical Theology*, Appendices).

During the last hundred years or so, however, a great change has taken place. What the minister previously dealt with has now become the province of the doctor. The role of the minister has been in fact taken over by the psychiatrist and he is sometimes viewed as a meddlesome and incompetent intruder if he attempts to exercise his responsibilities in this sphere in respect of his flock.

It is pertinent to ask how this change came about. One name comes to mind as of great importance, that of Sigmund Freud. Freud's influence has been incalculable. Not only in the field of psychiatry but also in education, penology, and the bringing up of children. There can be no doubt that from a Christian point of view much of his influence has been malevolent. There can also be little doubt that he has had great influence in procuring the general influence of his model of mental illness. It is true that he taught that there was no necessity for a man to be medically qualified in order to practise psychotherapy. It is also true that he himself used his prestige as a doctor to further his activities and work. We must view his influence in this sphere as being profound.

There is not time in this address to examine his teaching. From a Christian point of view it is relevant to consider what kind of man this was who has so affected man's thinking in this sphere. Freud was a Jew by birth but certainly not by religion. 'Freud called himself a "completely godless Jew" and a "hopeless pagan"' (Jay Adams, *Competent to Counsel*, p. 16). Bakan writes: 'In his rooms Freud surrounded himself with every heathen god he could find. As if in sheer spite, he pursued "idols" and their associated trappings with a deep fascination' (Bakan, *Freud and Jewish Mystical Tradition*, p. 134). He quotes Freud as saying, 'Do you know that I am the Devil? All my life I have had to play the Devil, in order that others would be able to build the most beautiful cathedrals with the materials I had produced' (p. 181), although he explains that 'Freud did not believe in the Devil superstitiously as a real personage. He believed in the Devil rather in the profound way in which a great mind might become immersed in metaphor.' Perhaps one last quotation from this book is significant. 'We find that Freud immerses himself in demoniacal literature and that the desired effects, the liberation from depression and ability to work, are achieved' (Bakan, p. 221).

What we have to ask ourselves is how we should regard the work of such a man. Surely we must approach with the greatest care and circumspection the work of a man whose habits and statements are, to say the least, so unusual.

It is significant that many writers, psychologists, and psychiatrists, have begun to question the whole notion of the Freudian system. Indeed, it is worth noting that great confusion seems to prevail in this area. A man has written a book describing thirty-six different systems of psychotherapy. The truth is that psychiatrists simply do not agree among themselves over many fundamental issues both of diagnosis and treatment. It will be helpful to list a number of typical comments on this matter.

We find Eysenck writing, 'The medical notion of mental disease entities is not, in fact, entertained seriously by most psychiatrists and it is proposed therefore that it should be formally relinquished' (Eysenck, *The Dynamics of Anxiety and Hysteria*, p. 10). 'Sigmund Freud did not discover a new form of mental illness. He discovered the troubled, disaffiliated modern individual in conflict' (Leifer, *In the Name of Mental Health*, p. 104). 'Although it has been evident for at least 20 years that classical Freudian psychoanalysis is a therapeutic fiasco, yet the assumptions concerning the nature of man from which this form of treatment was derived continue to be acclaimed as if one could move the world with them' (Mowrer, *Crisis in Psychiatry and Religion*, p. 158). 'The meaning of mental health is "desirable behaviour", mental illness is "undesirable behaviour" . . . Mental illness is a deviation from social standards of behaviour' (Leifer, p. 157). 'Apart from schizophrenia and manic depressive psychoses . . . I know of no evidence to do with personality disorders and the psychoneuroses which is not satisfactorily understood by regarding them basically as problems of early and recent interpersonal relationships and their effects upon the whole psycho-physical organism' (Lake, *Clinical Theology*, p. 65).

'Mental illness is a myth . . . psychiatrists are not concerned with mental illnesses and their treatment. In actual practice they deal with personal, social and ethical problems in living' (Szasz, *The Myth of Mental Illness*, p. 296). 'In many of its forms insanity is a religious problem rather than a medical problem and any treatment which fails to recognize that fact can hardly be effective' (Boisen, *Out of the Depths*, p. 111). Jay Adams whose work in this sphere is very significant and thought-provoking even goes so far as to say, 'There is therefore no place in a biblical scheme for a psychiatrist as a separate practitioner' (Adams, *Christian Counsellors' Manual*, p. 9).

Plainly, therefore, we must be very careful before we simply proceed as if this concept of mental illness is generally accepted. As Christian ministers we must apply our mind with diligence to this whole issue.

One fundamental issue raised by the idea of mental illness is that of responsibility. A Lutheran writer says: 'As far as mental illness is the result of sin, man is responsible to God' (*What Then Is Man?*, p. 263). If mental illness comes on us in the same way as cancer or other diseases, no one would hold the sufferer responsible. However, Menninger writes, 'Evil surrounds us, but when no one is responsible, no one is guilty, no moral questions are asked . . . we sink into despairing helplessness' (Hielema, *Pastoral or Christian Counselling*, p. 47). The refusal to admit man's responsibility for his own condition leads to apathy and despair, whereas when we assert man's responsibility we stir him up to repentance and activity.

In view of the confusion that seems to prevail in this area it is necessary for us to turn to the Bible. Confronted as we are with profound and grievous problems in this area, we must ask ourselves, What does the Bible say about this? Does Holy Scripture shed any light on these issues? Can we hear God speaking about these phenomena that occur in the lives of men? We believe God has spoken to us in his Word; let us hear what he has to say and submit our minds to his holy teaching.

AN OUTLINE OF BIBLICAL TEACHING

We now proceed to an examination of the main lines of biblical teaching in this area. What follows is only an outline. It is not in any sense an exhaustive account of what Scripture teaches on the subject. It is necessary to remember the Bible sets forth man as being in a state of rebellion against and being guilty before God's Word; he will not obey God's truth, he will not acknowledge God's Son as his Saviour.

First of all there is the attribution of madness to those in whom the Spirit of God is working mightily. 'And when his friends heard of it, they went out to lay hold on him: for they said, he is beside himself' (*Mark* 3:21). 'And many of them said, He hath a devil and is mad; why hear ye him?' (*John* 10:20). Here our blessed Saviour is accused of madness. So little do men understand goodness, holiness, truth, and obedience to God, that when they see it they call it madness. The Apostle Paul had a similar experience: 'And as he thus spoke for himself, Festus said with a loud voice, Paul, thou art beside thyself; much learning doth make thee mad. But he said, I am not mad, most noble Festus: but speak forth the words of truth and soberness' (*Acts* 26:24–25).

A modern illustration of this is provided by John Sung. John Sung was an evangelist notably used of God in China and the Far East before the Second World War. He was brought up in China and being academically brilliant went to the U.S.A. to study. He had an evangelical experience in China before he left. Whilst in the U.S.A. he felt called to the ministry and went to Union Theological Seminary, New York, to train. Union is a place noted for its liberalism, and understandably, under the influence of false teaching his soul became deadened. However, God in his mercy met with him and John Sung began once again to rejoice in Christ. He went around the corridors of the Seminary singing the praises of the Redeemer. As a man of some determination of character, at some stage he made a bonfire, in which he publicly burnt his books of liberal theology. All this proved too much for the authorities of the Seminary, who committed him to a psychiatric hospital. Whilst he was there, due to a disagreement with the authorities, he was committed to a ward where there were violent men. Nevertheless in his mercy God soon delivered him and he began a life of eminent usefulness. There seems little doubt that the joy of a salvation restored to him, and a zeal against error, was construed as madness.

Secondly, we have conviction of sin giving rise to symptoms, which today would be called mental illness. There are copious illustrations of this to be found in the Psalms (*Psa.* 6:3–7; 32:3–4; 38:1–10; 42:3; 51:8; 88; 130:1 and many others). It will be helpful to look at one or two of these passages in detail. 'When I kept silence, my bones waxed old through my roaring all the day long. For day and night thy hand was heavy upon me: my moisture is turned into the drought of summer. I acknowledged my sin unto thee, and mine iniquity have I not hid. I said, I will confess my transgression unto the Lord; and thou forgavest the iniquity of my sin' (*Psa.* 32:3–5). Here the guilt of unconfessed sin is a terrible burden producing pain in the soul, and from it there is neither respite nor peace. But when sin is acknowledged, through the mercy of God, peace comes to David's troubled soul. After his sin in the matter of Bathsheba David likens the convicting work of God to the breaking of his bones (*Psa.* 51:8). Similarly, in Psalm 38 a consciousness of God's displeasure has overwhelming and widespread consequences. But again in the end conviction of sin leads to confession, 'For I will declare mine iniquity; I will be sorry for my sin' (*Psa.* 38:18). The experiences of Luther and Bunyan in fairly recent history are illustrative of such conviction. There seems little doubt that today a person going through similar experiences could very well find himself in the hands of a psychiatrist. The extreme damage that could be done to such a person by a man of Freudian tendencies or atheistic viewpoint, hardly needs to be pointed out.

Thirdly, we have the possibility of malingering. 'And David laid up these words in his heart, and was sore afraid of Achish the king of Gath. And he changed his behaviour before them, and feigned himself mad in their hands, and scrabbled on the doors of the gate, and let his spittle fall down upon his beard. Then said Achish unto his servants, Lo, ye see the man is mad: wherefore then have ye brought him to me? Have I need of mad men, that ye have brought this fellow to play the mad man in my presence? Shall this fellow come into my house?' (*1 Sam.* 21:12-15). David was afraid, so he pretends to be mad, and in fact he attains the desired end, namely, to escape out of the hands of Achish. Plainly not all people who behave in a demented way are malingering; far from it! However, Jay Adams gives a number of instances from his experience in the United States where people had acted as if they were mad in order to avoid troubles or difficulties. They found their place of refuge in a mental hospital. People may behave in a bizarre way in order to obtain some end or to avoid trouble. Thus an elderly person, by threatening suicide, may be able to manipulate his family. Or a young person may act as if mad and thus avoid work which he hates.

Fourthly, we have mental illness or depression that has its roots in physical and mental exhaustion. After his victory at Carmel, in which God's honour was vindicated and false religion confounded, and after running to Jezreel, Elijah experiences some form of collapse when he hears Jezebel's threat upon his life. 'But he himself went a day's journey into the wilderness, and came and sat down under a juniper tree, and he requested for himself that he might die; and said, It is enough; now, O Lord, take away my life; for I am not better than my fathers' (*1 Kings* 19:4). Pastor Albert N. Martin, speaking about this, remarked that God recognized and understood his condition. He pointed out that his immediate need was rest and nourishment, and this God gave to him. God made no attempt to deal with the underlying spiritual trouble until he had first dealt with the physical exhaustion. Illustrating from his own experience, he remarked how lack of sleep can lead to great depression. This, in its turn, will sometimes depart when adequate rest is given. This is a very important matter. A man overworks for months or years; a minister disregards the principle of one day of rest in seven; in the end they break down. Plainly there must be a dealing with the exhaustion before any other underlying causes of stress can be dealt with. This it should be remarked may be a lengthy process. A man who has abused his body for years cannot rightly expect restoration in a few days.

Fifthly, we have mental illness as a result of sin and the judgment of God. When Ahab coveted Naboth's vineyard and could not get it, we read: 'He laid him down upon his bed, and turned away his face, and would eat no bread' (*1 Kings* 21:4). A person refuses to get up, refuses to eat; 'he must be mentally ill', you say. Not necessarily! Ahab was in a rage of frustrated covetousness and hurt pride. It is surprising how people behave when they cannot get their own way. Similarly we read that 'when Ahithophel saw that his counsel was not followed, he saddled his ass and arose, and gat him home to his house, to his city, and put his household in order, and hanged himself and died' (*2 Sam.* 17:23). Anger and despair turned against himself led to self-destruction. It seems generally recognized that in cases of melancholy and depression there is frequently if not always present an element of anger. This may not always be recognized or admitted. Nevertheless it is present. Underneath the outward symptoms there may be anger and bitterness against God and his dealings with us. This may be suppressed and be turned inwards, thus resulting in self-hatred.

But the Bible not only teaches that sin leads to such misery as a result of man's own constitution, it also asserts that madness may be the direct result of a judgment of God. Thus Isaiah makes the general and highly relevant statement: 'But the wicked are like the troubled sea, when it cannot rest, whose waters cast up mire and dirt. There is no peace, saith my God, to the wicked' (*Isa.* 57:20-21). In Deuteronomy 28 there is an enumeration of the consequences of Israel's disregard of the commandments of God: 'But it shall come to pass, if thou wilt not hearken unto the voice of the Lord thy God, to observe to do all his commandments and his statutes which I command thee this day; that all these curses shall come upon thee . . . The Lord shall smite thee with madness and blindness and astonishment of heart . . . so that thou shalt be mad for the sight of thine eyes which thou shalt see' (*Deut.* 28:15, 28, 34). It is, of course, characteristic of fallen man to minimize the consequences of sin and the penal justice of God. However, Scripture repeatedly tells us it is an evil and bitter thing to depart from God, and the consequences of such a departure are incalculable.

Perhaps the most significant passage in this respect is to be found in Daniel. In chapter 4 we read of Nebuchadnezzar's dream, the interpretation of it given by Daniel, and then its fulfilment. 'At the end of twelve months Nebuchadnezzar walked in the palace of the kingdom of Babylon. The king spake and said, Is not this great Babylon, that I have built for the house of the kingdom by the might of my power, and for the honour of my majesty? While the word was in the king's mouth, there fell a voice from heaven, saying, O king Nebuchadnezzar, to thee it is spoken; the kingdom is departed from thee. And they shall drive thee from men, and thy dwelling shall be with the beasts of the field: they shall make thee to eat grass as oxen, and seven times shall pass over thee, until thou know that the most High ruleth in the kingdom of men, and giveth it to whomsoever he will. The same hour was the thing fulfilled upon Nebuchadnezzar . . .' (*Dan.* 4:29–33). The king's insanity is stated unequivocally to be a judgment of God, to teach him about the sovereignty of God. It is stated that his insanity should last a predetermined time, and in due course his reason returned to him. The result of this seems to have been real spiritual blessing to Nebuchadnezzar. Although commentators are divided on this, a number think that he died a true believer. What is certain is that he rendered great honour and glory to God, and this chapter ends: 'Now I Nebuchadnezzar praise and extol and honour the King of heaven, all whose works are truth, and his ways judgment: and those that walk in pride he is able to abase.'

It is also to be seriously noted what use is made of this matter in chapter 5. Here Belshazzar is about to be judged for his wickedness, the writing is on the wall. From verse 18 onwards Daniel makes reference in detail to Nebuchadnezzar's madness, and concludes his rehearsal of these solemn events by saying: 'And thou his son, O Belshazzar, hast not humbled thine heart, though thou knewest all this . . . and the God in whose hand thy breath is, and whose are all thy ways, hast thou not glorified' (*Dan.* 5:22–23). Plainly, when we see insanity of this character in others we are required to humble ourselves, to turn from our own pride and wickedness. In no sense are we to think of such as being necessarily more sinful than ourselves; rather we are to humble ourselves and repent.

Sixthly, we have illustrations in Scripture of mental illness that is the result of sin and Satanic activity. There is a full and most sad illustration of this in the life of king Saul. After his failure to obey fully the Lord in the matter of the Amalekites, and the subsequent anointing of David by Samuel, we read: 'But the Spirit of the LORD departed from Saul, and an evil spirit from the Lord troubled him' (*1 Sam.* 16.14). Later on, after David's great victories, Saul begins to envy David and we read: 'And Saul eyed David from that day and forward. And it came to pass on the morrow, that the evil spirit from God came upon Saul, and he prophesied in the midst of the house: and David played with his hand as at other times: and there was a javelin in Saul's hand. And Saul cast the javelin; for he said, I will smite David even to the wall with it' (*1 Sam.* 18:9–11).

It seems quite wrong to discount the work of Satan in mental illness. Plainly it is equally wrong always to look for the work of Satan. As we have seen, there are many kinds of disturbance in which Satan is not directly mentioned. However, the great oppressor of men and enemy of the human race has real power and great malice. Paul warns us: 'Be ye angry and sin not; let not the sun go down upon your wrath: neither give place to the devil' (*Eph.* 4:26–27). Sin can plainly be the opportunity for Satan to act.

Seventhly, certain demon possession can produce symptoms akin to madness. Matthew 4:24 plainly distinguishes between demon possession and lunacy; 'And those which were possessed with devils and those that were lunatic, and those that had the palsy; and he healed them.' Other occurrences of demon possession occur in Matthew 17:14–21, Mark 5:1–20, and elsewhere in the New Testament. Plainly there is often violence and tendency to self-injury, behaviour that terrifies others; yet all is plainly terminated when Christ casts out the tormenting spirits. Evidently, the New Testament times were characterized by exceptional Satanic activity. Nevertheless, today it would be wrong to leave this out as an explanation of the symptoms of insanity and bizarre behaviour. We need balance and care in this area. (For a detailed study of biblical demonology, see Frederick S. Leahy, *Satan Cast Out*, Banner of Truth, 1975).

Eighthly and finally, we have situations that seem to be beyond human understanding. It is well to remember the incident of the blind man recorded in John 9: 'And as Jesus passed by, he saw a man which was blind from his birth. And his disciples asked him, saying, Master who did sin, this man or his parents, that he was born blind? Jesus answered, Neither hath this man sinned, nor his parents: but that the works of God should be made manifest in him.' The lessons of John 9 are substantial and of great interest.

No doubt we are all familiar with the facts of Job's experience. But let me briefly remind you of the most significant features of his history. Over all presides the Almighty God; he loves Job and commends his servant's integrity. But Satan seeks Job's overthrow, and obtains divine permission to attempt it, though limitations are placed upon him. He is responsible for much of the trouble that comes upon Job. Revelation lifts the veil and we see what part he plays and what purpose he has in Job's calamities. Then, also, we have the facts which form the background of Job's trials – the activities of his enemies resulting in the loss of his wealth, the ill-weather leading to the loss of his family, all the events in fact that result in the loss of Job's reputation and position. Then there are the various people involved – his wife who obviously is a great hindrance to him, and his so-called comforters. Anyone who is concerned to counsel others would do well to study the Book of Job, in particular the behaviour of his comforters, their words, their effect upon Job, and what God has to say about them in the end.

One noted commentator, Matthew Henry, remarks to the effect that the best thing Job's comforters did was to initially sit with him and say nothing. As soon as they opened their mouths they caused Job trouble. Their theology, says Henry, was excellent, their application of it very poor. All they could do was to impute secret sin to Job and explain his sufferings as God's judgments on his hypocrisy. It is impossible here to examine this story in any great depth. Nevertheless, it is essential we recognize its significance when we are faced with unexplained sufferings in believers.

When, to test our graces, God permits us to be tried by the devil and troubled by grievous calamities, it is no help for someone to rush in and accuse us of secret, unconfessed sins, as did Job's friends. Of course sin brings trouble, and we have seen that the Bible states this quite clearly. Nevertheless, the Book of Job has a significant place in the Old Testament and is put there as a warning. In the end God delivered Job, and rebuked his 'comforters' most sternly. Let us recognize there may be cases where it is not possible for us to discern what is going on. If this be so, by using the promises of God we are to encourage those who are afflicted, and must not push them deeper into the mire with our superficial solutions to their problems.

WHAT SHOULD WE DO WHEN WE MEET WITH MENTAL ILLNESS IN A CHRISTIAN?

Having given a brief outline of the biblical teaching involved, we have to ask a practical question: What should we do when confronted with symptoms of mental illness in a Christian? It is necessary first of all to state the reasons why we should seek medical help, preferably the help of a Christian doctor who has a thoroughly biblical understanding of the problems besetting sinful man, and not one who has capitulated to Freudian speculations and misrepresentations.

As we have seen, there may be a variety of physiological causes that underlie mental disturbance. As ministers we are not qualified in this field. Nor, of course, are we in a position to prescribe medication of any kind. Thus in some cases a few nights' good sleep resulting from judiciously prescribed sleeping tablets may work a definite improvement. We must also recognize that this is not an area to be treated lightly; it is sometimes a sphere in which 'fools rush in where angels fear to tread'. Certainly a sufferer is likely to be better off in the hands of an understanding Christian doctor, or a psychiatrist who has a biblical understanding of human nature, than in the hands of an incompetent minister who makes no real attempt to understand the real trouble and merely trots out in parrot fashion a few proof texts.

We must be careful here, for the results of wrong diagnosis can be most serious. Three illustrations to emphasize this will show us how careful we need to be. There was a report in a local paper of a lady who had gone on numerous occasions to her own doctor, complaining of stomach pains. He plainly thought she was a nuisance and diagnosed the trouble as 'nerves'. She got absolutely no help from him. In the end she took her own life. A post-mortem was held and it was revealed that she was suffering from an acute internal condition and would have only lived for another twenty-four hours if she had not taken her life. Again, a Christian lady was afflicted with stomach pains over a period of years. She went to her doctor who diagnosed the cause as 'nervous tension' and prescribed medication suitable for such a condition. After a number of years the pain became so acute that she was admitted to hospital for emergency surgery. This revealed the presence of a very large gallstone and that her gall bladder was on the point of rupturing. Lastly, a speaker at an evangelical conference narrated the recent case of a fine Christian lady of exemplary character and usefulness. She suffered however, from depression and this was kept under control by the use of drugs. On attending a neo-pentecostal type of meeting she announced she was delivered from drugs and would use them no more. Within a week she had taken her own life. Plainly, in this area the careless and self-confident are not fitted to operate.

There are reasons therefore for seeking medical help. However, it must be said that there are also substantial reasons for refusing and avoiding help from certain psychiatrists. Eysenck writes: 'A review of all available evidence by the present writer disclosed the sad fact that when comparing the effects of psychotherapy with the various estimates of spontaneous remission rates, there appeared to be no difference between cures accomplished' (Eysenck, *The Dynamics of Anxiety and Hysteria*, p. 8). In other words there is statistically as much hope of a cure without psychotherapy as with it. Furthermore it is well to bear in mind the statement of Szasz, 'All psychiatric therapies have as their aim the alteration of human behaviour' (*Myth of Mental Illness*, p. 205). We have to ask to what these alterations in behaviour tend and by what means are they to be accomplished? What are the values upon which the psychiatrist proceeds when seeking to change human behaviour? Furthermore we have to question how far a non-Christian psychiatrist is qualified to deal with conditions which may be the result of conviction of sin, guilt before God, and the work of Satan. How can such people proclaim forgiveness and salvation through the power of Christ?

It must be said that while there are a few psychiatrists who are Christian there are many who are not. Many people seem to have come across psychiatrists who have no hesitation in recommending blatantly sinful behaviour as a solution to inner problems and tensions. Such advice, plainly inimical to the spiritual well-being of the patient and directly contrary to God's Word, is not what we would wish for our people. Finally, today in some cases the treatment given seems to involve little attempt to get to the root of the problem and consists in prescribing large doses of drugs which often render any counselling by the minister virtually impossible.

It is now necessary to turn to the issue of how we ourselves should approach such problems.

First of all we require *humility*. Indeed we need repentance: often the church and its ministers have evaded their responsibilities in this area. If any servants of God feel that they are eminently qualified to operate here, all they show is that they are eminently disqualified by their pride and arrogance. We need to proceed in humble dependence upon God and his Spirit.

Secondly, we need *wisdom*. It is possible to make the issue sound very easy. While it is true that Christians should be able to help and encourage one another in their problems, yet it would seem that this is not the area in which the immature and unstable can operate. We have all seen people who, in trying to help others, have become upset themselves and done more harm than good. We need to ask wisdom of God, who gives liberally and upbraids not.

Thirdly, we need *compassion*. Jesus looked on the needy with great compassion, he saw them as sheep without a shepherd, and he was able to help them. We must avoid professionalism and be truly concerned to alleviate suffering.

Fourthly, we must have *confidence in God*. We must have confidence in his mercies, power, Spirit and his covenant. Let us remember 1 Corinthians 10:13 and other similar verses. Finally, we must be prepared to use spiritual weapons. We must learn to pray; others must be taught to pray for those afflicted in this way, that God may bless our feeble efforts and uphold and deliver those who are suffering.

The next issue is that of *diagnosis*. Plainly this is absolutely crucial. We must first try to find out what the symptoms are and what the patient thinks of his own state. We must gather information which is relevant and which will help us to understand the background and history of the patient. This will involve the asking of questions and doing a great deal of listening. We obviously cannot help people unless we are clear what the condition is from which they are suffering and what are the basic causes of it.

In this matter it is well to remember Luther's dictum, 'Prayer and temptation, Bible study, and meditation, make a minister.' Certainly ministers in the past seem to have had a gift of discerning the true state of those they were seeking to help (see Kennedy, *The Days of the Fathers in Ross-shire*). Knowing our own hearts and knowing Scripture should be a good basis on which to start. We must look to God to help us mightily so that we get right to the bottom of things. Superficial diagnoses and temporary palliatives are of little value; we must cultivate a real dealing with men in their deep needs. A word of warning is apposite at this point. There is much to be said for not doing this work on our own; this is obviously an imperative consideration when dealing with members of the opposite sex.

If we are able to come to some conclusion as to the cause of the situation we must then proceed to the issue of treatment.

'Were it possible to provide an adequate amount of genuine acceptance, love and security until maturity, emotional illness generally would be a minor problem for the human race' (Laughlin, *The Neuroses in Clinical Practice,* quoted in Lake, p. 114). Such a statement accords well with the biblical teaching of the church as the body of Christ. How good and pleasant it is for brethren to dwell together in unity! (*Psa.* 133:1). The church ought to be a place where afflicted persons can find sincere love and understanding. Alas, it is sometimes true that, through sin, churches become places more likely to disturb a person's peace of mind than to promote it. But we know that such things ought not so to be. It will surely be agreed by all, that the people of God should provide true care and affection for those afflicted in their minds.

We must never treat a person out of the context of his family. If someone is mentally troubled we can be virtually sure that his immediate family will be placed under stress and strain; hence we should have an eye to their need of comfort and support. Ideally it is best that people be kept within their families. Where this is not possible or where it is unsuitable, there are at least two places in England and Wales run by Christians where care can be provided if more supervision is necessary. Let us also see that physical help may be needed here. If a woman is utterly exhausted in caring for a young family, and is beginning to crack under the strain, we must be ready to help her and not merely to give advice.

What is most important is the application of the Word of God to the particular condition. This again is an issue in itself. Perhaps it is best to illustrate the relevance of Scripture from two Psalms. 'Thou, which hast shewed me great and sore troubles, shalt quicken me again, and shalt bring me up again from the depths of the earth . . . My tongue also shall talk of thy righteousness all the day long' (*Psa.* 71:20, 24). Here the importance of God's righteousness that justifies the believing sinner, is emphasized. At this point an apprehension of God's goodness is fundamental. In Psalm 73:17, 22–28 we see in a similar way how a man was brought out of great depression. Astonished at his own depravity and unspirituality he says: 'Thus my heart was grieved, and I was pricked in my reins. So foolish was I, and ignorant: I was as a beast before thee.' By consideration of the mercy of God as manifested in 'the sanctuary of God' he is delivered and restored to his joy in the Lord. This involves a deep knowledge of Scripture, but Scripture is very broad and deals perceptively with the great problems that afflict the human race.

CONCLUSION

In conclusion it is necessary to say something about prevention. Obviously many problems should be dealt with in the context of the preaching of the Word of God. If the preacher is preaching in a manner relevant to his hearers, many issues, which if left alone will cause great trouble, are certain to be dealt with. When God would deal with Job's difficulty he does so by his word and then reveals to him his glory. In Psalm 107 we read: 'He sent his word, and healed them and delivered them from their destructions' (verse 20). Counselling is no substitute for preaching and must not become one. When Job hears God's Word and meets with him, he bows down, repents in dust and ashes, and his inward turmoil is brought to a conclusion. Many, many are the troubles in man that should be dealt with in this way. Nevertheless, Scripture gives other examples where the Word of God is to be applied in the context of a personal meeting.

Let us be careful that our preaching is balanced. The age we live in desperately needs to hear the law of God. By the law is the knowledge of sin. Every mouth is to be stopped and all the world is to become guilty before God. Nevertheless, let us remember that there are sensitive souls who know of their sins only too well; what they need is the comfort of the gospel. Both Richard Baxter and John Colquhoun recognize this.

'I advise all men to take heed of placing religion too much in fears and tears and scruples, or in any other kind of sorrow, but such as tendeth to raise us to a high estimation of Christ, and to the magnifying of grace, and a sweeter taste of the love of God, and to the firmer resolution against sin. And that tears and grief be not commanded inordinately for themselves, nor as mere signs of a converted person' (*Autobiography of Richard Baxter*, Everyman, p. 217). 'Think as often of the righteousness of Jesus Christ as of your own sinfulness; as often of his fulness of grace as of your own emptiness of grace; and as frequently of the boundless love, grace, and mercy of your covenant God, as of his majesty, holiness, and justice' (Colquhoun, 'Directions to Christians Afflicted with Melancholy', *The Banner of Truth*, October 1971, p. 33). The exhibition of Christ in the glory of his offices and the graciousness of his Person is the great means God has ordained for the healing of man's soul, so desperately sick and wounded by sin and Satan. Let the mind be much taken up with the Redeemer, and much darkness and many troubles will be avoided.

If people would avoid mental trouble, let them lead a balanced life. There is a great place for hard work and minds thus taken up will avoid a preoccupation with themselves. But man needs rest and recreation too. The Sabbath was made for man, doubtless because he needed a day of rest from his labours. It is not sinful to have times of recreation, but let the Christian see that he does not abuse the body which God has given to him and which is the temple of the Holy Spirit.

Finally, we must remember the need for balance in our ministries. We have many things to do. What we have spoken about is only one aspect of our work. However, it is an important area, an area in which we are to seek to glorify God.

'Such as sit in darkness and in the shadow of death, being bound in affliction and iron: because they rebelled against the words of God, and contemned the counsel of the most High: therefore he brought down their heart with labour; they fell down and there was none to help. Then they cried unto the LORD in their trouble, and he saved them out of their distresses. He brought them out of darkness and the shadow of death, and brake their bands in sunder. Oh that men would praise the LORD for his goodness and for his wonderful works to the children of men! For he hath broken the gates of brass and cut the bars of iron in sunder' (*Psa.* 107:10–16).

May God use us in such a manner that the lips of men may be filled with the praises of our gracious Redeemer!

The Lord Jesus speaking in the synagogue at Nazareth at the beginning of his ministry said, 'The Spirit of the Lord is upon me, because he hath anointed me to preach the gospel to the poor; he hath sent me to heal the broken hearted, to preach deliverance to the captives, and recovering of sight to the blind, to set at liberty them that are bruised, to preach the acceptable year of the Lord' (*Luke* 4:18–19). Doubtless the primary reference here is to the salvation of sinners. Can we not believe, however, that Christ's ministry here designated also has reference to the poor souls so grievously affected in their minds and hearts that they are a burden to themselves and a desperate cause of sadness to those with whom they live? May God's Spirit enable us also to minister by the preaching of his word and the counselling of his people that great glory may be brought to his blessed and holy Name!

[1] An address given at the Leicester Ministers' Conference, 1976, and printed in *The Banner of Truth* magazine, no. 154.

7

THE PROPHET BALAAM[1]

In John's Gospel, chapter 10, our Lord Jesus Christ set forth
the glorious truths concerning the calling, feeding, and pres-
ervation of his sheep. This passage also gives great prominence
to the enemies that confront and threaten the welfare of God's
flock. In verse 1 we read about the person who climbs into the
sheepfold some other way. Mention is made in verse 8 of
'thieves and robbers' who came before the Lord Jesus. In verse
10 we read of the thief coming 'but for to steal, and to kill,
and to destroy'. He also speaks of the hireling who flees when
he sees the wolf coming. No under-shepherd of God's flock
could read this chapter without concluding that one of the
principal functions of his pastoral office must be the preser-
vation and keeping safe of the flock of God from those enemies
that confront it. You are aware, of course, that these words
would have come in a more powerful way to those to whom
they were originally spoken; flocks of sheep in those days were
threatened by literal wolves and bears and lions and so on,
which, given the opportunity (as we know from the story of
David), would ravage, plunder, and destroy the shepherd's
flock.

This subject that we are going to consider, the prophet
Balaam, is a subject that is very much connected to our Lord's
teaching concerning the hireling. A connection can also be made
to words found towards the end of the Sermon on the Mount,
where our Lord warns his people to 'Beware of false prophets,

which come to you in sheep's clothing, but inwardly they are ravening wolves' (*Matt.* 7:15).

IDENTIFYING THE FALSE PROPHET

I ought, perhaps, to give some brief account of how I was led to speak on this subject. Someone quizzed me the other day saying, 'Are you speaking on this subject because you reckon that there are many people like Balaam present at the conference?' Actually it never crossed my mind that that was the case. It is true that we, as ministers of the gospel, are no doubt tempted in varying ways as was Balaam. I very much doubt whether there is any minister here who has not at some time wondered about the smallness of his flock and the desirability of having a larger one; and, to be honest, I can imagine that many of you ministers might feel, from time to time, that an increase in your salary would be very welcome! And so the sort of temptations that came to Balaam on a large scale may come to us ministers in one way or another. However, that was not the reason why I decided to speak on this subject.

When you read such a verse as 'Beware of false prophets', or when you read a verse at the conclusion of the life of the Lord Jesus where he says, 'There shall arise false Christs and false prophets, and shall show great signs and wonders; insomuch that, if it were possible, they shall deceive the very elect' (*Matt.* 24:24), you have to ask yourself, how a false prophet, a wolf in sheep's clothing, is to be identified? I speak as a minister of the Word to ministers. If someone from your church comes to you and says, 'Tell me, how should I identify a wolf in sheep's clothing?', I want you to have a ready answer. But, as I have said to my own congregation on a number of occasions, false prophets do not come into the midst of the people of God with a large notice on their chest saying in bold letters: 'I am a false prophet, a wolf in sheep's clothing.' The false prophet is likely to be a plausible, agreeable, persuasive, pleasant and exceedingly deceptive person. You are no doubt familiar with the picture that is given us in the thirteenth chapter of Revelation, of one who is compared to the beast – a second beast – coming out of the earth. He looks like a lamb but speaks like a dragon; he does great wonders, making fire come down from heaven on the earth in the sight of men, and deceives those who dwell on the earth by the means of the miracles which he had the power to do. Now, brethren, I would suggest to you that it is a very difficult matter to identify false prophets. If it were not so, then they would not have done such enormous damage to the church of God.

If you read Spurgeon, you can see what the situation was like towards the end of the nineteenth century. But when you look at the situation in our own country today – I am speaking of the United Kingdom, of course – you say to yourself, 'How is it that the prosperity of the church towards the end of the nineteenth century has given place to the terrible chaos and confusion and ruin that prevails today?' This reversal of fortunes has not come about because of State persecution; rather, it has happened as the result of corruption within the church; certain people have got into the church and poisoned her life, bringing God's displeasure upon it. The ruination caused by such people is enormous, but I say their identification is exceedingly difficult. A similar problem confronted the New Testament church, and particularly towards the conclusion of the New Testament era, although undoubtedly there were such evil persons during the first Christian century. You will be aware, no doubt, of how Peter in his Second Epistle, says, 'There were false prophets also among the people, even as there shall be false teachers among you, who privily shall bring in damnable heresies, even denying the Lord that bought them, and bring upon themselves swift destruction' (2 *Pet.* 2:1). Peter is saying here that if you would understand the character of the false teachers who were threatening the church of Christ at that time, then you must examine the character, behaviour, and procedure of the false prophets in Old Testament days.

The apostle Peter also speaks of those who 'have forsaken the right way, and are gone astray, following the way of Balaam the son of Bosor, who loved the wages of unrighteousness; but was rebuked for his iniquity: the dumb ass speaking with man's voice forbad the madness of the prophet' (verses 15–16). In Joshua 13:22, Balaam is called a 'soothsayer' – the margin gives 'diviner' – a person who engaged in occult practices of some kind trying to discern the future. Here he is spoken about by Peter, writing under the inspiration of the Holy Spirit, as a 'prophet'. This is very strange. Again, in the Epistle of Jude, the same kind of subject is dealt with, as he writes of those who have 'crept in unawares', and those who 'ran greedily after the error of Balaam for reward' (verse 11). And again, in the second chapter of Revelation where the Lord Jesus is speaking to the church at Pergamos, he says this, 'I have a few things against thee, because thou hast there them that hold the doctrine of Balaam, who taught Balak to cast a stumblingblock before the children of Israel, to eat things sacrificed unto idols, and to commit fornication. So hast thou also them that hold the doctrine of the Nicolaitans, which thing I hate' (verses 14–15). These three references together with their contexts indicate quite clearly the kind of people who threatened the church at the close of the New Testament era; in some peculiar way they partook of the spirit of this man Balaam. If you want to understand the character of these men and the manner in which they proceed it is necessary to study Balaam. I have no doubt that what the Scriptures teach us about him is applicable to the church today. If you would understand the character of a false prophet at his most dangerous and subtle, then you need to think carefully about Balaam.

THE HISTORY OF BALAAM

So let us now turn to Numbers 22. Before we begin to look at Balaam there are two preliminary considerations to keep in mind. Firstly, Balak the king of Moab sees the children of Israel proceeding on their way with victories over the militarily very powerful kings Sihon and Og. As a consequence Balak becomes exceedingly troubled about the effect that the Israelites will have upon the people of Moab, and it is in this context that he seeks the help of Balaam. However, his fears were ungrounded, because in Deuteronomy 2:9 Moses says: 'And the LORD said unto me, Distress not the Moabites, neither contend with them in battle: for I will not give thee of their land for a possession; because I have given Ar unto the children of Lot for a possession.' Balak's fears were totally unwarranted. Is there not a lesson for us here? How many of the church's troubles arise because people or nations or rulers consider themselves threatened in some way by God's people; the church of Jesus Christ is not a threat to the 'powers that be'. Moses was told specifically to leave Moab alone, so Balak's whole policy arose out of a misconception on his part.

The second thing I would comment on in passing is Balak's willingness to pour vast sums of money into (as I understand it) manipulating God. Notice that he is prepared to spend much to get his own way in the matter of religion. I comment about this because I have read recently about some particular movement of which someone said, 'Look at all the money that organization has got; God must be blessing them.' Now, brethren, I have no doubt that if God does bless his church and, given a background of reasonable economic prosperity, Christians will give most willingly and generously, but it is a complete delusion to think that the greater the amount of money, the greater the blessing of God. The prosperity of an organization or movement does not indicate that God is behind it or that God is blessing it. Were not the children of Israel willing to give up their gold and jewellery to make the idolatrous golden calf? Balak is willing to pour large amounts of cash if only he can obtain the religious blessing he thinks he needs. This, then, is the setting into which Balaam comes.

Balaam appears on the scene in Numbers 22 but it seems that he already had built himself some kind of reputation. Balak speaks to Balaam and says: 'Come now therefore, I pray thee, curse me this people; for they are too mighty for me: peradventure I shall prevail . . . because I see that he whom thou blessest is blessed, and he whom thou cursest is cursed' (verse 6). So Balaam appears on the scene already with an established reputation for some kind of real, though unsaving, relationship (what exactly it is is hard to determine) with the God of Israel. He already has a reputation, and I think that he is very jealous of it. I think, too, that some of the things he says are meant to promote his reputation, because the greater his reputation as a prophet or soothsayer, the more likely it is that Balak will give him what he wants. If you were to come to Numbers 22 for the first time, and not reading it very carefully, you might come to the conclusion that, although Balaam was a man with faults and deficiencies, nevertheless he is basically a man in whom grace prevails. I assume you are familiar with these chapters, and have noted that Balaam keeps on saying, 'Well, I just cannot say anything else but what God tells me, and though you give me a house full of gold and silver I still will not say what you want.' Such words may lead you to think, 'What a goodly character; that is precisely what I would expect of a true man of God.' He speaks wise and true words and utters prophecies that are fulfilled - including wonderful prophecies about Christ, and apparently in the end holds on to his integrity, for Balaam goes off in one direction and Balak goes off in another. Balaam has acted as a minister who is faithful to God. Yes, he has his faults; yes, he fails; but surely here is a man of real integrity.

Later in Numbers 25, we read of how the Midianites and the Moabites corrupt the Israelites with their women and bring God's judgment upon them. Twenty-four thousand Israelites are slain, but this seems to have nothing to do with Balaam. Observe the way in which the Scriptures are written. We are not told that the events of chapter 25 had anything to do with Balaam. Balaam, having declared his oracles just disappears from view and some time later the children of Israel are corrupted. But when you reach chapter 31 you suddenly find these details in verse 8, 'And they slew the kings of Midian . . . Balaam also the son of Beor they slew with the sword.' And then it says: 'Behold, these caused the children of Israel, through the counsel of Balaam, to commit trespass against the LORD in the matter of Peor, and there was a plague among the congregation of the LORD' (verse 16). Now it is really strange, is it not?, that the Scriptures do not tell you immediately that Balaam was behind the policy that resulted in the corrupting of the children of Israel. But later, humanly-speaking almost incidentally, you are given this vital piece of information. It causes you to turn back and say to yourself, 'Well, I had better look more carefully into this matter. Here is a very strange man whom I, at first, thought to be a tempted servant of God, who had some personal failings, but when it came to the real issues spoke God's truth and would not be bought off by Balak at all.' And yet that judgment of Balaam's character would be totally wrong.

In some ways Balaam's conduct was exemplary. The enemies of God's people came to him and wanted to engage him to help them. When they came what does Balaam say?

'And he said unto them, Lodge here this night, and I will bring you word again, as the LORD shall speak unto me: and the princes of Moab abode with Balaam. And God came unto Balaam, and said, What men are these with thee? And Balaam said unto God, Balak the son of Zippor, king of Moab, hath sent unto me, saying, Behold, there is a people come out of Egypt, which covereth the face of the earth: come now, curse me them; peradventure I shall be able to overcome them, and drive them out. And God said unto Balaam, Thou shalt not go with them; thou shalt not curse the people: for they are blessed' (*Num.* 22:8–12).

It seems to me, as you examine this incident, that in one sense these words ought to have ended the whole matter; God told Balaam that the Moabites were endeavouring to use him against the people God was determined to bless. But 'Balaam rose up in the morning, and said unto the princes of Balak, Get you into your land: for the LORD refuseth to give me leave to go with you', which was not, strictly speaking, what God had said to him.

The fact is that they came to him with the glittering rewards of divination, they came with gifts, and it seems that Balaam was reluctant to lose the opportunity of obtaining that which the Moabites brought with them.

'And Balak sent yet again princes, more, and more honourable than they. And they came to Balaam, and said to him, Thus saith Balak the son of Zippor, Let nothing, I pray thee, hinder thee from coming unto me: For I will promote thee unto very great honour, and I will do whatsoever thou sayest unto me: come therefore, I pray thee, curse me this people. And Balaam answered and said unto the servants of Balak, If Balak would give me his house full of silver and gold, I cannot go beyond the word of the LORD my God, to do less or more. Now therefore, I pray you, tarry ye also here this night, that I may know what the LORD will say unto me' (*Num.* 22:15–19).

But the Lord had already said unto Balaam that these people were blessed and that Balaam was not to curse them. Why therefore does he go to God again? It is strange, is it not? It appears that he wants God to change his mind. You understand the phenomenon? God has made something perfectly clear to a person in your congregation through his Word, and the person then says, 'Well, I am going to pray about it.' And you say to him that the matter is clear and that the proposed action is not right. But the person replies: 'I am going to pray about it and really seek God's will about it' – as if somehow it will become right!

This is the way Balaam was thinking. We read, 'God came unto Balaam at night, and said unto him, if the men come to call thee, rise up, and go with-them; but yet the word which I shall say unto thee, that shalt thou do' (*Num.* 22:20). Commentators vary in their comments, but I think the commentators are right who point out that Balaam did not wait for them to come to him. The Scriptures say, 'Balaam rose up in the morning, and saddled his ass, and went with the princes of Moab.' In other words, he shows a strange willingness to go along with the enemies of God's people. As we go through this chapter, all I can do is to point you to certain places which seem to me to illustrate the lessons that God intends us to learn from this. As Balaam goes, Balak meets him, and says: 'Did I not earnestly send unto thee to call thee? Wherefore camest thou not unto me? Am I not able indeed to promote thee to honour?' (*Num.* 22:37). I said Balak is willing to pour his money into this scheme and Balaam has big ears to hear all about it. If he can do what Balak desires, he is going to do it. But God, of course, will over-rule and restrain him. God will turn the curse into a blessing and Balaam will be subject to the sovereign will of God.

So, off Balaam goes. I have no time to go through all the occasions when he goes up to offer his sacrifice and meet with God. The Lord meets with him, speaks to him, his Spirit descends upon him, and Balaam speaks only what God tells him. His words are meticulous in their accuracy and he is meticulous in his obedience. He speaks of his experiences, wonderful experiences, as in Numbers 24:2:

'Balaam lifted up his eyes, and he saw Israel abiding in his tents according to their tribes; and the spirit of God came upon him. And he took up his parable, and said, Balaam the son of Beor hath said, and the man whose eyes are open hath said: He hath said, which heard the words of God, which saw the vision of the Almighty, falling into a trance, but having his eyes open.'

Balaam was not speaking falsely; he did have experiences of God. God met with him, and the Spirit came upon him. Moreover, he spoke of Christ, and some of the most exalted and glorious testimonies concerning the coming of the Messiah are to be found here. I will quote one of them: 'I shall see him, but not now: I shall behold him, but not nigh: there shall come a Star out of Jacob, and a Sceptre shall rise out of Israel, and shall smite the corners of Moab, and destroy all the children of Sheth' (*Num.* 24:17). But all the time it seems that Balaam has this hankering to please Balak, the avowed enemy of God's people. He keeps on saying, 'I will go to another place and will offer more sacrifices and see what happens.' Now why does he do this? Because – and this comes out in the details of the subsequent history and the reference to him particularly in 2 Peter – Balak's rewards, honour, power, and position drew him on. How could he get his hands on them? The only way was by pleasing Balak. God over-ruled the attempt to curse and turned it into a blessing, but in the end Balaam would find a way by which he could obtain those things for which his heart really longed.

THE LESSONS

These things deserve far more detailed attention than I have been able to give to them, but the lessons supplied by Balaam certainly need to be noted by and applied to all of us. Consider again what happens in Numbers 25.

'Israel abode in Shittim, and the people began to commit whoredom with the daughters of Moab. And they called the people unto the sacrifices of their gods: and the people did eat, and bowed down to their gods. And Israel joined himself unto Baal-peor: and the anger of the LORD was kindled against Israel. And the LORD said unto Moses, Take all the heads of the people, and hang them up before the LORD against the sun, that the fierce anger of the LORD may be turned away from Israel' (verses 1–4).

Balaam's counsel is most effective in procuring the temporary ruin of God's people, the temporary corruption of God's people, and it was Balaam who had the understanding – albeit, perverse understanding – that since God was holy, the way to destroy the people of God was to lead them into sin which would cause God's displeasure to come upon them and they would cease to be an effective menace to others. That is 'the counsel of Balaam'.

What lessons may we learn from Balaam's character? Dare I say it, I have got ten lessons – and then a few more after those! First of all, *Balaam had great gifts*. He had great gifts, yes, but no grace. Let me make some passing comments. We live in an age when people are boastful of their gifts. Frankly, I am not persuaded by these 'gifts' either biblically or pragmatically. But even if a person comes to you able to boast of genuine gifts, this does not provide an adequate reason to follow him. Remember, Judas had gifts; he was an apostle, but also a devil (*John* 6:70). The Bible says that genuine gifts may co-exist with a wicked heart.

Now, this is not a new phenomenon. We read about it in Scripture. John Owen in the third chapter of his work, *Of Spiritual Mindedness*, remarks on this. He is actually speaking about the gift of prayer, but that does not really matter because what he is saying applies in a general sense.

> No persons are in greater danger of walking at hazard with God than those who live in the exercise of spiritual gifts in duties unto their own satisfaction and that of others, for they may countenance themselves with an appearance of everything that should be in them in reality and power, when there is nothing of it in them. And so it has fallen out. We have seen many earnest in the exercise of this gift who have turned vile and debauched apostates' (vol. 7, p. 287).

So, first of all, Balaam was a man with great gifts, but no grace.

Secondly, he was a man of *great enthusiasm*, but he had no grace. He is very active, is he not? 'Balaam rose up in the morning, and saddled his ass, and went with the princes of Moab' (*Num.* 22:21). He is very active, he is doing lots of things, he is very zealous. There is no slackness in Balaam. Whatever his motivation may have been, there is no slackness in him. Look what he does. He goes on his rounds, he sacrifices, he goes up into the high places, he seeks the face of God in some manner – but still he is a man without grace. There can be great enthusiasm, there can be great zeal, where no grace exists. The New Testament teaches us that the Jews had a zeal of God, but that zeal did them no good because it was not according to knowledge. The existence of zeal in matters of religion and spiritual devotion is not an indisputable evidence of saving grace.

Thirdly, Balaam was a man of *great experiences*. After all, an ass spoke to him. If I may paraphrase a comment made by John Calvin: 'God spoke to Balaam through an ass to show that God could speak through a man like Balaam who was an ass!' Can you imagine the reaction of some people today if an ass spoke to them? Can you imagine the capital they would make out of it? And let us be clear about this; the ass genuinely spoke, and God spoke to Balaam too; he saw an angel, an angel with a flaming sword. And let me just remind you that in Numbers 23:4 we read, 'And God met Balaam.' The Almighty God met Balaam! In Numbers 24:4 we read: 'He hath said, which heard the words of God, which saw the vision of the Almighty.' In verse 16 of the same chapter says: 'He hath said, which heard the words of God, and knew the knowledge of the most High, which saw the vision of the Almighty, falling into a trance, but having his eyes open.'

These were not spurious experiences, they were genuine experiences brought about by Almighty God according to his sovereign purposes - but Balaam was without grace. We ought to observe here that he spoke much about his experiences. Now, of course, there is a place for speaking about experiences, a place for saying what great things the Lord has done for us. We know this. But we learn also that bragging about one's spiritual experiences is a very unspiritual thing to do. Paul would not speak about the things that he was privileged to hear when caught up to the third heaven (2 *Cor.* 12). The fact is that if you belong to a certain circle and a certain kind of constituency, and you wish to be advanced, you had better get some experiences of an extraordinary nature, then talk about them, and everybody will be most impressed and promote you to a position of great honour. It has been pointed out that the more Balak was impressed with Balaam's knowledge of God, the more potentially useful Balaam would be to Balak and, therefore, the more money Balak would part with to obtain the spiritual help of this 'great man'.

Fourthly, Balaam had great *orthodoxy*, but no grace. Now do not get me wrong; we are all for orthodoxy and really want to be orthodox. We believe in sound doctrine – make no mistake about that whatever! We will have little to do with people who decry doctrine or speak lightly of it. But it is a fact, given to us, for instance, in Numbers 23:19, that Balaam was very orthodox in his statements: 'God is not a man, that he should lie; neither the son of man, that he should repent: hath he said, and shall he not do it? or hath he spoken, and shall he not make it good?' This is very sound doctrine, is it not? I have also pointed out to you Numbers 24:17. Indeed, you could go through all of Balaam's prophecies and observe how orthodox and true are his comments about God. He speaks the truth, but he had no grace!

Fifthly, Balaam had *pious sentiments*, but no saving grace in his heart. In Numbers 23:10 he said: 'Let me die the death of the righteous, and let my last end be like his!' In verse 26 we read: 'Balaam answered and said unto Balak, Told not I thee, saying, All that the LORD speaketh, that I must do?' If you hear a man speak like that, you are inclined to say, 'What a pious person he is!' It is not simply that he speaks the truth. He says,

'Oh, I desire to be with the righteous and I desire to do the will of God.' In verse 13, he repeats this: 'If Balak would give me his house full of silver and gold, I cannot go beyond the commandment of the LORD , to do either good or bad of mine own mind; but what the LORD saith, that will I speak.' He has pious sentiments – but no grace.

Sixthly, he was *useful* for the people of God. Down through the succeeding centuries people would look back to the prophecies of Balaam concerning the Messiah. If you want to learn about the Messiah, and the glorious blessings and purposes of God in his covenant and his kingdom, then read Balaam's oracles and you are sure to be blessed. Balaam was a great blessing to the people of God! Very useful, but no grace!

Seventhly, although Balaam was orthodox, he had *little true understanding* about God! There is a mystery here. He knows certain things, he is orthodox as we have seen, he meets with God, and yet you say, 'How can a man who seems to know so much about God be found among the enemies of God, promoting their aims against God's people?' You say, 'What madness, utter madness!' Balaam lacked understanding; his knowledge of God was not saving.

Eighthly, Balaam was a *great enemy* of God's people and God's purposes concerning them. He is really a very wicked man, a very bad and dangerous man. And those positive things that I have said concerning him make him all the more dangerous.

Ninthly, Balaam had great *desires for money and honour*. Now this has got nothing to do with ministers being properly remunerated; we are not addressing that particular subject here. Balaam was controlled by the desire for honour and position. And you will remember how the Lord Jesus said, 'I am come in my Father's name, and ye receive me not: if another shall come in his own name, him ye will receive. How can ye believe, which receive honour one of another, and seek not the honour that cometh from God only?' (*John* 5:43–44).

Remember the words of John 12:42–43: 'Nevertheless among the chief rulers also many believed on him; but because of the Pharisees they did not confess him, lest they should be put out of the synagogue: for they loved the praise of men more than the praise of God'. My brethren, I do not believe that you are as Balaam, but I do believe that we as ministers are sometimes tempted along this line. We can be tempted to tailor our message to win the favour of people who fundamentally are at enmity with God. This is to be like Balaam.

My tenth point is this: Balaam had *great subtlety* and his actions ultimately contradicted his sentiments and his theology.

THE OUTCOME

Let me mention a few further lessons concerning the procedure and the character of Balaam and the manner in which he promoted the injury of the people of God. What is the significance of his advice, what is the fearful and evil character of this man? First of all, he mixes truth with a measure of very dangerous poison. In *The Log College* by Archibald Alexander, mention is made of a Mr William Tennent.

At New York Mr Tennent went to hear a sermon delivered by a transient clergyman who was often and well spoken of but whose manner was singular and who frequently introduced odd conceits into his sermons, which tended to excite mirth rather than edification. Upon leaving the church a friend asked Mr Tennent's opinion of the sermon. He said it made him think of a man who should take a bag and put into it some of the very best superfine wheatflour, a greater quantity of Indian meal, and some arsenic, and mix them all together. A part of the sermon was of the very best quality, more of it was coarse but very wholesome food, and some of it rank poison (p. 141).

Such words remind us of Balaam. Balaam, it seems was the man behind the mixing of the children of Israel with the daughters of Moab. What is the significance of this? I turn again to John Owen on this matter, and quote from *Of Spiritual Mindedness*:

This proved the great means of the apostasy of the Christian church also, for, to maintain some appearance of spiritual affections, men introduced carnal incitations of them into evangelical worship, such as singing, with music and pompous ceremonies, for they find such things needful to reconcile the worship of God unto their minds and affections, and through them they appear to have great delight therein. Could some men but in their thoughts separate divine service from that outward order, those methods of variety, show and melody wherewith they are affected, they would have no delight in it, but look upon it as a thing that must be endured. How can it be otherwise conceived of among the Papists? They will with much earnestness, many evidences of devotion, sometimes with difficulty and danger, repair unto their solemn worship, and when they are present understand not one word whereby their minds might be excited unto the real actings of faith, love and delight in God! Only order, ceremony, music and other incentives of carnal affections make great impression on them. Affections spiritually renewed are not concerned in these things. Yea, if those in whom they are should be engaged in the use of them, they would find them means of diverting their minds from the proper work of divine worship rather than an advantage therein (vol. 7, pp. 424–5).

What, it seems to me, is being said here by Balaam is, 'You give the people what they want. There is in man, (and perhaps there is to be found in the professed people of God) a carnality. Feed their carnality! That will destroy them.' Do you understand? Owen says again and again here that error comes into the church because of the carnality of people who want some kind of excitement, something to replace that which is really spiritual. It seems to me that this is one of the ways in which Balaam is operating: 'Give them what they want.'

Secondly, there is here, I fear, terrible corruption on a sexual level. I do not really want to go into this, but I recently heard a discussion on the subject of dancing in worship, and someone made the comment: 'Isn't it interesting that you don't find the lady dancers in these worship services are women of 55 or over – women who have passed the flower of their youth; no, you find that they are young and attractive women.' My friends, if you were to take an ordinary, healthy, hot-blooded man into such a congregation and ask him what he thinks is going on, he will give you a more sensible answer than some of the supposedly pious and super-spiritual people in the church! Sadly, today, certain kinds of evangelicalism are getting mixed up with the most appalling sensuality, and you can find people, (God have mercy on us!), who are professed evangelicals who in the church services are dancing around with half-naked women. You hear about these things and do you not say to yourself, 'This is precisely the way that Balaam operated; this is the way that Balaam corrupted the people of God. He introduced women into prominence, and he used the sexual proclivities of the people of God to destroy them. All this arises from his lust for the wages of unrighteousness.'

Balaam's advice elicited the inward corruption that was present within the people of God. As we know from 1 Corinthians 1 it must needs be that divisions, heresies come about that those who are approved within the church may be made manifest. And Balaam's advice brought out the true character of many people. The corruption of the people was openly displayed: 'And, behold, one of the children of Israel came and brought unto his brethren a Midianitish woman in the sight of Moses, and in the sight of all the congregation of the children of Israel, who were weeping before the door of the tabernacle of the congregation' (*Num.* 25:6). This man showed great defiance and contempt for God and great hostility to any who would stand in the way of the fulfilment of his lustful desires; he was filled with contempt.

Thirdly, this occasion of Israel's sin gave Phinehas the opportunity to show his zeal for God and true holiness. We ministers may often think to ourselves that we have been harsh and unkind on occasions when we should have been loving and encouraging. Although we do not use Phinehas' methods, there are occasions when it is necessary for those who are zealous in God's cause to take radical action against evil. Remember how Paul writes to Titus. He warns of the dangers confronting the church in Crete and says: 'For there are many unruly and vain talkers and deceivers, specially they of the circumcision: whose mouths must be stopped.' My brothers, part of your job-description is to shut the mouths of certain people. There are some people who need this kind of a response from us. But, do not think that they will pat you on the back, or compliment you, if you try to shut them up. They will try to kill you and eliminate you in some way. There are times when a great battle rages among the people of God. Balaam's wickedness was the occasion of the manifestation of Phinehas' zeal. And I would remind you of this. It says here,

'And the LORD spake unto Moses, saying, Phinehas, the son of Eleazer, the son of Aaron the priest, hath turned my wrath away from the children of Israel, while he was zealous for my sake among them, that I consumed not the children of Israel in my jealousy. Wherefore say, Behold, I give unto him my covenant of peace: and he shall have it, and his seed after him, even the covenant of an everlasting priesthood; because he was zealous for his God, and made an atonement for the children of Israel' (*Num.* 25:10–13).

So the occasion of such corruption in the church manifests those who are inwardly rotten and also reveals those who are zealous for God and holiness. In conclusion, I mention Nehemiah 13. We have to look at the overall, sovereign mercy of God in this situation. God confounds those who are enemies of his people.

'They read in the book of Moses [that] . . . the Moabite should not come into the congregation of God for ever; because they met not the children of Israel with bread and with water, but hired Balaam against them, that he should curse them: howbeit our God turned the curse into a blessing' (*Neh.* 13:2).

Then, let us, my brethren, be found with Phinehas, not with the Midianites. Let us be found with those who are the friends of God, upholders of his truth and holiness, and not with those whose policies, actions, corruptions, and worldliness will destroy the church of God.

Finally, people like Balaam and the corrupting of God's people that ensued from his counsel can be very depressing for good Christian people. This is why we began by referring to John 10. Brethren, let us always remember that we are only under-shepherds. We have a Great and Good Shepherd, One who is aware of the enemies of God's people. He died to overcome the wolf, to destroy the thief, and to prevail against the murderer. We can, therefore, entrust our congregations and our churches to his sovereign, powerful, faithful love. He, *He*, HE will destroy all his and our enemies, for he shall reign till all his enemies are made a footstool for his feet. 'Thanks be to God, which giveth us the victory through our Lord Jesus Christ' (*1 Cor.* 15:57). Amen.

---

[1] An address given at the Leicester Ministers' Conference, 1986, and printed in *The Banner of Truth* magazine, no. 275.

8

SLAYING GIANTS: A SERMON ON 1 SAMUEL 17:42–47[1]

The fact that I am preaching on this very familiar passage does not mean that I am presuming to say anything new or original about it. Also, if you think you may now opt out and say, 'Well, I know what is going to happen at the end: this man is going to tell me to go off and slay all the local Goliaths' – well, I am not! You can rest assured that that is not going to be the main thrust of what I have to say. It would most certainly be out of place to tell Christian ministers to go and slay their enemies, although you may, on occasions, have a desire in your sinful nature to do so!

'And the Philistine said unto David, Am I a dog that thou comest to me with staves?' We meet with dogs in various places in the Bible. In that great Psalm that prophesies the sufferings and death of Christ we read: 'For dogs have compassed me: the assembly of the wicked have enclosed me: they pierced my hands and feet' (*Psa.* 22:16). Such dogs are filled with enmity towards Jesus Christ. You read about them also in Psalm 59:6–7. Even the author of 1 Corinthians 13 – and I sometimes wonder whether I have misunderstood that chapter of the Bible when I read what the same man wrote in Philippians chapter 3: 'Beware of dogs' (*Phil.* 3.2). We are all supposed to be very loving today, are we not? But Paul calls people dogs here, precisely because that is what they are like. You see, they behave

281

like dogs, snarling, vicious enemies of our Lord Jesus Christ. And finally, you meet with dogs (I say you meet with them, but I hope you will never meet with them or be among them!) in Revelation 22:13: 'For without are dogs and sorcerers and whoremongers and murderers and idolaters and whosoever loveth and maketh a lie.' Dogs are excluded and shut out from the presence of God in heaven. These are men and women whose nature is dog-like.

So, here in 1 Samuel 17 we are dealing with a dog whom God slew. Goliath was full of boasting against the Almighty, the God of Israel, and he was slain in the midst of his boasting, clothed as he was in all his armour and feted in the praises of the Philistines. One moment he is full of boasting, the next he is lying on the ground, a decapitated corpse.

THE BACKGROUND

Let us look very briefly at the background to this famous incident. Let me remind you of the previous history of Israel as recorded in 1 Samuel. Here we are informed about Eli the priest, his two sons Hophni and Phineas, and the immorality that lay at the very heart of Israel's worship. Eli's sons were wicked men who lay with women at the door of the tabernacle and the old priest took no disciplinary action against them. This depravity led on to the misguided bearing of the ark into battle in which the Israelites were defeated and the Ark of the Covenant was taken into captivity. Hophni and Phineas were slain and Eli himself collapsed and died when he heard the tragic news. These events were followed by the ministry of Samuel, under whose prophetic ministry God blessed the nation. But at the end of Samuel's life there is still corruption in Israel; Samuel's sons were corrupt judges who perverted justice by receiving bribes. Under God's direction, Samuel anoints Saul to be the nation's first king.

Saul was a kind of mixed blessing to Israel. His case is a very solemn one. He was a man who was clearly used by God.

Anointed by the Spirit, he delivered the men of Jabesh Gilead from the Philistines and many other victories were granted to him and to his son Jonathan. Nevertheless, Saul was a man of misplaced zeal and inadequate repentance. This is the man who slew the Gibeonites to whom the children of Israel had given their word to preserve them. In his misplaced zeal, this was the man who would have killed his own son for eating a little bit of honey in the midst of the battle because of an oath Saul had unwisely made and of which Jonathan knew nothing. Saul was hard on others but soft on himself; zealous against other people's sins but soft on his own. Do you recognize this kind of syndrome? When the fault is in Jonathan he says 'He shall die'; when it is in himself, he pleads his case with Samuel and begs for blessing.

This is the context of chapter 17. The way in which Goliath defied the people of Israel and caused consternation among them seems so relevant to our situation today: 'When Saul and all Israel heard these words of the Philistines they were dismayed and greatly afraid' (verse 11). 'And all the men of Israel, when they saw the man, fled from him and were sore afraid' (verse 24). Even Jonathan was not able, or willing to do anything about this threat to the people of God. As I look at the situation in which I live, is it not true that the depraved elite of our land laugh at the people of God? Sexual perversions, which I had never heard of until I went into the army, are being taught to our school children today. This is laughing at God, mocking God.

Now there are people opposing these things – like those in the Christian Institute, as also are many of you here today. But does it not strike you that in 1 Samuel 17 we have a parallel with the situation facing us today? We have been powerless, have we not? Do we not feel intimidated? Who is there who can stand against these people of grand power, these brazen mockers of God? Almost the last thing I did in my twenty-eight years of service as the governor of a large comprehensive school in England was to oppose this trend. Towards the end of the agenda at a meeting of the board they said to us, 'Now we have to consider whether to distribute contraceptives to the students.' Most of the school's students are under the age of consent, and I said (these were actually my last words), 'I am opposed to this.' A stunned silence followed before the chairman said, 'Right, let us go on to the next matter.' My brethren, this is the situation in which you and I live today. The Goliath of our day is saying, 'I defy the armies of the living God.' See how the media defies God? See how they dishonour our Lord Jesus Christ? Do you not find that Allah is given more respect because people are afraid of the zeal of the Muslims? Our Lord Jesus Christ is not given respect, partly because of the apathy and the indifference and the lukewarmness and the silence of many Christians. Jesus Christ is dishonoured while others are honoured to whom honour should never be given.

DAVID'S COMING

Into this situation comes this young man David. Who is David? We know from Acts 13:36 that God said that David 'was a man after my own heart, which shall fulfil all my will'. David was a very exceptional young man. The other thing I would say about David is that he has already been anointed with the Holy Spirit. Samuel took the horn of oil (1 *Sam.* 16.13) and anointed him with it in the midst of his brethren; the Spirit of the LORD came upon David from that day forward. Here, then, is a man empowered by the Holy Spirit. In the providence of God David comes into the camp of Israel's fighting men. His father sent him to take some necessary supplies to his brothers and to bring him news of how they fared. In the camp David hears what Goliath has been saying and he is filled with indignation against him. David is full of zeal for the honour of God. He is willing to lay down his life for the honour of God.

What zeal David displays for God's holy name! 'Who is this uncircumcised Philistine that he should defy the armies of the living God?' he asks. And so the young shepherd boy is brought to King Saul, before whom he recounts the previous dealings of God with him. It is important to consider carefully the words of 1 Samuel 17:37: 'The LORD that delivered me out of the paw of the lion and out of the paw of the bear, he will deliver me out of the hand of this Philistine.' It also says in verses 34–35: 'Thy servant kept his father's sheep, and there came a lion, and a bear, and took a lamb out of the flock. And I went out after him and smote him and delivered it out of his mouth: and when he arose against me, I caught him by his beard, and smote him, and slew him.' Remember, at that time David was alone; there were no crowds to encourage him in his battle against the lion and the bear. It may well have been at night, in the darkness when these killer animals attacked the flock. David faced the very real danger of the lion and the bear on his own.

There is something very striking about this thought. Have you ever really considered the kind of animals David faced? I know that we have heard this story many times and, if we are not careful, it can all seem so frightfully romantic. I remember visiting Woburn Wildlife Park some time ago. It is one of those places you drive into with your car, and there we were in the middle of the lions' enclosure, surrounded by these wild animals. A lioness came up and stood about two feet from the window of the driving seat and I thought I will try and stare her out. This is absolutely true, but I tell you, I found it far more difficult than I had imagined. Have you ever taken your children to the zoo? I have and when we go we love to watch the animals at feeding time. The keepers bring out these great joints of meat and throw them to the lions. And there is the lion with his claws round it, sniffing it, and biting it. In such circumstances, have you ever thought to yourself, Shall I go into this cage and 'do a David'? Shall I rescue this lump of meat from the jaws of the lion? How do you think you would get on? It is all very well to say David went after the lion, but in David's case, we need to remember that he went after it in accordance with the will of God. He went in faith; David says, 'the LORD delivered me'. On the basis of these words I understand that he went with God's blessing.

But this leads us on to consider another point. What would Jesse, David's father, have thought about David's actions in protecting the flock? Oh yes, I am sure he was very proud of his brave and courageous son. But would he not also have thought that David his son was more precious to him than a lamb of the flock? Surely, his father would rather lose a lamb or a sheep than his own dear son? David, why risk your life for the sake of one of your lambs? This encounter of David the shepherd with the lion and the bear reminds us of John chapter 10 and especially verses ten to fifteen:

I am the good shepherd. The good shepherd giveth his life for the sheep. But he that is an hireling and not the shepherd, whose own the sheep are not seeth the wolf coming and leaveth the sheep and fleeth and the wolf catcheth them, and scattereth the sheep. The hireling fleeth because he is an hireling and careth not for the sheep. I am the good shepherd and know my sheep and am known of mine. As the Father knoweth me even so know I the Father and I lay down my life for the sheep.

O Lord God, will you let your Son be mangled by the lions and the dogs to save a sinner like me? I cannot understand why David should risk his life for a lamb. There were many other lambs. Why should he risk his life?

David the shepherd is a type and picture of the Lord Jesus Christ. The shepherd loves the sheep and will suffer and die for those he loves so well. David was delivered from death; the Lord Jesus was not. Jesus died that his sheep should not be torn and killed. Do you ever think of resigning? When someone asked me that question I replied, 'Yes, I have thought of resigning about once a month for the last twenty years!' I mean that, brothers. But then I ask myself, 'Are you a hireling? Will you leave the sheep unprotected? Will you leave them to be torn just because people are cruel to you? Why should you resign because people are cruel to you?' Do you know that the word 'eviscerate' means to tear out the guts? The merciless character of some people needs to be experienced to be believed! And the devil is behind it and says, 'We will get rid of this pastor, we will get rid of this shepherd, and then we can get in among the sheep.' Now, it may be necessary for us to resign on occasions but I think we need to be careful here because some people I know have a resigning syndrome. Where in the Bible do we get illustrations of good men resigning? Do you find good precedent for resignation? David did not say, 'I am resigning from being a shepherd because there are lions and bears out there'!

I will tell you a story that is particularly relevant to Christian ministers. In the Second World War an engineer in the Merchant Navy is on duty in the engine room, right down in the belly of the ship, when for the third time the ship on which he is sailing is torpedoed. The ship quickly catches fire and begins to list heavily. The engineer manages to get up on deck but the lifeboats have already been launched and the davits (the supports from which the lifeboats hang) are swinging around uncontrollably. One of them hits him on the head and knocks him onto the burning deck unconscious. When he recovers consciousness the side of his thigh is burnt. In one of the life boats into which the crew have scrambled there is a Scottish engineering officer. We do not know for sure but I like to think he was a Christian. This officer hearing that his comrade is lying unconscious on deck, climbs back up the scrambling net, picks him up, puts him over his shoulder, and carries him down into the boat. When the man recovers consciousness he has no idea how he has got into the boat. The brave Scotsman goes back on board and tries to rescue somebody else, but in the process he goes down with the ship.

When I read about that incident I thought to myself, how many of us would go back on to a burning, sinking ship when we were in a relatively safe lifeboat? But the extraordinary thing is that here was a man who was willing to lay down his life to save somebody else.

Well, brethren, are we not *pusillanimous*? When I was a little boy I used to love collecting long words and would put them down in a book. One of the words I jotted down was *pusillanimous*; it means weak and wet. You know the sort of man that is pusillanimate with no manliness. David was a *man*. He will go and he will risk his life in order to save one of his sheep from the jaw of the lion and the paw of the bear so that his father suffers no loss. What faithfulness to the shepherd's task! What amazing love for his father's sheep!

DAVID'S STRATEGY

We have to understand that somewhere in this incident David saw Goliath's weakness. There was one weak spot in Goliath's armour and David saw it. Goliath's defeat was in some way connected to this weakness and David's great skill in exploiting it. The shepherd boy had taught himself how to use the sling as an effective weapon. Some commentators say that a good slinger can sling a stone up to one hundred miles an hour! David saw the weakness, one spot, where the giant's helmet did not protect his forehead. So he goes forward in the name of the living God. He slings the stone and Goliath is slain.

But I ask you to think for a moment about David's tactics. He had better get it right and hit the target first time, or else! As I sit in my study's chair and eat a sweet or a chocolate biscuit I sometimes attempt to throw the wrapping into a waste-paper basket at the other side of the room. Sometimes it goes in and sometimes it does not. But what does it matter? Have

you ever read about those sadistic people in the Gulag Archi-
pelago who used to kill people at will? 'Here is a piece of waste
paper', they say. 'Throw it into the waste-paper basket over
there and you will live. If you miss the target we will blow off
your head.' They have got to toss it. If they miss they are dead
men. Now as far as I can understand this story of David, if he
misses with his slingshot Goliath will have his head off. So
David goes in the Name of God; he goes in faith, and God
honours his faith, and Goliath is slain. But if I may say so, it is
a risky business.

My dear friends, how do you approach your enemies? How
do you deal with people who are trying to destroy you and
overcome you? Yes, there are people like that around; people
who want to get you out of the ministry or to destroy you in
some other way. Are we willing to suffer? We had better be
willing to suffer! God may, and very often does, deliver us –
praise his holy Name! – but we have to be ready to suffer.
Someone told me recently about people who did not want to
go into the ministry because of all the troubles associated with
it. But are we not supposed to suffer? Did not our Saviour
suffer? Did not the apostle Paul and the prophets of the Old
Testament suffer? Do you really think that you can exercise a
ministry without saying with Paul 'For we which live are
always delivered unto death for Jesus' sake' (2 *Cor.* 4:11). The
apostle was willing to die in his service for Christ.

So God has mercy upon Israel and gives David a great
victory over the giant. The Philistines turn tail and flee. How
shall we apply this to ourselves? Do we think that it is telling
us to go out and kill our enemies? Do you expect to go and 'do
a David'? David slew Goliath, yes, but we are not being told
to do that kind of thing at all. The Bible commands us to love
our enemies. That is the right thing for us to do. How can you
love your enemies if you go forth to slay them? It is one thing
for God to remove certain people, as no doubt he has done all
down through the ages, but what are we to do about these

dogs that confront us? 'Am I a dog?' To help us to answer this question may I quickly show you two dogs in the New Testament.

DOGS IN THE NEW TESTAMENT

In Acts 22 we have a dog who gives an account of himself: 'I persecuted this way unto death, binding and delivering into prisons both men and women. As also the high priest doth bear me witness.' (verses 4–5). Saul willingly and gladly sent people to prison and to death. He was willing to orphan children. He consented to the stoning of Stephen (*Acts* 8.1). What a vicious dog he was! Stoning a man to death is an unpleasant thing to say the least; smashing in his brain, his face, and his body with great lumps of stone. Saul of Tarsus was a very cruel man. He stood there supervising the execution of Stephen and said, 'Brothers, you are doing a good job.' Surely we have a dog here? His words and actions certainly reveal his dog-like nature. Yet the Lord Jesus on the road to Damascus met with this dog, not as it were with a sling and a stone, but with a divine and gracious salvation. Saul of Tarsus gave every appearance of being a dog but Christ had mercy on him. He was one of Christ's sheep: 'When it pleased God who separated me from my mother's womb and called me by his grace . . .' (*Gal.* 1:15). What is our New Testament equivalent of David? Surely it is seeing those who once opposed Christ becoming his faithful and obedient servants.

Let me show you another dog. In Matthew 15:21 we are told that Jesus 'departed to the coasts of Tyre and Sidon. And behold a woman of Canaan came out of the same coasts and cried unto him saying, Have mercy on me, O Lord, Thou Son of David: my daughter is grievously vexed with a devil.' Is this not remarkable? When you have trouble and sorrow and pain in your family and among your children, did you ever find that it tended to alienate you from God? And do you not meet people who say, 'Look at what God has allowed, look at my child dying of leukaemia. How can I believe in God?' Well, here is a woman whom Jesus will describe as a dog who is afflicted because her daughter is grievously vexed with a devil. And yet this draws her to Jesus Christ. The devil is trying to destroy her and her family, but cannot understand the secret and merciful workings of God in her heart.

However, before help comes, she runs into further trouble: 'And his disciples came and besought him, saying, Send her away; for she crieth after us.' Some commentators, I know, say this means that she should be healed and sent away. I am not really persuaded by that interpretation. But the disciples were certainly not very sympathetic to her at all. She receives no encouragement whatsoever from the professed leaders of the people of God at that time. Even Jesus does not answer her. He says nothing. He does not say, 'Pray and God will hear your prayers.' He does not answer her at all. She says, 'Have mercy on me, O Lord.' But he does not say anything. Then eventually he says, 'I am not sent but to the lost sheep of the house of Israel.' She knows she does not belong to the house of Israel. 'You are excluded from my present ministry.' 'Then came she and worshipped him, saying, Lord, help me.'

You see, she is always pressing nearer. But then what does Jesus say? 'It is not meet to take the children's bread and cast it to dogs.' I cannot go into all these issues just now for there is no time. The little dogs are the family pets under the table, but would you really like to be addressed as a dog? Jesus says to her, 'It is not meet to take the children's bread and give it unto dogs.' What will she do? Jesus is calling her a dog. 'She said, Truth, Lord: yet the dogs eat of the crumbs which fall from their master's table.' Ah! She sounds like one of Jesus' sheep to me. It is lovely the way in which the Lord Jesus comments on her humble response: 'O woman, great is thy faith: be it unto thee even as thou wilt.'

Brethren, am I going to send you forth from this conference to slay Goliaths? No, no, my brethren, I am going to send you forth to preach the gospel so that Christ's sheep whom, as you know, we cannot discern because there is nothing outward to distinguish them, and who presently may give every appearance of being dogs, may be recovered and saved and become servants of the Most High God. You remember that Paul behaved like a dog, and yet he says: 'This is a faithful saying and worthy of all acceptation that Christ Jesus came into the world to save sinners of whom I am chief. Howbeit for this cause I obtained mercy, that in me first Jesus Christ might show forth all longsuffering, for a pattern to them which should hereafter believe on him to life everlasting' (*1 Tim.* 1:15).

O my friends, the prophet Micah tells us that God 'delighteth in mercy'. Judgment is God's strange work. God has no delight in the death of a sinner. Certainly sinners will go to hell, and so will those who continue in their dog-like ways unless they repent and believe the gospel. Nevertheless, Paul and the Syro-Phoenician woman are examples of the extraordinary mercy of God to those one would least expect to be saved – the one 'breathing out threatenings and slaughter against the disciples of the Lord' and the other with her poor daughter given over for a time to the works of the devil.

CONCLUSIONS

Let me draw some conclusions from what we have been considering together. First of all, going back to 1 Samuel 17 and the preceding verses, I want to remind you that *God ordained this situation in which we find ourselves today.* We need to be very careful about this lesson, however. One of the dangers of reading too much history (and I am all for reading history and love reading Christian biographies), is to feel sometimes that one would rather be alive in the age of Whitefield or Spurgeon. But God put you and me into this age. Yes, it is a difficult age but we can draw comfort and strength from realizing that God has put us here. We believe in the sovereignty of God, do we not, so why do we let our minds wander off into better days and more prosperous situations? Do we not all at times feel like this in such an age of disappointment? But God has put us into this situation just as he put David into the situation where he was looking after his father's sheep in great obscurity. We must not underestimate the power of pride in us. I have been a minister in the same church for nearly forty-five years. Sometimes people ask me, 'How have you got on?' Well, I have survived. I am still here. But often people come in and look around at the small congregation and say, 'What has this incompetent idiot been doing for the last forty-four years? Where is everybody? Where are all his converts?' And I feel humiliated. Have you ever felt humiliated because of the paucity of the fruit that God has been pleased to give you? He has given us fruit and I have seen people converted and I believe there are people in heaven who were converted through my ministry. I am not denying that God has helped us and blessed us, but it has all been on a very small scale.

I imagine for many of you, my brethren, the congregation to which you preach is relatively small. In such circumstances we get restless and the thought crosses our minds as to whether we should go somewhere else and whether we have come to the end of our ministry. People say to me as I get older, 'Why do you not seek a wider ministry?' I do not want a wider ministry! I would prefer to see the ministry I am exercising more fruitful. I desire that God might bless my labours in the place where he has appointed for me. At the same time I know what it is to get restless. Brothers, be very careful about resigning. Accept God's ordained place for you. If he changes your position, as he certainly did with David, well and good. If not, accept his will with a submissive and joyful heart.

The second thing I want to say is that *God supplies our need*. God supplied David's need when he fought Goliath just as he had supplied David's need when he was a shepherd boy looking after his father's sheep. It was God who enabled him to slay Goliath. That is what God called him to do, and if there is someone here who is called to do some great thing for God, praise God for that. But remember, there was only one David in the whole of the Old Testament. And even should there be a David here, there is only likely to be one, leaving three hundred and forty other men who are not going to be Davids. But, brethren, whatever you are called to do, God will enable you. Oh how I need, again and again, to teach myself about the most basic things that belong to the Christian life! I need to pray especially that God would help me to listen to his Word as I ought.

God evidently knew that David had taken heed to his Word, for David said 'the Lord delivered me'. Here is a man of faith who trusted God. The Bible teaches us that 'faith comes by hearing and hearing by the word of God'. Faith is not just some notion in our mind. It is trusting what God has said. If David went out according to the will of God against the bear and the lion then he must have gone out as God had directed him and he faithfully served God in his capacity as an obscure shepherd boy. Are you serving God in some obscure situation? God wants you to serve him faithfully just where you are. Beware of Satan trying to drive you out, either by throwing difficulties in your way or by ensnaring ambitions which lead you to think that you could do something more grand. Again, if you are truly called to do something more grand then do it. All I am saying is that God always enables us to do what we are required to do. Go back to your homes and your churches, brethren, and serve God faithfully.

How solemn a thought it is that we will have to give an account of ourselves to God. Do you think often about the Day of Judgment? I suppose we ought to have an address at the conference on this very subject. Do you know what will happen on that Day? 'Every one of us shall give an account of himself to God.' There are some very sobering things said in Scripture about the Day of Judgment but among them is thus: you are going to give an account of yourself and that will include giving an account of your ministry. A pastor once wrote a letter to John Brown of Haddington in which he complained that he only had twenty-eight people in his congregation. John Brown replied, 'I think you will find that quite enough to account for on the Day of Judgment.' What a true and solemn word!

Thirdly, my friends, *God is full of mercy.* Who would have thought that the situation should have been transformed so suddenly? I am not saying such turn-a-rounds always take place. Some of God's people, including such fine examples as Moses, Caleb and Joshua, have spent forty years in a wilderness because of their parents' sins. Some of God's people have spent seventy years in captivity because of the sins of their fathers. There was no release from this captivity until the seventy years were accomplished. So things may not turn all at once. And yet they may turn. You see, if God Almighty chooses to intervene, he can change and overthrow a situation in a moment. Goliath is boasting one day and all the children of Israel are in terror and consternation; the next he is dead. The enemies of God are triumphing for Jesus is dead and finished, or so they think. But then the resurrection and Pentecost come and thousands are converted. The gospel begins to spread with tremendous power. It is nothing to God to change our situation. But even if he does not change our situation we will still serve him. This is what Shadrach, Meshach and Abednego said: 'Our God whom we serve is able to deliver us' (*Dan.* 3:17). And he will deliver us if he chooses; but if he will not then we are still not going to worship the gods of Babylon, even if it means being thrown into a burning fiery furnace. As we know, God did deliver them. Though they were thrown into a burning fiery furnace they came out alive, untouched by the fire. God is full of mercy.

Someone came to me recently to be baptized and proceeded to tell me how over the last two years God had evidently been working quietly and silently in his life. This made me tremendously happy. He was a reticent man who was not given to speaking much about anything; but when I did speak to him it was quite clear that God had been working secretly in his heart. God had mercy on this man; he opened his eyes, opened his heart, and changed his life.

Do you believe in the mercy of God? 'Go ye into all the world and preach the gospel to every creature.' My brothers, have confidence in the message and have confidence in the method of delivering it! In his letter to the Romans Paul says, 'As much as in me is, I am ready to preach the gospel to you that are at Rome also. For I am not ashamed of the gospel of Christ; for it is the power of God unto salvation to every one that believeth, to the Jew first and also to the Greek.' You can read what Rome was like in the rest of Romans chapter 1 and 1 Corinthians 6. Yet Paul says, I am not ashamed of the gospel of Christ, and I am ready to preach it in the midst of such a sinful world as this.

Finally, my friends, may God give you courage. If truth be told, we are all cowards. I have often feared that the enemies of the gospel might get me in the end. You, too, may be afraid that certain people will destroy you. Being afraid does not mean that you are a creep and a weakling. David fled from Saul because he was afraid. But our God strengthened him and may he also strengthen you and give you courage! What God said to Joshua, he would say to us:

'Have not I commanded thee, be strong and of a good courage; be not afraid, neither be thou dismayed: for the LORD thy God is with thee whithersoever thou goest' (*Josh.* 1:9).

God will be with you, my friend. You can go back home and know that 'Immanuel' – 'God with us' – is with *you*. Amen.

---

[1] An edited version of the final sermon at the Leicester Ministers' Conference, April 2003.